THE CONCEPT
OF THE GODDESS

———— :•: ————

D1270348

THE CONCEPT
OF THE GODDESS

Edited by
Sandra Billington and
Miranda Green

London and New York

First published 1996
by Routledge
11 New Fetter Lane, London EC4P 4EE

Simultaneously published in the USA and Canada
by Routledge
29 West 35th Street, New York, NY 10001

Selection and editorial matter © 1996 Sandra Billington and Miranda Green
Individual chapters © 1996 The contributors

Typeset in Stempel Garamond by
Florencetype, Stoodleigh, Devon

Printed and bound in Great Britain by
Biddles Ltd, Guildford and King's Lynn

British Library Cataloguing in Publication Data
A catalogue record for this book is available from the British Library

Library of Congress Cataloguing in Publication Data
A catalogue record for this book has been requested

ISBN 0-415-14421-3

CONTENTS

——— •◆• ———

— Contents —

ILLUSTRATIONS

———— •◆• ————

FIGURES

TABLE

CONTRIBUTORS

———— •❖• ————

Lindsay Allason-Jones Archaeological Museum Officer for the University of Newcastle upon Tyne.

Sandra Billington Reader in Medieval and Renaissance Theatre, University of Glasgow.

Carmen Blacker Fellow of the British Academy, former Lecturer in Japanese, Cambridge University and former President of the Folklore Society.

Anna Chaudri Researcher in Caucasian Studies, Cambridge University

Hilda Ellis Davidson Former Vice-President of Lucy Cavendish College, Cambridge University and President of the Folklore Society.

Miranda Green Head of Research in Humanities, University of Wales College, Newport.

Stephan Grundy Researcher at Uppsala University.

Máire Herbert Associate Professor, Department of Early and Medieval Irish, University College, Cork.

Glenys Lloyd-Morgan Fellow of the Society of Antiquaries.

Patricia Lysaght Lecturer in Irish Folklore and Ethnology in the Department of Irish Folklore, University College, Dublin.

Samuel Pyeatt Menefee Fellow of the Faculty of Advocates and Fellow of the Society of Antiquaries.

Britt-Mari Näsström Associate Professor at the Institute of Religious Studies, University of Göteborg.

Catharina Raudvere Associate Professor, Department of History of Religions, University of Linköping.

Dr Juliette Wood Honorary Lecturer in the Department of Welsh at University of Wales College, Cardiff and President of the Folklore Society.

PREFACE:
THE LIFE AND WORKS OF
HILDA ELLIS DAVIDSON

———— •◆• ————

Hilda Ellis Davidson is one of those rare scholars whom one finds it hard, sometimes, to believe can really exist. Her publications include the very full commentary to *The History of the Danes: Saxo Grammaticus* (1979–80); *The Road to Hel* (1943; reprinted 1968); *Gods and Myths of Northern Europe* (1964); *Pagan Scandinavia* (1967); *Scandinavian Mythology* (1969); *The Viking Road to Byzantium* (1976); *Myths and Symbols of Pagan Europe* (1988) and *The Lost Beliefs of Northern Europe* (1993). These erudite and readable books have helped extend popular as well as scholarly interest in the fields of Norse, Germanic and British myth and folklore, with translations into Swedish, Norwegian, Danish, Dutch and Japanese. Indefatigable in her own work, Hilda is equally energetic in the support of other good work, wherever she comes across it: sometimes gathering up valuable and neglected papers to find them a publisher, sometimes advising a promising student on their approach to research. For many a young scholar Hilda has been, if not quite a goddess, then at least a fairy godmother. As Jacqueline Simpson, the current President of the Folklore Society, has said, Hilda's first great gift is enthusiasm which communicates itself to all who work with her.

Her second great gift is in combining different fields of study, bridging gaps between the disciplines of archaeology, literature, folklore and history. Two fine examples of this can be found in her presidential addresses to the Folklore Society in 1975 and 1976: 'Folklore and Literature' and 'Folklore and History', which are touchstones for rigorous scholasticism within interdisciplinary material. They warn against any distorting tunnel-vision which selects only what fits one's own argument, or a reductive, motif-collecting attitude to the subject in which the mythology appears. Further, there are the equal dangers of pursuit of an 'archetype' figure or tale. Instead, these papers remind us, it is essential to acknowledge a variety of possibilities and complications: the fluidity of myths, and their interplay with changing situations or contexts, are a part of their longevity.

Hilda's association with the Folklore Society has been long and distinguished: from 1949 to 1986, serving on the Council (later Committee) from 1956 to 1986. The shifts and conflicts of these times have been captured in her article 'Changes in the Folklore Society, 1949–1986', in *Folklore* (1987). Vividly appreciative of the work of others, this paper does not of course consider the important role Hilda herself played, first in rescuing folklore studies from an eccentric postwar image, typified by a would-be magician and ladies in 'large and depressing hats' (Davidson 1987: 124), and later in maintaining against the pressures of modern bureaucracy, 'the pursuit of truth in the company of friends' (ibid.: 129).

It was during the 1960s that Hilda and others, notably Katharine Briggs and Venetia Newall, began to counter the indiscipline of the postwar years with papers to the Society which punctured 'false assumptions' (ibid.: 127). Some, taken up by the media, helped over the next ten years to raise the profile of the Folklore Society to a level nearer to that of its continental equivalents and without the outside financial help which many of those receive; the Society's journal, *Folklore*, began to publish serious, investigative papers on British and international subjects. Underpinning the change was the 'palace revolution' between 1967 and 1970 (ibid.: 127), led by Katharine Briggs as President, with the support of Hilda and others. Real power at the time was held by the Society's Treasurer; two Presidents had already resigned on discovering the illusory nature of their title, with the result that 'the Presidential Office had assumed something of the menace of the Dangerous Quest in the fairytale; few were bold enough to accept it' (Davidson 1986: 144), and the Folklore Society itself appeared to be without any future; but Katharine Briggs's combination of dignity, determination and personal resources restored the balance. Under her presidency it became possible to rewrite the Society's constitution under democratic and convivial conditions. Hilda's own period as President was from 1973 to 1976, following on from that of Stewart Sanderson. In these four years she not only sustained the period of efficient teamwork but also enlarged the range of the Society's contacts through, for example, overseas speakers at Society meetings. Despite the financial problems of the mid-1970s, members look back on it as a highly successful time: *Folklore* continued uninterrupted, and publication of the Mistletoe Series, begun in 1974 with Hilda as general editor, continued until 1984. British folklore had become a subject which one could at last call a discipline, open to both academics and amateurs, but with a demand for the scrupulous criteria outlined above. One high point was the Centenary Conference of the Folklore Society held at Royal Holloway College in 1978, when British scholars hosted a highly successful international meeting to explore areas of worldwide interest in the twentieth century (see Newall 1980). Much of this purposeful reorientation of the Society in the second half of this century has been due to Hilda's abilities both to conceptualize and to grapple with the practical details necessary for ideas to be carried out. There can be few people with such a gift for negotiating setbacks so skilfully that in retrospect they look like springboards to achievement.

The early 1970s also saw the burgeoning of Lucy Cavendish College, in Cambridge, from a dining club for postgraduate women members of the University who were not fellows of other colleges, to college status, able to tutor mature women students as undergraduates. Hilda joined the College in 1969 as a Calouste Gulbenkian Research Fellow, and in 1971 was appointed a College Lecturer. She was elected a Fellow in 1974, and made Vice-President between 1975 and 1980.

The women students coming into the College from 1972 needed to adjust to a new way of life, often combining family commitments with, for the first time, the possibility of seeing themselves as career women. Hilda's experience in just such a combination, and her warm and sensible advice, were an invaluable support for many overcoming the difficulties of such a change. Her enthusiasm for all areas of academic work made it seem that much more accessible to the newcomer and, as Vice-President at a time of growth in numbers, and before burdens of administration weighed the post down, she infected the whole College with her enthusiasm. Particularly valuable was her gift of perceiving specific needs of individual students, which was never lost among more general responsibilities. The gift of a bibliography of key works brought many a student's objectives that much closer.

When Katharine Briggs died in 1980, Hilda's first concern was that her contribution to the growth of British folklore studies was not forgotten. Despite the demands of her own writing, she travelled through Britain collecting papers and recollections from family, friends and colleagues, and in 1986 published an inspiring biography of her. In 1984 Hilda's tireless spirit of enquiry had received just recognition in the award of the Coote Lake Medal for Folklore Research – an award only occasionally bestowed – and in 1989 *Myths and Symbols of Pagan Europe* appropriately won the Katharine Briggs Prize, endowed in 1982.

Since 1985 Hilda has been an Honorary Member of the Folklore Society; but retirement from its Committee has not meant inactivity. The Katharine Briggs Club, founded by her in January 1987 has developed into another flourishing academic enterprise. The beginnings in 1987 were already encouraging, with fifteen dining and seventeen corresponding members who wanted a convivial forum for discussion, untrammelled by distractions of committee meetings or a proliferation of paperwork. The use of Katharine Briggs's name is to keep alive what she stood for: the pursuit of truth in the company of friends, which is also very much a part of Hilda's own instinct, and she still maintains it as the Club's convener, keeping in touch with existing members and inviting new ones. Meetings are held twice yearly in London, the focal point being lectures by members on the many aspects of folklore Katharine was herself involved in. Subjects have ranged from flower symbolism in German literature to the consecration ceremony of the Japanese emperor, from connections between dragons and saffron to funerary practices in the nineteenth century. Corresponding members are now widely scattered from the USA to Finland, Sweden and Japan. Total membership stands at fifty–three, and since 1989 biennial day-conferences have given birth to three publications: *The Seer in Celtic and Other Traditions* (Edinburgh, 1989) and *Boundaries and Thresholds* (Stroud, 1993), both edited by Hilda. This present third volume, dedicated to her, has a title which is itself an appropriate tribute to Hilda's contribution to the subjects of mythology and folklore.

Throughout her life, academic work has happily coexisted with a full family life and participation in local church affairs: a comprehensive list of Hilda's titles includes those of churchwarden and bellringer; while a further Cambridge branch of the Folklore Society has thrived under her care since the mid-1970s. Nor has academic study blunted her general interest in people: with her intellectual curiosity and generosity, and talents of the practical combined with the imaginative, not to mention astuteness without cunning, Hilda Ellis Davidson is the living proof that for a woman to be successful as an academic she does not have to sacrifice other aspects of her identity.

Sandra Billington
Glasgow 1994

REFERENCES

Davidson, H.E. 1943. *The Road to Hel*. Cambridge: Cambridge University Press. (Repr. Westport, Conn.: Greenwood Press, 1968).
—— 1964. *Gods and Myths of Northern Europe*. Harmondsworth: Penguin.
—— 1967 *Pagan Scandinavia*. London: Thames and Hudson.
—— 1969. *Scandinavian Mythology*. London: Hamlyn.
—— 1976. *The Viking Road to Byzantium*. London: Allen and Unwin.
—— 1979–80. *The History of the Danes: Saxo Grammaticus*. Cambridge: D.S. Brewer.
—— 1986. *Katharine Briggs: Story-Teller*. Lutterworth Press, Cambridge.
—— 1987. 'Changes in the Folklore Society, 1949–1986' *Folklore* 98, 123–30.
—— 1988. *Myths and Symbols of Pagan Europe*. Manchester: Manchester University Press.
—— ed. 1989. *The Seer in Celtic and Other Traditions*. John Donald, Edinburgh.
—— 1993a. *The Lost Beliefs of Northern Europe*. London: Routledge.
—— ed. 1993. *Boundaries and Thresholds*. Thimble Press, Stroud.
Newall, V. ed. 1980: *Folklore Studies in the Twentieth Century: Proceedings of the Centenary Conference of the Folklore Society*. D.S. Brewer, Cambridge.

INTRODUCTION

—— •◆• ——

Miranda Green

Sandra Billington has paid apt and fitting tribute to the work of Hilda Ellis Davidson. What I wish to do here is to introduce the present volume. The subject-matter is diverse, reflecting the wide range of interests and special-izations both of the contributors and of Hilda Ellis Davidson herself. The varied approaches that have been adopted embrace the disciplines of anthro-pology, archaeology, mythic literature, and folklore. Despite this diversity, two important general points emerge: first, the enormous powers and wide-ranging responsibilities of the goddesses; and, second, the inadvisability of making inferences from the status of female divinities about the position of women in society. A valuable aspect of the approach taken here is that the contributions have not been biased by specifically feminist attitudes but are based entirely upon observations resulting from research. It is neces-sary to exercise a rigorous approach to scholarship in this emotive subject, and, in a book which explores the veneration of goddesses belonging to many divergent times and cultures, it is essential not to fall into the trap of using evidence from one area and period to account for phenomena observed in another. If comparisons between beliefs and perceptions of differing peoples are made, they must be based upon genuine evidence for similarities rather than on generalizing theory.

Juliette Wood's opening chapter addresses the problems just outlined, arguing against half-baked ideas of an archetypal and all-powerful Goddess-image. She introduces the concept of the Goddess in terms of modern interest in the 'feminine aspects of the sacred' and the importance to this of New Age thinking. Wood examines theoretical models upon which Goddess-studies are sometimes based and, in this context, stresses the significance of the folklorist's perspective.

Wood's paper explores the prominence accorded to Goddess-studies by the feminist movement of the past few decades, and the idea held by this group that, since formal religion has repressed the female aspect of holiness, it has been necessary to seek this missing dimension outside the mainstream of current religious systems. The author's analysis of such a perspective points out the ill-founded nature of arguments that worship of a Goddess

I

as a supreme sacred entity implies high status for the women in those societies. She presents a critical appraisal of the current debate concerning the apparent historical pedigree of the Goddess which is accepted by some students of modern female cults. There is a distinction to be made between an interpretation of the Goddess as a result of ancient, matriarchal belief-systems and the use of the Goddess-concept as a symbolic or archetype image. Wood examines the problems that the former approach can produce.

A key element in modern feminist studies of the Goddess is the concept of revitalization and reconstruction, the desire for a reorientation of culture towards the centrality of the female. Marija Gimbutas, in particular, has espoused theories based on archaeological evidence as a springboard for the construction of a model in which cultures of the remote past are linked with the present and even the future. What often happens in current Goddess-theories is a conflation of material evidence and metaphoric concept: thus the construct of a modern divine female principle is based upon evidence for Goddess-cults in the past. Wood challenges the validity of such a methodology. However, this opening chapter concludes on a positive note, by exploring not only the shortcomings but also the strengths of survivalist thinking, suggesting that one way forward in the debate is to impose the academic rigour of folklore studies to the survivalist model. This discipline has the dual merit of exposing the false arguments of the model and of enhancing our understanding of modern concepts of the goddess.

The contributions of Miranda Green and Catharina Raudvere explore two specific aspects of the sacred female in past European cultures, each of them combining a theoretical perspective with analysis of particular source-material. Green's study takes an archaeological approach and examines the evidence for healer-goddesses in Celtic Europe from the first to the fifth century AD. The main discussion is preceded by a comment on the sanctity of water in later European prehistory, a reverence which subsequently manifested itself in curative cults centred on sacred springs and pools: all the healer-goddesses surveyed here had a close link with water. Green points to the dominance of healing divinities, particularly goddesses, at a time when the rudimentary nature of empirical medicine must have driven sick people to seek divine aid in preference to visiting the doctor. Close scrutiny of both the iconography of the water-goddesses and the offerings made to them reflect a belief-system in which such divinities were perceived as possessing complex roles, not only associated with physical suffering. These female spirits were responsible also for the fertility and general well-being of their worshippers; they provided them with spiritual refreshment, and guided them in life, cherishing them even in the grave and beyond. But studies of the great healing sanctuary of Sulis at Bath reveal that here, at least, the goddess was not simply a benefactress but also had the power to harm.

Raudvere's contribution examines the supernatural symbolism of female shape-shifters in the Scandinavian mythic tradition and discusses the principles and reasons behind the concept of shape-changing, the function of such a concept and the actual beliefs that underpinned this tradition. The author questions whether such characters were thought to have genuinely existed or whether they were, perhaps, metaphors representing, for example, evil. The central focus of the chapter is the *mara*, a group of females who possessed suprahuman knowledge and powers, 'night-hags' who engendered anxiety and terror. Raudvere observes that 'Norse mythology is by no means a map of a concrete world, rather it is a guide to a mental universe'. Belief, she argues, may exist on many levels, both empirical and conceptual. Shape-shifting is used to explain things, like strength or sexual vigour. But belief in 'witches' and in the ability of certain entities to change their shape may well have been real. In Norse myth, such shape-shifters could be either divine or human. The transformation of the *mara* could come about as punishment, perhaps as a result of jealousy (the same thing occurs in Irish myth), but the change was always for ill. Most of the female shape-shifters were associated in some manner with witchcraft. The *mara* could be an envious neighbour, transfigured for this vice; or the envy itself (regarded as a powerful force for evil) could take on a specific and personified guise of its own. In the Scandinavian shape-shifting myths it was the soul that assumed a temporary new shape. In this context, Raudvere points out an interesting gender-issue, in that action against female shape-shifters was normally taken by men. The texts with which the author is working present perceptions of the shape-shifters as 'reasonable truth'. The *mara* was an experience of anxiety or a cause of ill-luck; at one and the same time a specific entity and a personified cause/effect.

There follow two papers concerned with analysis of the Norse goddess Freyja. Stephan Grundy explores the dual or single entity represented by Freyja and Frigg, while Britt-Mari Näsström examines the multiple identity of Freyja, as represented by her names. In his discussion of Freyja and Frigg, Grundy points out that, although both deities have a close link with Óðinn, each has a discrete function. Frigg possesses a clear domestic role as Óðinn's wife, a mother and the spirit of hearth and home; by contrast, Freyja is presented in the myths as flighty and promiscuous. Thus, the distinct character of each would seem to reflect their separate identities. Yet detailed study of the sources reveals similarities between them which are sufficiently significant to suggest that they may originally have been a single goddess. The author presents the arguments for and against this thesis: he concludes in support of an original distinction between them but suggests that the blurring of their identities may have come about because, at an early stage in the development of the mythology, they were perhaps both wives of Óðinn in a polygynous union.

Näsström's concerns with Freyja lie particularly with the multiplicity of names by which she was identified in Scandinavian mythic texts. As is the case with many divinities of European antiquity, Freyja's several names must be related, in origin, to aspects of her myth, functions or image. Some of these names refer specifically to Freyja's responsibilities for fertility. But most important to an understanding of this multifaceted character is the recognition that her many names aptly reflect her multifarious concerns.

Samuel Pyeatt Menefee's and Hilda Ellis Davidson's contributions examine aspects of North European folklore. Menefee's paper is concerned with tracing a curious British tradition, that of Meg, who turns up in many guises, from a Stone Age monument to a fifteenth-century cannon. The author looks at a folkloric tradition which links Meg with certain mega-lithic monuments, focusing upon the particular phenomenon of prehistoric stone structures in Cumbria which are known as Long Meg and Little Meg, and exploring the derivation of the name. Tradition has it that Long Meg and her daughters were witches or loose women, turned into stone for their wickedness. But the name is also associated with other folklore: there are sixteenth-century references to a lady known as Long Meg of Westminster, a name also given to a great tombstone in Westminster Abbey. Finally, Meg's name was given to a series of great guns which were so called between the fifteenth and the seventeenth century. Menefee has set himself the diffi-cult task of unravelling these folkloric threads to see whether it is possible to establish a genuine myth behind the 'Meg' tradition of Britain.

In 'Milk and the Northern Goddess', Davidson seeks to identify a North European goddess whose primary responsibility was the dairy and, conse-quently, the production of milk, butter and cheese. The keeping of milk-yielding animals in Northern Europe was such a fundamental element in later prehistory that it would be surprising if there were no divine power associated specifically with milk products. Many ancient rituals are recorded but, until Davidson turned her attention to the problem, no particular divinity had been identified. Since dairying is traditionally women's work, it is very likely that a goddess rather than a male deity should be sought for such a role. Davidson suggests that some Romano-British iconography may point to the presence of an indigenous dairy-goddess. The author goes on to explore apotropaic dairy symbols and milking rites, linking her discussion with the great Irish goddess Brigid, whose concerns included cattle-herding and dairy produce. She examines Irish and Scandinavian references to Otherworld cows and their association with supernatural females. Davidson concludes by alluding to the numerous references in British folklore to spirits of the herd, dairy and home who could help or harm humans, depending on how they were treated.

Lindsay Allason-Jones, Glenys Lloyd-Morgan and Sandra Billington all take as their themes named goddesses of European antiquity. Allason-Jones's subject is the Romano-British goddess Coventina, who was an apparently localized British deity venerated at a sacred spring during the Roman period at the fort of Carrawburgh on Hadrian's Wall. The evidence for Coventina's presence here takes the forms of iconography and of epigraphic dedications. The author has previously published a detailed study of the site and its goddess; here she is particularly concerned with the identity and function of Coventina. The derivation of her name is an enigma, though various interpretations have been posited. Allason-Jones considers the question of Coventina as a purely British goddess, since inscriptions from north-west Spain and the south of France have been claimed as referring to the same divinity. The ritual associated with the site and its offerings is examined, with a view to establishing the nature of the cult. That Coventina was a water-deity is beyond doubt: the presence of the spring and cistern, and the imagery of the goddess, make this identification clear. But although her association with a spring has led to the assumption that she was a healer, the gifts of her devotees do not substantiate such a claim. What is interesting is that her titles *augusta* and *sancta* betray a higher status for Coventina than was appropriate for a purely local spirit. The author argues that Carrawburgh may not even have been the centre of her cult, since the worshippers mentioned on some of the inscriptions came from the Low Countries.

Lloyd-Morgan explores the evidence for two hitherto largely neglected classical goddesses, Nemesis and Bellona, information about whom comes from ancient literature, epigraphy and iconography. The cult of Nemesis is of considerable antiquity: she is mentioned in a text of the eighth century BC. She was associated with other goddesses, notably Themis and Aphrodite; her symbols or emblems include a winged wheel and a tiller (similar to the attributes of the Roman Fortuna). The most interesting evidence for the cult and its devotees comes from inscriptions, which record her high rank and that of some of her dedicants. The worship of Nemesis was often linked with amphitheatres – an appropriate association for a goddess who represented inexorable fate, moderation and justice. Compared with Nemesis, Bellona was a simpler goddess, with a less ancient pedigree. She was a Roman spirit of war, and a number of inscribed dedications attest her cult in Rome and the provinces. In some of these she is associated with the war-god Mars and with Virtus (the spirit of courage and integrity).

Billington's topic is the Roman goddess Fors (Chance) Fortuna, and her cult in the city of Rome itself. The author examines her multi-layered roles as portrayed in ancient literature and discusses how attitudes to the interpretation of her have altered in different periods, possibly through conflating more positive aspects of Fortuna with aspects of Fors. In isolating the latter, Billington shows that her presentation in contemporary documents is as an ambiguous, capricious and unpredictable spirit. Fors may have been the first aspect of Fortuna to have been venerated at Rome: in origin she may have been associated with agriculture and the caprices of the weather. Fors was, predominantly, a fickle deity who could aid or harm, give or destroy.

Aspects of the goddess in Irish mythic literature are the subjects of the next two contributions. Máire Herbert takes up the theme of the Irish goddesses of war, death and sovereignty; her perspective is that of the image of the supernatural, as expressed in the early Insular mythic stories. She is particularly interested both in how representations of the Irish goddesses change and develop in the texts, and in the relationship between various sets of 'war'-goddesses, like the Badb and the Mórrígan, who have different names but apparently interchangeable functions. All these goddesses share the ability to metamorphose, both between human and animal shape and between youth and old age. Medieval clerics, themselves influenced by classical writings, have biased the presentation of the Insular goddesses so that their demonic character is emphasized.

Patricia Lysaght's paper is the result of the author's current research interest in the theme of the female death-messenger in Celtic folklore. She is the banshee, though she is known by many different names. The chapter examines the connection between this supernatural female and the goddesses of Insular mythology, especially those associated with sovereignty and the land. The banshee particularly attended the male members of noble families, and she conveyed her message of death by means of a scream. She could appear as an old woman, a young girl, or a washerwoman prophet. In these respects, she bears close resemblance to such Irish goddesses as the Mórrígan and the Badb.

The two final contributions widen the scope of this volume by their choice of subject, which takes the discussion outside Europe, via Eurasia to Asia, on the related subjects of hunting-goddesses. Using material only recently accessible, Anna Chaudhri's paper examines Caucasian hunting divinities, beginning with the hunting culture of the Ossetes in the central Caucasus, and the traces of its old hunting religion, which, although it has largely died out as an active belief-system, is none the less well remembered by some older villagers. The whole hunting landscape is perceived as sacred, the property of the divine; hunters are only permitted to kill wild creatures if they observe the proper rituals, even using a special, arcane, hunting language. The hunting-deity may be perceived as male or female, and some Caucasian peoples worship an ambivalent spirit, of which the male aspect promotes the hunt, and the female protects the hunted beasts. One manifestation of the divine huntress is as a shape-shifter who is able to assume the form of one of her animals. She is young and frighteningly beautiful but, like the goddess of Irish myth, can present herself as an aged hag; she is always dangerous.

Carmen Blacker's contribution takes us to Japan: her theme is Yamanokami, goddess of the mountain, wild nature and the hunt. In Japan, the mountains are now the only wild regions, and they are regarded as an

Otherworld, separate from the flat, cultivated land. Yamanokami is mistress of the forests and their animals; she combines the guardianship of her creatures with that of their hunters and she is the special goddess of the *matagi*, the game-hunters of the forest. These *matagi* are a special, marginal people, bound by precise rituals. When hunting, the *matagi* are segregated from their communities and live together on the mountain. The hunt itself is prescribed by strict rules. The *matagi*'s particular relationship with Yamanokami results from an episode in the remote past when they gave her help. Like so many of the goddesses described in this book, this Japanese deity is perceived as a shape-changer, who can adopt human shape or that of one of her beasts; she can be a young, lovely girl or a hideous crone. Significantly, and perhaps curiously, she harbours a jealous hatred of women!

This book presents the reader with a kaleidoscope of images and personalities associated with the Goddess in European tradition and beyond, and ranging from the first century AD almost to modern times. The powers, responsibilities and forms of the goddesses reflect a wide range of perceptions and beliefs. Yet ways of expressing these ideas of the divine female display some remarkable features in common, even though they may belong to very separate cultures. For me, perhaps the most interesting recurrent image is the ambivalence of so many of the goddesses: they could help or harm, cure or curse, promote life or destroy it. They were formidable forces of energy which could only be controlled, if at all, by due respect and acknowledgement of their power.

Miranda Green
University of Wales College, Newport

CHAPTER ONE

THE CONCEPT OF THE GODDESS

————— •◆• —————

Juliette Wood

The last ten years have seen an upsurge in the study of the feminine aspect of the sacred. Archaeologists, theologians, feminist critics, psychologists and popular writers have produced analyses of every type imaginable, and 'the Goddess' has become one of the buzz words of New Age, neo-pagan and certain feminist writers. By no means everything discussed here fits under the umbrella of the New Age: much of the scholarship dates from before the term was coined, and many of the writers would reject such a title. However, in its emphasis on the necessity to revitalize culture, New Age thinking in its broadest sense provides a good starting-point for examining both the historical background and the current range of thought about the Goddess.[1]

The importance of New Age thinking in the late twentieth century has been widely recognized, and despite recent media attention to some of its more dramatic features, it is a phenomenon which cannot be written off as trivial (Ellwood 1992: 59–60). Critics and historians stress the similarity of New Age thinking to the kind of alternative spirituality that has reappeared regularly in Western societies. Despite the essentially discrete nature of these spiritual movements, certain themes recur: for example, belief in the perfectibility of human kind, at least on the non-material plane; the direct access of all to enlightenment without the need of institutions such as priesthoods. Spirit and matter are viewed as intimately connected in a basically hierarchical, ordered, complexly integrated world (often presided over by a benign but impersonal force such as the Numen or Gaia). Priority is nevertheless given to the spiritual, and one of the aims of these movements is to open the individual's consciousness to some kind of non-material understanding. This understanding of the complexities of the cosmos comes about through a process of initiation which, although not directed by an institutionalized priesthood, is often facilitated by contact with an intermediary being. These intermediaries take various forms: the psychopomps of the Neo platonists, the angelic beings of ritual magic, the spirit guides of theosophy, the aliens of modern Ufologists, and the neo-pagan gods which are a feature of late twentieth-century alternative thought. This brings us to the subject of the Goddess.

The hierarchical world-view, the link between matter and spirit, the use of personalized beings as intermediaries in initiation have an old and distinguished pedigree in this type of spirituality, and their validity depends on intuition and belief. However, at least since the eighteenth century, many alternative spiritual movements have also sought empirical validation. For example, mesmerism explained itself in terms of the theory of electricity; spiritualism sought validation in parapsychology; alternative healing frequently draws on quantum physics; and, to bring us back to the Goddess once again, much contemporary neo-pagan study draws on archaeological and anthropological work, as well as on the work of comparative mythologists. The scholarship itself is not, of course, part of the alternative world-view, but it does make significant contributions to the conceptual framework, especially in regard to notions of antiquity, and the nature of myth and how it relates to the present. My argument here is that a number of modern Goddess-studies resemble influential nineteenth-century models of culture in their use of archaeology and anthropology, in the assumptions they draw about early society, in their definition of myth, and in their conception of the relationship of the past to the present. Folklorists can make a special contribution to this debate. Ideas about the nature of culture as embodied in the writings of such men as E.B. Tylor and J.G. Frazer were crucial to the discipline of folklore for over fifty years, and this gives folklore a unique perspective on the conceptual models that underpin aspects of Goddess-studies. In addition, folklore studies are much more concerned with the nature of belief and can provide a framework for understanding some of the assumptions of these studies (see Dorson 1968, 1972; Wilson 1979).[2]

Modern feminism provides the context for study of the Goddess in the last few decades. Within the context of religion, it has attempted to rebalance or redefine the relationship between male/female aspects of the deity. Typical of this more radical feminist theology is the belief that the feminine has somehow been 'lost', or deliberately repressed by institutional religions with their overwhelming focus on patriarchal male deities (McCance 1990: 167–73). The feminine is therefore sought outside the context of organized religion and/or historically prior to its appearance. In addition, religion and society are linked in a very direct way; the assumption being that where 'goddesses' are worshipped, women are empowered with a status equal to if not higher than that of men, and, further, that feminine power is ecologically harmonious and pacifistic (Gimbutas 1991: vi–xi, 324; Gadon 1989: 341–4, 353, 359–60; Baring and Cashford 1991: 9).

Opinion varies widely, although a number of writers express disquiet with the extreme historicism of many Goddess-studies and suggest alternatives. In an article which surveys the concept of Goddess-worship in contemporary feminist thinking, Dawn McCance considers Rosemary

9

Reuter's position, which dismisses the cult of the mother-goddess as a false understanding of origins and states that such feminist spiritualities succumb to the suppressed animus of paternal religion (McCance 1990: 172, quoting Reuter). Writers such as Carol Christ suggest that neither biblical nor prehistoric traditions of ancient goddesses are needed but that new traditions must be created (Christ 1989: 240–51; McCance 1990: 171). A recent study by Ross Kraemer focuses on women's role in actual religious contexts rather than in the context of theories of primal matriarchies. Kraemer points out that the dilemma of gynocentric myths in patriarchal societies is not resolved by seeing them as a reflection of earlier, less repressive, more gynocentric societies (Kraemer 1992: 208). The existence or non-existence of a unified Goddess-religion is an important issue even among writers who reject or offer an alternative (Barstow 1983: 7–15; Ehrenburg 1989: 63–76; Fleming 1969: 246–61).

Many scholars distinguish clearly, and quite rightly, between a literal interpretation of the Goddess, and metaphorical use of the Goddess paradigm. The former accepts as historical fact that an ancient and unified system of belief and practice characterized by a matriarchal culture and centred on a powerful goddess figure existed at some identifiable historical period. The latter sees the Goddess as a non-historical archetype or a poetic metaphor. The focus here is on the former literal position, which is currently widely held.

Robert Graves's classic *The White Goddess*, an influential and oft-quoted work in modern studies, provides a good illustration of some of the ideas about early culture, and of the methodology that supports these ideas.[3] The work is an exposition of Graves's poetic ideas: namely, that the inspiration for all poetry has been the feminine principle, which the author calls 'the White Goddess' (Musgrove 1962: 3), although Graves never makes clear whether the 'goddess' is a metaphor or a reality (ibid.: 19). As an exposition of a personal mythology it has much in common with William Blake, but Graves's premise that history and mythology reflect the conflict between patriarchal and matriarchal cultures coincides with an important stream in modern Goddess-studies. His work is in the tradition of Victorian synthesists – sweeping through enormous quantities of data for the pattern which informs it all. He entitled his book a 'historical grammar of poetic myth', in which myth is a kind of universal poetic discourse, a highly imaginative and, to a poet such as Graves, highly valued impulse of the human mind. His working methods are those of the comparativist strongly rooted in the classics. He was influenced, as perhaps no other poet at the time, by the work of Sir James Frazer (Vickery 1972: 1–25). The popularity of Graves's work stems not just from its subject-matter but from the fact that it shares, in its orientation to the past and in its attitude to myth, many of the concepts and assumptions that underpin much neo-pagan Goddess-study (Hutton 1991: 145).

A good illustration of Graves's methodology is his use of Welsh material in the discussion of the figure of Ceridwen. Welsh tradition was an important influence on his work (Musgrove 1962: 56). He does not suffer from the druidic fantasies of Nash and Spence and takes account of current Welsh scholarship, such as the suggestion that Welsh poetry had a prose context similar to Irish (Graves 1961: 74–8) – an innovative theory for its day. He is aware of Iolo Morganwg's dubious sources and of W.J. Gruffydd's theories on the relationship between medieval Welsh tales and Irish hero-tales. His command of the scholarship is impressive, and still he gets it wrong. Part of the problem with his analysis of the character of Ceridwen, a powerful supernatural female who appears in *Hanes Taliesin*, and with his study of some of the poems ascribed to the historical poet Taliesin, derives from Graves's wildly inaccurate philological speculation. His suggestion that Ceridwen is an avatar of the White Goddess is supported by analysing the name as *cerdd* – translated as song/inspiration – and *wen* as white. Graves is depending on Macculloch here and so is not entirely to blame (ibid.: 27–30, 67). However, *cerdd* meaning inspiration is not actually attested in any of the citings in modern Welsh dictionaries, and *cerdd > cerid* is an extremely unlikely development in any case.[4] A more fundamental problem is his attitude to the dating of the material. Graves's source is the translation that appears at the end of Charlotte Guest's *Mabinogion*. The texts of *Hanes Taliesin* are much later than those of the *Mabinogion*, dating from the sixteenth to the eighteenth century, while the poems appear in an earlier manuscript, *Llyfr Taliesin*. Graves had no way of knowing this, but he automatically assumed the texts to be centuries older than their first appearance in manuscript. The prose material associated with Taliesin contains a number of wonder-tale episodes, local legends and a saucy novella tale. Nevertheless, scholars who have examined this material have persistently ignored its early modern narrative context and read it as pertaining to an ancient period in which it had a more meaningful cohesion, embodying ideas relating to metempsychosis (Scott 1930), druidic doctrine (Nash 1848), shamanism (Ford 1992) or, as here, a Goddess-myth. The assumption that non-rational features of certain texts – in this instance the shape-changing and magical activities of the characters – must belong to the past is a basic premise in nineteenth-century approaches to culture. It is rooted in the conception of contemporary rationality; therefore the non-rational features of texts such as these cannot be contemporary and need to be explained by some feature of the past. Myth for Graves is a creative impulse behind all literature, not a narrative genre. The result is a very evocative but rather imprecise category which can, particularly when applied to material with an oral or traditional dimension, become the sum of valued literary qualities or valued narrative themes and motifs. In this context the term 'myth' no longer relates to a category of narrative but becomes an affirmation of a story's importance: a linguistically positive sign rather than a description.

Elsewhere Graves suggests that this myth of Mother-goddess and son, which he sees as basic to all European literature, was found among peoples living in an area Graves calls 'the Aegean world' prior to the second millennium BC. At this time a number of invasions occurred, resulting in a synthesis rather than a displacement, and

> the connection between the early myths of the Hebrews, the Greeks and the Celts is that all three races were civilized by the same Aegean people whom they conquered and absorbed ... the popular appeal of modern Catholicism, despite the patriarchal Trinity and all-male priesthood, is based rather on the Aegean Mother and Son religious tradition, to which it has slowly reverted, than on ... Indo-European warrior-god elements.
>
> (Graves 1948)

Fascinating as Graves is, the combination of poor philology, inadequate texts and out-of-date archaeology needs to be pointed out. When, as with Graves, one has a highly speculative model based on very open-ended data, the danger is that the writer may follow personal imagination rather than provide insight into the culture from which the data comes. Nevertheless, Graves articulates a continuity between past and present; a past where the Goddess was worshipped in a unified and harmonious society and which, despite the restrictiveness of subsequent historical developments, reaches out to inform the present.

The similarity between Graves's methodology and ideas and nineteenth-century models of social organization and myth is an important one, linking recent interest in the Goddess with a particular approach to culture (Hutton 1991: 325–8). E. B. Tylor proposed a universal model for culture in which every society progresses from savagery through barbarism to civilization; from irrationality to rationality. He drew heavily on ethnological data which was becoming available in the nineteenth century, often as a by-product of imperial expansion, and he was influenced by the then current legal debate on whether early society was patriarchal or matriarchal. Tylor viewed a whole range of behaviour (e.g. folktales and folk-customs) as survivals from an earlier and less rational stage of culture which lingered on in rural areas and among primitive people (Tambiah 1990: 42–51; Dorson 1968). Sir James Frazer worked within a framework of strict rationally-based cultural progression similar to Tylor's but applied it more specifically to religious thought. Frazer located the religious impulse in the universal experience of an annually repeated agricultural cycle whose meaning was expressed in myths and rituals which reflected the yearly death and rebirth of a vegetation god. Ethnological data, here too a by-product of imperial expansion, classical literature and even the Bible, was examined for traces of this 'primitive' world-view. As with Tylor, this world-view gave way to a rational understanding of the world, at least among educated, urban Europeans. However, the survivals of these primitive myths and rituals could be found among the rural folk of Europe as well as among technologically simple societies the world over (Vickery 1973: 38–67).

What both evolutionary models and modern Goddess-paradigms have in common is a view of early society as an organic whole whose cultural pattern is predictable, universal and progressive. Society evolves from simpler to more complex forms. The process of transition does not always eradicate all modes of thought characteristic of an earlier stage. They can still be identified at a later stage as non-rational survivals, obvious because they do not conform, or at least do not appear to conform, to the prevailing world-view of the culture. Indeed, so similar are the assumptions and the methodology of many modern Goddess-studies that, in her universality and persistence, the Goddess resembles Frazer's Dying God, resuscitated once again and cross-dressed. However, there is an important difference. Whereas Tylor and Frazer both espoused models of culture which were rational and progressive, many twentieth-century studies of the Goddess view cultural change as loss of the integrity that the Goddess represents. As a consequence, cultural change becomes essentially de-evolutionary, with the past seen in terms of a lost paradise, and the future in terms of a possible utopia. Revitalization is an important aspect of feminist Goddess-theory (Townsend 1990: 179–80), with archaeology and history becoming the basis for millenarian reconstruction. Gimbutas's archaeological theories are central to this position (Gimbutas 1974; 1989; 1991). Earlier writers who espoused either cultural evolutionism or matriarchal theories are frequently quoted. Gadon, for example, puts Frazer in the matriarchal tradition by asserting that his work completes Bachofen's task of assembling the evidence for matricity among world cultures (Gadon 1989: 226). Ideas about Jungian archetypes also come into play, applying these archetypes not just to individual psyches but to culture as a whole (Baring and Cashford 1991). This need for a concrete historical and cultural context seems quite unaffected by scholarly questions about the acceptability of its assertions.[5] The flow continues and causes one to question why writers should continue to espouse a model that rests on assumptions which are at best speculative and, at worst 'built on sand' (Townsend 1990: 198).

It may be that in shifting the focus from 'primitive' societies to ancient cultures, the model is less vulnerable to assaults from 'fieldwork'; after all, one is talking not about a living 'primitive' culture, whose members may reveal a world-view at variance with the assumptions of such evolutionary models, but about a 'primal stage' of culture whose characteristics have to be extrapolated from archaeological and historical data. However, this shift from the ethnographic to the historical alters the model very little and still demands a number of *a priori* assumptions about culture which are highly speculative (Townsend 1990: 188–94; Hutton 1991: 37–42). Goddess-religion is located in an ancient 'Ur-culture', no longer accessible through direct experience (see Figure 1.1). Whether a 'primitive culture' located in ethnographic space or an 'Ur-culture' located in historic time, these models deal with the question of how past relates to the present and, by implication, how self and other are related in cultural terms. In terms of ethnographic space, the model is articulating the nature of the boundary between self and other. In terms of historical time, the focus is the boundary between past and present. We can, perhaps, better understand why these models should persist if we look at the nature of cultural boundary. Contact

Figure 1.1 Stillnessa and medieval trappings lend an aura of mystery to this supernatural female in Theaker's Edwardian illustration.

between groups usually results in the delineation of a boundary. Not infre-
quently, this delineation is uneven, with the dominant group applying
categories related to its own idea of *status quo* to the weaker group, with
the result that the dominant group, to a degree, determines the identity of
the weaker. In effect one becomes a centre, the other a periphery.

Denys Hay has examined the historical development of European
boundaries and attendant attitudes (Hay 1968), while Fredrik Barth has
looked at the phenomenon in his classic study of ethnicity (Barth 1969);
most recently Malcolm Chapman has applied it to ideas of cultural and
historical identity among modern Celtic nations (Chapman 1992). A
striking feature of their observations is that they so often ascribe ambiguous
qualities to peripheral groups; qualities which can then be characterized in
a positive or a negative way, but always dependent on the dominant group.
For a centre which perceives itself as organized, the periphery may be
chaotic (negative) or the place of free and untrammelled behaviour (positive). Similarly, a centre which defines itself as rational may define the
periphery as irrational or, more positively, as emotional or intuitive. In the
context of gender, a group dominated by masculine categories may emphasize feminine ones at the periphery. A good illustration of how the
periphery is dependent on the attitudes of the centre is the figure of the
warrior-woman, a female who crosses into a male category. Amazons were
located at geographical extremes in situations of earthly paradise or precar-
ious utopia. A key feature in this kind of ethnographic description is that
the dominant group imposes an identity based on its own sense of right-
ness. What happens when the present attempts to link itself to the past,
when one ethnic group describes another, or when the centre confronts the
periphery is that the dominant identity is seen in a distorting mirror (to
paraphrase Kuper), and the past, the foreign or the periphery becomes an
image of what one was or has left behind and of what once was and could
be again. In the context of Goddess-studies, the past becomes a template
for possible renewal in the future.

Peter Burke, in his assessment of centre-and-periphery dialectic in historical writing, emphasizes that one of the problems is that it is used sometimes
in a geographic context and sometimes in a metaphorical one (Burke 1992:
79–84). Boudica and Cleopatra in their different ways indicate peripheral
dependence on central, in this case Roman, attitudes, and how metaphorical and actual peripheries can become intermingled. Boudica's geographical
context takes on a metaphorical dimension. As Celt, she reflects ambiguous
Roman attitudes to the Celts as a whole. Although dangerous, a woman
warrior, there is something of the glamorous, seductive female and the noble
savage about her. Her anger is, after all, sparked off by the rape. Cleopatra's
character is less ambiguous but equally mixes geography and metaphor.
Her geographical context has overtones of luxury and decadence. She is
not a victim of aggression but is, rather, a menace to the Roman males who

come within her orbit. There is a clear gender dimension as well in that both women usurp male roles, leading (male) armies against (male) Romans. Both stories are told from the Roman point of view and therefore control the characterization of the periphery, which is geographical, metaphorical and gendered.

This fusion of actual and metaphorical is prevalent among writers on the Goddess. What is basically a metaphorical periphery – alienation of the feminine – is being given historical reality in the so-called Goddess religion of the past. Validation of a perceived need to emphasize the feminine is being expressed in terms of historical actuality, and the need for validation too often outweighs other factors. A kind of metaphorical myth is created in which the sense of female alienation within a male-dominated culture is reversed. Alienated feminine sensibility and survivals of Goddess-worship may be marginalized by modern male-dominated society, but the survival of the Goddess and her religion links this periphery with the past, in which the feminine and all it embodies were central. Because the feminine was central before, it possesses the ability to be central again:

> The new knowledge of our past now being reclaimed signals a way out of our alienation from one another and from nature ... this new spirituality [and] reconnection with millennia-long traditions of respect and reverence for our Earth Mother ... may be a key to the more evolved consciousness.
>
> (Campbell and Musés 1991: 19–20)

The history of the discipline of folklore presents a salutary experience of the tenacity of such models. Many critics emphasize that there can be no objection to the Goddess-myth as an image for women. The problem is with the reification of the model in cultural/historical time, the assertion that the Goddess once existed in a more feminine, more pacifistic, more ecologically sound world (Gadon 1989: 226, 228). One historian has noticed how quickly the two sides reach an impasse (Hutton 1991: 144); it is nearly always on whether the Goddess actually existed in particular historical contexts and whether the sources used can legitimately constitute proof for her existence (Fleming 1969: 252). The historical dimension in Goddess-studies is supplied by archaeology, often controversial, but certainly up to date. The ethnographic data, however, is still folklore-as-survival, usually drawn from rural areas or from areas remote from mainstream cultures, a method no longer acceptable to professional folklorists.

Even more problematic is the fact that the sources for this material are the very nineteenth-century works that created the evolutionary approach. These evolutionary/survivalist explanations of human society have been superseded by modern anthropological research. As Kuper says:

The rapid establishment and the endurance of a theory is not particularly remarkable if the theory is substantially correct. But hardly any anthropologist today would accept that this classic account of primitive society can be sustained ... The term implies some historical point of reference ... a type of society ancestral to more advanced forms and there is no way of reconstructing prehistoric social forms, classifying them and aligning them in a time series. There are no fossils of social organization.

(Kuper 1988: 7)

Yet the publication of books which say exactly this has continued unabated. Margaret Murray's Neolithic fantasies border on the absurd when looked at in the light of the actual documents of witchcraft (Russell 1972: 20–43). Murray suggested that witchcraft was the survival of a Neolithic religion centring around the worship of a god and attendant goddess whose followers were persecuted by the Christian Church. Yet this has had little effect on the development of modern *wicca*, or its adoption of the Goddess-paradigm (Starhawk 1989: 199, 213; Gimbutas 1991: 209–10; Adler 1986: 41–135, 176–232, 445).

Modern folklore theory suggests a reason why this *impasse* occurs which can present a somewhat more positive approach than the catalogue of

Prologue.

Figure 1.2 Sorcery depicted as a powerful female by Howard Pyle (1903). Such images have been taken in a more positive direction in modern feminist interpretations of the Goddess.

Figure 1.3 In Batten's illustration (1892), the giant's daughter, as Mistress of Nature,
protects the hero and commands the birds to do her bidding.

outmoded theories and poor methodology so often levelled at Goddess-
studies. The Goddess is only the latest manifestation of a view of culture
which suggests a Golden Age whose real meaning was suppressed subsequently by some powerful, restrictive force, but whose message has
managed to survive and to reveal itself to the favoured few. This combination of lost paradise, conspiracy theory and remnant of initiates who can
bring about transformation is heady stuff. What seems to be happening
here comes very close to classic definitions of superstition, in that these
models present an alternative causality and are dealing with belief but are
not in any real sense a cognitive description of culture. This is not to
say that such descriptions are not valuable or stimulating. The historiciza-
tion of the Goddess-metaphor presents conceptual and methodological

problems, but the fact that the Goddess-metaphor is described in terms of cultural actualities is a fascinating example of identity creation. The centre/periphery dialectic establishes boundaries and, by extension, a sense of identity, and presents a framework in which it is possible to understand why these models mix ethnographic and historical material. Locating the Goddess in an actual past provides an apparently factual and secure basis for revival, and survival through time is the link (Townsend 1990: 180–2; Gadon 1989: 369–77; Baring and Cashford 1991: 666–81). Attitudes to the past affect the delineation of the feminine in the present, and its proposed development in the future. The temporal boundary of past and future is breached by the alleged existence of a past Goddess and her survival into the present. The spatial boundary of feminine alienation can also be breached by the same means. Survivals of 'goddess-religion' among modern peripheral groups are an assurance that the feminine has not been completely repressed and can provide a link between past and future.

Space does not permit a thorough examination of all, or even a representative sample, of contemporary Goddess-studies, but one of the most influential writers in this debate is undoubtedly the late Marija Gimbutas. The first systematic, book-length exposition of Gimbutas's ideas appeared in 1974, entitled *The Gods and Goddesses of Old Europe*. It was one of several important works which argued for the indigenous identity of European culture. Various factors had begun to call into question the idea of diffusion from cradles of civilization, and Gimbutas gave archaeological credence to some of these new ideas. She drew heavily on Neumann's study *The Great Mother* (1955), although, unlike him, she located the Goddess in a concrete cultural context and suggested that late Palaeolithic religion was dominated by powerful mother-goddesses and that women were prominent in that culture. Controversy continues as to the extent to which one can reconstruct complex religious ideas from archaeological sources, and indeed how far some of these artefacts can be interpreted at all (Ehrenburg 1989: 23–38; Hutton 1991: 32–44; Mallory 1989: 234–43). Gimbutas, however, presents a coherent, stimulating and vigorously argued synthesis even though academic criticism of the evidence for a mother-goddess had been voiced by archaeologists several years prior to Gimbutas's first book (Fleming 1969: 255) and that evidence continues to be reassessed (Ehrenburg 1989: 63–76).

Gimbutas, however, expanded her argument, placing increasing emphasis on a unified Goddess, more powerful than any male god, who dominated Palaeolithic and Neolithic religion prior to a series of invasions by Indo-European peoples with their patriarchal institutions. In *The Language of the Goddess* Gimbutas claims to have 'Widened the scope of descriptive archaeology into interdisciplinary research [leaning] heavily on comparative mythology, early historical sources, linguistics ... folklore and historical ethnography' (1989: xv, 342). These last two categories include 'the ancient beliefs that were recorded in historical times or those that are still extant in rural and peripheral areas of Europe removed from the turbulence of European history, particularly in Basque, Breton, Welsh, Irish and Scandinavian countries (ibid.: xvii). Her use of 'ancient beliefs' – i.e. folklore – is frankly problematic for the reasons outlined above. Few references are supported by documentation, and the bibliography contains very little modern and mainstream folklore research, and far too much fringe and outmoded nineteenth-century material.

This has an all-too-familiar ring to the folklorist. It focuses on rural and fringe societies as preserving survivals of earlier periods because they are outside mainstream culture, which, by implication, is dominated by patriarchal institutions: 'Belief in the Deer-Mother ... was strong for many thousands of years. In European folklore, especially the Irish and the Scots, we can still find references to supernatural deer and deer-goddesses etc' (Gimbutas 1991: 225-6). This mirrors a technique favoured by Victorian synthesists, flitting from period to period and from culture to culture with no indication of context. The argument uses analogy and suggestion but offers no supporting evidence, simply assuming agreement on the reader's part. This tendency is, not surprisingly, more pronounced in recent popular works than in Gimbutas's scholarly articles, but it is these popular works that are so influential on other studies on the Goddess.[6] In discussing the bear-goddess imagery in *Gods and Goddesses*, Gimbutas merely hints at survivals in modern European folklore (1974: 190, 200). Her discussion of the same image in *Language of the Goddess* is more pointed. Examples of 'folk-memories' mix in with archaeological finds, with no attempt to establish a logical timeline. Because they are folk-memories, they can be listed together and become evidence for survival of the overriding image of the Goddess (Gimbutas 1989: 116, 134). No consideration is given to the possibility that customs can originate in modern times; nor is there any attempt to establish the reliability of information. References to sources are absent; nor does the writer question how widely these customs and beliefs were practised. References to stories and customs taken out of context from second- or third-hand sources is simply not acceptable in the context of modern folklore studies. Similarity of form across culture and through time does not necessarily mean similarity of function, and the assumption of survival of belief and practice, *ipso facto*, down through the centuries is questionable. For a folklorist aware of the history of the discipline, this is very much re-inventing the wheel, and one which proved square the first time. For Gimbutas, the world of the Goddess, firmly set in Palaeolithic/Neolithic Europe, was an organic egalitarian one ruptured by the Indo-European/Kurgan invasion. Inherent is an idea of early cultural unity comparable to that of the evolutionists. On this point Gimbutas seems to shift ground. Cultural unity is not universal *per se*, as the ostensible context of her researches is European, but, at least in her popular books, she ultimately adopts a universalist approach (see Gimbutas 1991: 324).[7]

The structure of this argument is very revealing. Gimbutas's folklore references are either from areas on the fringe of modern Europe, or remote in time. Although she is arguing for a pre-Indo-European Goddess-culture, she nevertheless manages to include people like the Celts among those who are at the periphery, away from the turbulences of European history, despite the fact that other scholarly arguments see the Celts as central to the Indo-European way of life (Chapman 1992: 14–23). What is happening here is the construction of a periphery which embodies all the positive factors of the 'lost paradise' of the Goddess – an insistence that it did survive on the margins of patriarchal culture. In this way a context is set up from which the lost paradise can be revitalized as the centre. The revitalization elements in this model, and the historical/cultural dimension, depend on each other: the historical reality of the Goddess needs to be established, because if the Goddess did not exist she cannot survive and there is little basis for revitalization.

One of the effects of survivalist models is that the data is not really assessed but fitted into a pre-existing framework. For a number of Goddess-studies this is perfectly acceptable, since the model of egalitarian past and future revival is what is important, rather than the details. The past becomes a template for the future, and this self-contained position need only build on its assumptions, not question them. In her analysis of attitudes to calendar customs, Georgina Boyes points out that one of the effects of survivalist models was to seek for the meaning of custom not in its socio-cultural context but in an undocumented area of the past. In effect, this gives precedence to the hypothetical 'prehistoric' form over the actuality of contemporary performance (Boyes 1987/8: 88–96). This may help to explain why such uncritical methodology characterizes Goddess-scholarship, despite the fact that it is so often thoughtful and positive towards 'folk'-groups. Because a particular aspect (the prehistoric origin) is given *a priori* status, a consideration of the modern context is redundant. The right to endow meaning is wholly in the hands of the observer (ibid.: 88–96), and therefore Goddess-studies can point out so-called folk-survivals without even considering other factors. For the researcher such as a folklorist, used to dealing with the whole context, this use of material appears uncritical. Indeed, in many Goddess-studies scholarship from the last two decades, where just these objections to nineteenth-century cultural models have been discussed, is noticeable by its almost total absence.

A recent article on the influence of cultural-evolution theory on the development of folklore studies in Britain makes this point in a slightly different context (Bennett 1994: 3). Cultural evolution gave British folklorists a genuine basis for the scientific validity of folklore. Folk-tradition was a kind of fossil record of primitive culture on the analogy of geology or anthropology (ibid.: 15–17). The dilemma Bennett identifies is that space (contemporary folk-traditions) had to be treated as time (primitive culture); modern folk-traditions were the survivals of primitive culture. Once this link was broken, folklorists had to re-think completely the theoretical basis of their discipline.

An analogous dilemma seems to exist in Goddess-studies. An actual Goddess-religion in the past is the basis for revitalization in the future. The 'evidence' for the Goddess presents many of the same problems as the existence of 'survivals' did for nineteenth-century folklorists. Located spatially in the remote corners of the present, survivals, whether of primitive custom or of benign Goddess, are the assurances of the validity, indeed the very existence, of the past. The use of the metalinguistically positive term 'ancient' in these writings is too common to need exemplification. When these ancient practices can be linked to customs practised by, for example, Celts, who have long held an important place in discussions of cultural antiquity, or to native American cultures, with their overtones of noble savagery, the discourse itself carries the argument. Thus the imagined past and the surviving present become a hope for the future. Only when one begins to look at the kind of specifics mentioned above is the flow interrupted and the shortcomings of this model as a description of actual culture revealed. Perhaps this is why, as Hutton points out in his study of modern paganism, the same writers appear time and again in the bibliographies (Hutton 1991: 144), and why, as Clark, Luhrmann and Adler have noted, modern fantasy fiction plays a large part in the conceptual landscape of the neo-pagan world (Clark 1991: 188–9; Luhrmann 1989: 87–92; Adler 1986: 445).

Here, perhaps, some resolution between the demands of scholarship and the elegiac quality of this writing is possible. The Goddess-model operates on the level of symbolic discourse (Tambiah 1990: 23). The periphery is metaphorical rather than historical. If we look at the Goddess-paradigm as an exercise in creative history, then we are looking at a view of the past which, however it may fail academic criteria, presents a powerful image of feminine cultural identity. In the case of the Goddess, the fact of survival, followed by suppression and then transformation, is extended to the gender she represents. Her original context embodies the qualities lacking in some current situation, and her restoration transposes these qualities to her present. The link is her survival, the assurance that her power is eclipsed but not really diminished. Once something becomes a survival it is automatically powerful and mysterious. Emphasis upon the past in any form strengthens the notion that the corporate nature of society is the result of historical process. Groups often attempt to lengthen their historical traditions as a means of validating a cultural identity, and dissatisfaction with present situations can be expressed imaginatively by recreating a past (Wilson 1979: 446). Vickery demonstrates in his study of Frazer's work that, whatever its shortcomings as anthropology, it continues to be a compelling literary statement (Vickery 1973: 132–44). The same may be said of the Goddess: survivalist thinking is about preserving the power of the past.

The mechanics of this argument will undoubtedly always cause disagreement. However, the discipline of folklore can contribute much to the debates engendered by modern Goddess-studies. It can, and indeed must, identify the fallacies of the model, both in its *a priori* assumptions about the nature of culture and in its uncritical methodology; but, in its concern with the mechanisms of belief, it can provide a more positive understanding of the conceptual framework of modern Goddess-studies.

NOTES

1 Different writers attribute somewhat different qualities to this figure, but there is widespread agreement that she represents a universal concept of some kind. For this reason I use upper case for her supposed title, the Goddess.
2 The most influential works have been E.B. Tylor's *Primitive Culture* and J.G. Frazer's *The Golden Bough* vol. III: *The Dying God*. Frazer is more directly relevent here as he is still cited as an authoritative source in many works on the Goddess, despite the availability of other pertinent consideration of his assumptions and working methods. See Downie 1970: 85–93; Ackerman 1987; Fontenrose 1971: 25, 34–5, 50–60.
3 Equally popular among modern Goddess studies are Bachofen 1967, and Neumann 1955 on matriarchy. Graves is used here because he, more than the others, relies on material that can be considered folklore.
4 For the various meanings of the name 'Keritwen', see Bromwich, 1978: 308. Although a possible explanation for the element of the name could be 'fair and loved', Ifor Williams pointed out that the original form may have been *cyrridfen*, *cyrridben*: i.e. hooked or crooked woman. See Thomas, 1966: s.v. *cerdd*.
5 Lauri Honko discusses just this problem in relation to the *Kalevala*: see Honko 1990: 182.
6 Space does not permit a critique of these models, but see Harris 1968: 142–216; Lowie 1937: 63–127; Fontenrose 1971: 25, 34–5, 50–60. For archaeology and neo-paganism generally, see Hutton 1991; Bennett 1994; Boyes 1987/8: 5–11; and Wood 1992 for folklore categories applied to the problem.
7 A list of Professor Gimbutas's publications can be found in Palomé 1987: 384–96.

REFERENCES

Ackerman, D.R. 1987. *J.G. Frazer: His Life and Work*. Cambridge.
Adler, M. 1986. *Drawing Down the Moon: Witches, Druids, Goddess-Worshippers and Other Pagans in America Today*, rev. edn. Boston, Mass.
Bachofen J.J. 1967. *Myths, Religion and Mother Right: Selected Writings*, trans. R. Mannheim. London.
Baring A., and J. Cashford 1991. *The Myth of the Goddess. Evolution of an Image*, London.

Barstow, A.L. 1983. 'The Prehistoric Goddess' in C. Olsen (ed.), *The Book of the Goddess, Past and Present: An Introduction to her Religion*. New York. 7–15.

Barth, F. ed. 1969. *Ethnic Groups and Boundaries: The Social Organization of Culture Difference*. Oslo.

Bennett, G. 1994. '"Geologists" and Folklorists: Cultural Evolution and "The Science of Folklore"', *Folklore* 105, 25–38.

Boyes, G. 1987/8. 'Cultural Survivals: Theory and Traditional Customs. An Examination of the Effects of Privileging on the Form and Perception of some English Calendar Customs', *Folklife* 26, 5–11.

Bromwich, R. ed. 1978. *Trioedd Ynys Prydein: The Welsh Triads*. 2nd edn. Cardiff.

Brunvand, J. ed. 1979. *Readings in American Folklore*. New York.

Burke, P. 1992. *History and Social Theory*. Cambridge.

Campbell, J., and C. Musés eds 1991. *In all her Names: Explorations of the Feminine in Divinity*. San Francisco, Calif.

Chapman, M. 1992. *The Celts: The Construction of a Myth*. Basingstoke.

Christ, P.C. 1989. 'Symbols of Goddess and God in Feminist Theology', in C. Olsen, (ed.), *The Book of the Goddess, Past and Present: An Introduction to her Religion*. New York. 231–51.

Clark, R. 1991. *The Great Queens: Irish Goddesses from the Morrígan to Cathleen ní Houlihan*. Gerrards Cross.

Dorson, R. 1968. *The British Folklorists: A History*. London.

—— 1972: 'Current Theories of Folklore', in R. Dorson (ed.), *Folklore and Folklife: An Introduction*. Chicago. 7–33.

Downie, R.A. 1970. *Frazer and the Golden Bough*. London.

Ehrenburg, M. 1989. *Women in Prehistory*. London.

Ellwood, R. 1992. 'How New is the New Age?', in J.R. Lewis and J.G. Melton (eds), *Perspectives on the New Age*. Albany, NY. 59–67.

Fleming, A. 1969. 'The Myth of the Mother-Goddess', *World Archaeology* 1:2, 247–61.

Fontenrose, J. 1971. *The Ritual Theory of Myth*. Berkeley, Calif.

Ford, P. ed. 1992. *Ystorya Taliesin*. Cardiff.

Frazer, J.G. 1911–15: *The Golden Bough*. 8 vols. London.

Gadon, E.W. 1989. *The Once and Future Goddess; Symbol for Our Time*. San Francisco, Calif.

Gimbutas, M. 1974. *The Gods and Goddesses of Old Europe 6500–3500; Myth, Legends and Cult Images* (rev. 1982 as *The Goddesses and Gods of Old Europe*). London.

—— 1989. *The Language of the Goddess*. London.

—— 1991. *The Civilization of the Goddess*. San Francisco, Calif.

Graves, R. 1948. *The White Goddess; A Historical Grammar of Poetic Myth* (rev. 1961). London.

Harris, M. 1968. *The Rise of Anthropological Theory*. London.

Hay, D. 1968. *Europe: The Emergence of an Idea*. Edinburgh.

Honko, L. 1990. 'The *Kalevala*: The Processual View', in L. Honko (ed.), *Religion, Myth and Folklore in the World's Epics*, Religion and Society 30. Berlin and New York. 181–230.

Hurtado, L.W. ed. 1990. *Goddesses in Religions and Modern Debate*. University of Manitoba Studies in Religion 1. Atlanta, Ga.

Hutton, R. 1991. *The Pagan Religions of the Ancient British Isles: Their Nature and Legacy*. Oxford.

Kraemer, R.S. 1992. *Her Share of the Blessings: Women's Religions among Pagans, Jews and Christians in the Greco-Roman World*. Oxford.

Kuper, A. 1988. *The Invention of Primitive Society: Transformations of an Illusion.* London.

Lewis, J.R., and J.G. Melton eds. 1992. *Perspectives on the New Age.* Suny Series in Religious Studies. Albany, NY.

Lowie, R. 1937. *The History of Ethnological Thought.* London.

Luhrmann, T.M. 1989. *Persuasions of the Witches' Craft: Ritual Magic and Witchcraft in Present-Day England.* Oxford.

Mallory, J.P. 1989. *In Search of the Indo-Europeans.* London.

McCance, D. 1990. 'Understandings of "the Goddess" in Contemporary Feminist Scholarship', in L.W. Hurtado (ed.), *Goddesses in Religions and Modern Debate.* University of Manitoba Studies in Religion 1. Atlanta, Ga. 165–78.

Musgrove, S. 1949: *Anthropological Themes in the Modern Novel,* Auckland University College Bulletin 35, English Series 3. Auckland.

—— 1962. *The Ancestry of the White Goddess.* Auckland University College Bulletin 62, English Series 11. Auckland.

Nash, D.W. 1848. *Taliesin: or, The Bards and Druids of Britain.* London.

Neumann, E. 1955. *The Great Mother: An Analysis of the Archetype,* trans. R. Mannheim, Bollingen Services 47. New York.

Olsen, C. ed. 1983. *The Book of the Goddess, Past and Present: An Introduction to her Religion.* New York.

Palomé, E. ed. 1987. *Proto-Indo European: The Archaeology of a Linguistic Problem: Studies in Honor of Maria Gimbutas,* Washington, DC.

Russell, J.B. 1972. *Witchcraft in the Middle Ages.* Ithaca, NY.

Scott, R.D. 1930. *The Thumb of Knowledge in the Legends of Finn, Sigurd and Taliesin.* New York.

Starhawk 1989. *The Spiral Dance: A Rebirth of the Ancient Religion of the Great Goddess.* 10th anniversary edn. San Francisco, Calif.

Tambiah, S.J. 1990. *Magic, Science, Religion and the Scope of Rationality.* Cambridge.

Thomas, R.J. ed. 1966. *Geiriadur Prifysgol Cymru: A Dictionary of the Welsh Language.* Cardiff.

Townsend, J.B. 1990. 'The Goddess: Fact, Fallacy and Revitalization Movement', in L.W. Hurtado (ed.), *Goddesses in Religions and Modern Debate,* University of Manitoba Studies in Religion 1. Atlanta, Ga. 179–203.

Tylor, E.B. 1871. *Primitive Culture,* 2 vols. London.

Vickery, J. 1972. *Robert Graves and the White Goddess.* Lincoln, Nebr.

—— 1973. *The Literary Impact of the Golden Bough.* Princeton, NJ.

Wilson, W.A. 1979. 'Folklore and History: Fact amid the Legends' in J. Brunvand (ed.), *Readings in American Folklore.* New York.

Wood J. 1992. 'Celtic Goddesses: Myths and Mythology' in C. Larrington (ed.), *The Feminist Companion to Mythology.* London. 118–36.

CHAPTER TWO

THE CELTIC GODDESS AS HEALER

———— ·◆· ————

Miranda Green

INTRODUCTION

The evidence for a healer-goddess in Celtic Europe during the early first millennium AD is based almost entirely upon iconographical and epigraphic evidence. Certain concepts need to be introduced here in order that the role of the Goddess as healer may be better understood. First, there is a strong link between religion and medicine: this is something that is evidenced both in the classical and in the Celtic world. Sick people in antiquity relied upon the healing skills of the supernatural powers at least as much as upon empirical medicine (Allason-Jones 1989: 156). Indeed, at many therapeutic sanctuaries in Gaul and Britain, doctors were present as well as priests, for example at *Fontes Sequanae* (Deyts 1985) and Bath (Cunliffe 1988: 359–62); it is even possible that the two roles were sometimes combined in the one individual. Second, the perception of the numinous in water is important. There is abundant evidence in non-Mediterranean Europe from at least the later Bronze Age – say around 1300 BC – that water was a central focus of ritual activity (Bradley 1990; Fitzpatrick 1984). During the later Iron Age this activity began to manifest itself in the development of healing sanctuaries on the sites of thermal springs, a phenomenon which burgeoned in the Romano-Celtic phase in the Rhineland, Gaul and Britain (Green 1986: 138–66; 1989: 155–64).

Third, the evidence for healing cults in Celtic Europe demonstrates a very close link between healing, regeneration and fertility, which may account for the fact that many Celtic divine healers were perceived as female, and for the strong association between curative cult establishments and the mother-goddesses. There is evidence that many devotees of healing-deities were women; the fact that most stone altars were dedicated by men probably does not reflect anything other than economic or social factors, as Lindsay Allason-Jones has suggested (1989: 152). Women may not normally have had the means to erect expensive stone monuments as readily as their male counterparts. However, the cult of Apollo Vindonnus at Essarois in Burgundy seems – from the ex-votoes – to have been patronized by women (Pelletier 1984: pl. 1). The lady wearing a torc whose wooden image was dedicated at the thermal shrine of Chamalières in the

Figure 2.1 Wooden carving of a goddess, priestess or pilgrim, first century AD; from the healing-spring shrine at Chamalières, Puy-de-Dôme, France. (Musée Archéologique, Clermont-Ferrand.)

first century AD was probably a devotee, but it is just possible that she may have been the goddess herself (see Figure 2.1). There is a small amount of evidence for the association of women with the healing professions: at Grand in the Vosges, a stone of Romano-Celtic date depicts the inside of a chemist's shop with a female chemist at work with mortar and herbs. An inscription and image on a tombstone at Metz betray the presence of a female doctor in the first century AD (Pelletier 1984: pls 39, 40).

Fourth, we must be wary of positing theories about the status of women in Celtic society from the importance of the Goddess. Margaret Ehrenberg (1989: 11) has shown how invalid such assumptions may be. Having sounded this note of caution, it is, however, interesting that classical literary references to Celtic women contain many allusions to the contrast between their status and that of their more lowly Mediterranean sisters (Ehrenberg 1989: 151–2; Ammianus Marcellinus/Page 1935: XV, 12; Diodorus Siculus/Warmington 1968: V, 32, 2).

SEQUANA OF BURGUNDY

Sequana was a water-spirit, the personification of the River Seine at its source, *Fontes Sequanae*. Here, in the valley of the Châtillon Plateau, a spring of fresh, pure water wells up from the ground and was the focus of religious devotion from the later first century BC. The spring is pure but it contains no genuine mineral properties. Sequana is special in that she is not paired with any Roman goddess; her name is known from about ten inscriptions, and there is a bronze cult-statue of Sequana herself. In 1963, during the excavation of buildings dating to the Roman period, more than 200 wooden votives were discovered in water-logged ground, apparently pre-dating Roman levels and originally set up perhaps around the sacred pool (Deyts 1983; 1985). The pre-Roman activity centred upon the pool itself; there is no evidence of permanent structures at this time. Shortly after the Roman occupation of the region the sanctuary was monumental-ized and the spring canalized. It was now an extensive religious complex, containing two temples, porticoes, a dormitory and reservoirs, still centred on the sacred spring and pool. The votive images were now of stone. In common with the activities at classical healing shrines, sick pilgrims visited the sanctuary bearing offerings – possibly bought at the shrine shop – bathed, slept, and asked for a cure with gifts of models of themselves or their afflictions. Eyes, chest, genitals, limbs – these were just a few of the complaints represented by the votives (Figure 2.2). The eye problems so prevalent at many shrines could have been due to poor hygiene or malnu-trition: a lack of animal fat can cause night-blindness (Allason-Jones 1989: 49). The votive model breasts in bronze and silver may denote milk defi-ciency, a serious problem for child-rearing in antiquity. Sequana was not a specialist: she healed all afflictions (Deyts 1985; Green 1986: 150–51; Sandars 1984: 148).

SIRONA AND HER PEERS

There is a group of continental healer-goddesses who have a common char-acteristic: namely, the possession of a male partner. It is the case with the healers, as with other divine couples like Mercury and Rosmerta, that the native goddess seems often to possess a wider variety of functions and concerns than her consort and, in addition, is the less influenced by Graeco-Roman traditions (Green 1989: 45–73). These goddesses usually have completely native names, and symbolism which is less influenced by Graeco-Roman art-forms than their male companions. In addition, they show evidence of independent identity: they are not mere female ciphers attached to the cults of male divinities.

Figure 2.2 Stone carving of a blind pilgrim, from the Roman phase of the sanctuary of Sequana, at *Fontes Sequanae*, near Dijon. (Musée Archéologique, Dijon.)

SIRONA

Sirona is the divine partner of the Celtic healing Apollo, normally called Apollo Grannus (a native epithet associated with Grand in the Vosges). But she occurs alone, for example at Corseul in Brittany, where she is called Tsirona (Marache 1979: 15); her high rank is shown by inscriptions where she is linked with the spirit of the emperor. Sirona was venerated alone also at Baumburg in Noricum (Austria). Her cult was widely distributed and may well have pre-dated the Roman occupation of Gaul and elsewhere (Thevenot 1969: 103–4, 110; Green 1989: 61–3). Sirona was at her most popular among the Terveri: the main cult-centre was at Hochscheid, a spring sanctuary in the Moselle Basin, to which we shall return. But, elsewhere among the Treveri, Sirona was invoked at Nietaldorf, Bitburg and Sainte-Fontaine, and among the neighbouring Mediomatrici at Sablon, Metz (Thevenot 1968: 103–4; Musée Archéologique de Metz 1981). Sirona's spring-cult is evidenced at Wiesbaden, Mainz and Luxeuil and even at Brigetio in Hungary, where, in the third century AD, a temple was set up to Apollo Grannus and Sarana (Szabó 1971: 66).

In the second century AD a temple was erected at Hochscheid, on the site of a spring whose waters supplied a cistern. The evidence of coins suggests that this building replaced an earlier shrine, perhaps of wood. Pilgrims offered presents of coins, figurines, etc. It seems to have been a wealthy shrine for so remote a region, perhaps a personal endowment by a prosperous trader or villa-owner who had occasion to be grateful to the guardians of the spring (Dehn 1941: 104ff; Schindler 1977: 33, fig. 92). The imagery here is interesting and Sirona's is the more informative. There were large stone statues of Apollo and Sirona; he is entirely Classical, but Sirona is represented as a woman in a long robe and a diadem, a snake round her right forearm, and a bowl of three eggs held in her left hand (Figure 2.3). The serpent/egg symbolism is essentially regenerative as well as curative. The snake's skin-sloughing habit gives it symbolism of rebirth and perhaps also the idea of sloughing off disease. Clay figurines brought to the shrine as gifts show Sirona seated, like a mother-goddess, with a small lapdog (Jenkins 1957: 60–76), which is perhaps indicative of healing. There is an Irish historical link between women and lapdogs which is suggested by Cormick as being possibly associated with the use of these animals as 'hot-water bottles' to comfort period pains (Cormick 1991: 7–9). The imagery of the couple in bronze at Malain in Burgundy is essentially similar to that at Hochscheid: this group has a dedicatory inscription beneath the images (Green 1992a: 225). On other sites, the fertility aspect of Sirona's cult is evidenced by the imagery; for example, at Sainte-Fontaine, where the goddess bears corn and fruit, and at Mainz and Baumburg where she is accompanied by ears of corn. This symbolism of the earth's abundance bears out the association between healing springs and the mother-goddess cult.

Sirona's name is interesting: it is philologically related to 'star', so perhaps associated with night and darkness. There could be a link with the moon, the female menstrual cycle and the darkness of the womb.

ANCAMNA AND DAMONA

These two continental goddesses are distinctive in their apparent polyandry, changing partners from site to site. Ancamna is known only from epigraphy. She was a Treveran deity, partner of Lenus Mars at Trier. But at Moehn, a rural sanctuary where Lenus was also venerated, Ancamna was

Figure 2.3 Stone statue of Sirona, second century AD; from the healing shrine at Hochscheid, Germany. (Illustrator Paul Jenkins.)

coupled with Mars Smertrius, another native version of the Roman god (Wightman 1970: 211–23; Mommsen et al. 1863– : XIII, 4119; Green 1992b: 28). Is this the same deity with two names, or are they separate entities? Mars's association with healing is common in the Celtic world, where his war role was transmuted into that of a guardian-protector against disease, as at Mavilly, where he appears (with a goddess) dressed as a warrior, but accompanied by a ram-horned snake, symbol of regeneration. Mavilly was particularly renowned for the cure of eye disease (Deyts 1976: nos 284, 285; Espérandieu 1907–66: nos 2067, 2072).

Damona's name means 'divine cow' or 'great cow', and this may reflect her role as a goddess of wealth and fertility. But first and foremost she was a healer, worshipped especially in Burgundy; she had a number of partners, but her main sanctuary was at Alesia, where she was coupled with Apollo Moritasgus. The two were venerated at a shrine with a pool in which sick pilgrims bathed in the hope of a cure (Le Gall 1963: 157–9; Thevenot 1969: 104–7). No image of Moritasgus survives but there is a fragment of Damona's statue, showing a strong link between her iconography and that of Sirona: a carved stone head is crowned with corn-ears and a hand entwined with a serpent's coils. At Bourbonne-Lancy, Damona's consort was Borvo, another spring-god, and an inscription from the curative shrine relates to Damona's association with the therapeutic sleep enjoyed by pilgrims seeking a healing dream or vision from the divine healers. The names of both Borvo and Moritasgus mean 'bubbling' or 'seething' water. At another Burgundian shrine, Arnay-le-Duc, Damona's partner is yet another god, Abilus (Duval 1976: 77, 177). Again a fragmentary image of the goddess represents her with a stone snake curled round a human arm. It is worth remembering that the Graeco-Roman healer-god, Asklepios, is often depicted with a coiled serpent.

The polyandrous nature of Damona's cult supports her status as an independent native divinity whose identity was not based on her association with any one god. Her rank is further enhanced by epigraphic evidence from the curative sanctuary of Bourbonne-les-Bains, where Damona was worshipped alone.

OTHER GAULISH SPRING GODDESSES

Many other spring-goddesses are recorded only on inscriptions, often again associated with male partners: Bormana and Bormanus were venerated in southern Gaul (Vallentin 1879–80: 1-36); Luxovius and Bricta at Luxeuil (Duval 1976: 117; Wuilleumier 1984: no. 403). Others were lone goddesses: Telo was the eponymous spring-spirit of Toulon in the Dordogne (Aebischer 1930: 427–41); Januaria at Beire-le-Châtel in Burgundy is mentioned on a statue of a figure playing pan-pipes (Deyts 1976: no. 9; 1992: 73–84). We have little clue as to Januaria's precise function, though she was worshipped at a curative shrine. The musical instrument may indeed be a symbol of healing sleep, just as in vernacular myth healing deities such as Cliodna were associated with music – this time with singing birds (Mac

Cana 1970: 86). The name of the Treveran goddess Icovellauna may be linked with water-imagery: she was venerated at Trier and at the thermal springs of Sablon, Metz (Toussaint 1948: 207–8; Green 1992b: 125). Aveta was a spring goddess of the Treveri, to whom pilgrims at Trier offered small clay figurines of mother-goddesses with baskets of fruit, with dogs or with babies (Wightman 1970: 217; Green 1992b: 36).

SULIS: HEALER AND AVENGER

The site of Bath, *Aquae Sulis*, was sacred before the Roman period: this is implied by the presence of eighteen Celtic Iron Age coins from the lowest levels (Cunliffe 1988: 1), although Colin Haselgrove has argued that many late Iron Age coins from temple sites may well have been deposited post-conquest (Haselgrove 1989: 73-88). Early in the Roman period – just fifteen years or so after the occupation – a great temple, baths and a huge religious precinct were constructed around the great spring, which pumps out hot water beside the River Avon at a rate of a quarter of a million gallons a day; a huge altar was set up in front of the temple, and a reservoir containing the main spring enclosed by a low stone wall. This was a great Neronian or Flavian building programme using Roman engineers. There were major alterations c. AD 200, which argue for a new slant to the cult: the temple was enlarged but the reservoir, which had been visible all over the precinct, including the baths, was enclosed in a huge vaulted hall, restricting both physical and visual access to it, and making the water more remote and mysterious. Pilgrims could now only approach the spring through a dim passageway – does this imply Otherworld symbolism?

The goddess at Bath was Sulis, a native deity (Figure 2.4), but she was equated with Minerva, which seems a curious conflation. If Sulis really is a healer-goddess, as her presence at the hot spring implies, then she may be linked with Minerva because the latter was perceived as goddess of the craft of medicine. But in addition there is a philological link between the name Sulis and the sun – the sun and healing were closely linked in the Celtic world (Green 1991: 119–21). Indeed the solar association may have come about at least partly because Sulis's springs were hot. The cult of Sulis flourished until the mid-fourth century AD. The springs have genuine medicinal properties which are good for such ailments as arthritis and gout; this must have gained Sulis a reputation for being able to cure everything. There were many devotees who donated ivory and bronze model breasts, spindle-whorls and jewellery. But unlike – say – Sequana's shrine, very few anatomical votives have been found. Pilgrims visited the shrine perhaps for a physical cure, or perhaps more often for spiritual refreshment. Immersion, purification, imbibing the water and thus the spirit of the goddess, the healing sleep, sacrifice, festivals and prayers all must have taken place here,

Figure 2.4 Life-size gilded head of the goddess Sulis Minerva, from the temple at Bath, Avon. (By kind permission of the Roman Baths Museum).

as well as the offering of gifts. The spring appears to have been the focus of personal contact with the goddess, to whom prayers, vows, requests and thanks were made. Stone altars record gratitude for Sulis's help. Money, rings, brooches and combs as well as other personal offerings were cast in, some by women, perhaps sometimes on impulse (Allason-Jones 1989: 156ff; Cunliffe 1978; 1988; 1990; Cunliffe and Davenport 1985; Henig 1988: 5–28; Potter and Johns 1992: 107–8).

Ritual activity is represented at Bath: a priest of Sulis, Calpurnius Receptus, died here aged 75. A *haruspex* (literally 'gut-gazer') may have been present in a personal rather than an official capacity. Part of a head-dress was found, suggesting liturgical regalia. About 12,000 coins come from the reservoir. This seems a large quantity but it works out as only an average of c. 24–48 coins a year (Walker 1988: 281–350). The presence of silver, pewter and bronze vessels could represent a ritual purpose (the drinking or pouring of the sacred water), but they could also have been offerings.

The question needs to be asked as to whether the assumption that Sulis is primarily a healer-goddess is valid. The only real evidence is her presence at the site of a major thermal spring. The third-century Roman writer Solinus refers to Bath having springs 'furnished luxuriously for human use ... over them Minerva presides'. There is no mention of healing. The inscriptions dedicating altars to the goddess do not specifically mention the curing of disease, whilst this does occur at *Fontes Sequanae*. Most importantly, there is a significant lack of anatomical votives, which are such clear indications of healing cults elsewhere. Certainly, I think, we have to reconsider Sulis's role, even though the hot springs must have played a genuine part in the establishment of the cult.

The diversity of Sulis's cult is nowhere shown more clearly than in the extraordinary group of 130 lead and pewter curses or *defixiones* from Bath found in the reservoir where they had been cast by vengeful devotees (Tomlin 1988: 58–277). This aspect of the goddess's nature and powers is seemingly at variance with the role of benevolent healer. Sulis was clearly perceived as an avenger of wrongs. Water and curses have a well-established link; as late as the nineteenth century in Wales, a man was imprisoned for inscribing a curse on a lead sheet and throwing it into a well. In a sense the named or unnamed malefactor was being symbolically sacrificed to the goddess. The 'fixing' was an important element of the *defixio*, so that the curse would not rebound on the curser. The choice of lead or pewter is significant both practically and symbolically The curses are very harsh, associated with fertility, sleep, blood and internal disorders (Figure 2.5). So there is a strong link with disease in this negative aspect of Sulis's cult:

> Docimedes has lost two gloves. He asks that the person who has stolen them should lose his mind and his eyes in the temple where she appoints.
>
> (Tomlin 1938: curse no. 5)
>
> Docilianus, son of Brucerus to the most holy goddess Sulis. I curse him who has stolen my hooded cloak, whether man or woman, slave or free, that the goddess inflict death upon him, and not allow him sleep or children, now and in the future, until he has brought my hooded cloak to the temple of her divinity.
>
> (ibid.: curse no. 10)

The cult of Sulis, whatever its precise nature, was popular and successful, attracting people over a wide area and over long periods of time – nearly

Figure 2.5 The 'Vilbia' curse, inscribed on a tablet of lead; from the sacred spring and reservoir of the goddess Sulis Minerva, Bath. (By kind permission of the Roman Baths Museum.)

four centuries. If we are right to interpret her cult as primarily that of a healer, then the reversal of benevolence and vengeance is interesting. What the goddess could give she could also take away, especially if the evil deed was perpetrated within her sacred space.

HEALING AND THE MOTHER-GODDESSES

The symbolism of the divine female healers has already demonstrated a close link between curing, fertility and regeneration. The mother-goddesses themselves, often in their distinctive triadic form, appear at thermal spring-sanctuaries, presumably as healers themselves. There is a natural link between the mother, childbirth and women's health before, during and after pregnancy. The Mothers were perceived as protectors and nourishers of children. Good examples of mother-goddesses at spring-shrines include those at Vertault and Bath (Deyts 1976: no. 222; Green 1989: figs 84, 88). At Aix-les-Bains, pilgrims at the curative shrine worshipped the *Matres Comedovae*, the *med* element perhaps referring specifically to health (de Vries 1963: 130). The *Matres Griselicae* were the eponymous healers at Greoulx, the *Glanicae* at Glanum, and the *Nemausicae* at Nîmes, all in Provence (Clébert 1970: 254). At Arrington in Cambridgeshire, a recent discovery consists of the burial of an infant who died of hydrocephalus: he was placed in a coffin on top of which was a group of clay figurines, including a mother-goddess of distinctively Rhenish type (Green 1992c). Was she placed in his grave as a symbolic mother but also as a healer, so that he would be whole in his life in the Otherworld?

The association between mothers and healers is enhanced by certain aspects of their symbolism, notably the presence with them of such animals as dogs and snakes. Dogs were associated with self-healing, and there were sacred dogs at the great healing sanctuary of Asklepios at Epidaurus in Greece. In Britain, images of dogs were notable occurrences at the healing shrine of Nodens at Lydney. We have seen the association between dogs, Sirona and Aveta. Snakes were potent symbols of rebirth and fertility, again associated with healing.

CONCLUSION

From our own experience in modern times we know that health figures prominently in, for example, governmental responsibility and spending. Health is a fundamental concern to humankind and must always have been so. In antiquity, many diseases that to us are commonplace and curable were neither understood nor capable of effective treatment. So the gods played a crucial role in the physical and spiritual well-being of the community. In the Celtic world, we know of many great healing-cults which were more or less influenced by the imagery and belief-systems of the Classical world. But I think it fair to say that some of the most interesting cults were those centred upon the goddesses; Sulis, Sequana, Sirona and their sisters in healing all presided over important popular sanctuaries to which pilgrims were attracted from far afield, drawn by the successful reputations of the goddesses. The links between healing and fertility are interesting, and these appear to be specific to the female healers. Perhaps more fascinating still is the reversal of beneficence and malignancy in Sulis's cult, where curing and cursing were both under the goddess's jurisdiction.

The healing deities may have played a large part in people's lives not only because they attended to their physical well-being but also perhaps because they offered spiritual renewal. This is not usually evidenced archaeologically but it is more than likely that pilgrims prayed to these divinities for many and complex reasons other than those of pure health.

Perhaps the most fascinating aspect of the healing-goddess cult is the manner in which it has survived into modern Christianity all over Europe. There are numerous instances of shrines to the Virgin Mary as a healer to whom pilgrims have come in recent years as suppliants, bearing gifts identical to those found in such sanctuaries as *Fontes Sequanae*. I will give just one example, from Malta, where Melleiha Bay, a subterranean shrine to Mary, cut into the rock, is associated with a natural spring (Badger 1838: 286–7). The gifts which decorate the walls include wax or silver models of limbs, hearts or eyes, baby clothes, shoes, crutches, plaster-casts, X-rays, pictures of children, even crash-helmets: all offered to Mary in hope or thanksgiving. There is a legend that the statue of Mary was often moved to a more respectable place within the main church later built above the original shrine but that, during the night, she always moved back down the forty steps to her old position by the spring. The dedications have been taking place for more than two hundred years and probably much longer; the shrine itself is said to be eight hundred years old. The link between divine female presence, spring-water and healing, shown here, is indistinguishable from perceptions of pagan Celtic pilgrims in the early first millennium AD.

REFERENCES

Aebischer, P. 1930. 'La Divinité aquatiquae Telo et l'hydronomie de la Gaule', *Revue celtique* 47, 427–41.

Allason-Jones, L. 1989. *Women in Roman Britain*. London.

Ammianus Marcellinus. trans. J.C. Rolfe, ed. T.E. Page 1935. *Histories*. LCL. London and Cambridge, Mass.

Badger, G.P. 1838. *Description of Malta and Gozo*. Valleta.

Bradley, R. 1990. *The Passage of Arms*. Cambridge.

Clébert, J-P. 1970. *Provence antique 2: L'époque gallo-romaine*. Paris.

Cormick, F.M.C. 1991. 'The Dog in Prehistoric and Early Christian Ireland', *Archaeology Ireland* 5: 4, 7–9.

Cunliffe B.W. 1978. *The Roman Baths: A Guide to the Baths and Roman Museum*. Bath.

—— ed. 1988. *The Temple of Sulis Minerva at Bath 2: The Finds from the Sacred Spring*. Oxford University Committee for Archaeology 16. Oxford.

—— 1990. *The Roman Baths: A Guide to the Baths and Roman Museum*. Bath.

Cunliffe, B.W., and D. Davenport. 1985. *The Temple of Sulis Minerva at Bath 1: The Site*. Oxford University Committee for Archaeology 7. Oxford.

de Vries, J. 1963. *La Religion des Celtes*. Paris.

Dehn, W. 1941. 'Ein Quelheiligtum des Apollo und der Sirona bei Hochscheid', *Germania* 25, 104–11.

Deyts, S. 1976. *Dijon, Musée Archéologique: Sculptures gallo-romaines mythologiques et religieuses*. Paris.

—— 1983. *Les Bois sculptés des sources de la Seine, 42è supplément à Gallia*. Paris.

—— 1985. *Le Sanctuaire des sources de la Seine*. Dijon.

—— 1992. *Images des dieux de la Gaule*. Paris.

Diodorus Siculus, trans. C.H. Oldfather 1968. LCL. London and Cambridge, Mass.

Duval, P-M. 1976. *Les Dieux de la Gaule*. Paris.

Ehrenberg, M. 1989. *Women in Prehistory*. London.

Espérandieu, E. 1907–66. *Recueil général des bas-reliefs de la Gaule romaine et pré-romaine*. Paris.

Fitzpatrick, A.P. 1984. 'The Deposition of La Tène Iron Age Metalwork in Watery Contexts in Southern England', in B.W. Cunliffe & D. Miles (eds) *Aspects of the Iron Age in Central Southern England*. Oxford University Committee for Archaeology 2. Oxford. 178–90.

Green, M.J. 1986. *The Gods of the Celts*. Gloucester.

—— 1989. *Symbol and Image in Celtic Religious Art*. London.

—— 1991. *The Sun-Gods of Ancient Europe*. London.

—— 1992a: *Animals in Celtic Life and Myth*. London.

—— 1992b: *Dictionary of Celtic Myth and Legend*. London.

—— 1992c: 'The Pipeclay Figurines', in A. Taylor (ed.), *A Roman Lead Coffin with Pipeclay Figurines from Arrington*. Cambridgeshire Archeaology, Report no. 2. Cambridge.

Haselgrove, C. 1989. 'Iron Age Coin-Deposition at Harlow Temple, Essex', *Oxford Journal of Archaeology* 8: 1: 73–88.

Henig, M. 1988. 'Objects from the Sacred Spring', in B.W. Cunliffe (ed.), *The Temple of Sulis Minerva at Bath 2: The Finds from the Sacred Spring*, Oxford University Committee for Archaeology 16. Oxford. 5–26.

Jenkins, F. 1957. 'The Role of the Dog in Romano-Gaulish Religion', *Collection Latomus* 16; 60–76.

Jones, F. 1954. *The Holy Wells of Wales*. Cardiff.

Le Gall, J. 1963: *Alésia: Archéologie et histoire*. Paris.

MacCana, P. 1970. *Celtic Mythology*. London.

Marache, R. 1979. *Les Romains en Bretagne*. Rennes.

Mommsen, T. et al., eds 1863 – *Corpus inscriptionum Latinarum*. Berlin.

Musée Archéologique de Metz 1981. *La Civilisation gallo-romaine dans la cité des Médiomatriques*. Metz.

Pelletier, A. 1984. *La Femme dans la société gallo-romaine*. Paris.

Potter, T.W., & C.M. Johns. 1992: *Roman Britain*. London.

Sandars, N.K. 1984. Review of S. Deyts, *Les Bois sculptés des sources de la Seine*, in *Antiquity* 58, 148.

Schindler, R. 1977. *Führer durch des Landesmuseum, Trier*. Trier.

Szabó, M. 1971. *The Celtic Heritage in Hungary*. Budapest.

Thevenot, E. 1969. *Divinités et sanctuaires de la Gaule*. Paris.

Tomlin, R.S.O. 1988. 'Curse Tablets', in B.W. Cunliffe (ed.) *The Temple of Sulis Minerva at Bath 2: The Finds from the Sacred Spring*. Oxford University Committee for Archaeology 16. Oxford. 58–277.

Toussaint, M. 1948. *Metz à l'époque gallo-romaine*. Metz.

Valletin, F. 1879–80. 'Les Dieux de la cité des Allobroges, d'après les monuments épigraphiques', *Revue celtique* 4, 1–36.

Walker, D.R. 1988. 'The Roman Coins', in B.W. Cunliffe (ed.) *The Temple of Sulis*

Minerva at Bath 2: The Finds from the Sacred Spring. Oxford University Committee for Archaeology 16. Oxford. 281–358.

Wightman, E. 1970. *Roman Trier and the Treveri*. London.

Wuilleumier, P. 1984. *Inscriptions latines des trois Gaules*, 17è supplément à *Gallia*. Paris.

CHAPTER THREE

NOW YOU SEE HER, NOW YOU DON'T: SOME NOTES ON THE CONCEPTION OF FEMALE SHAPE-SHIFTERS IN SCANDINAVIAN TRADITION

—— •◆• ——

Catharina Raudvere

The abilities to change shape, and to act out of the body in its temporal guise, were vital to many different Norse myths and conceptions. Materialized will, power or lust was a common theme in many texts. Óðinn changed his shape to perform deeds for himself and others; witches and strong-minded women took revenge as night-hags on reluctant husbands and lovers.

We can ask with the French historian Paul Veyne whether the people of the North really believed in their myths. Were the stories of transformation considered realistic truths? Did people believe that a woman could act at night while her physical body lay sleeping at home, and in what sense might this be thought true? Writing of ancient Greek mythology, Veyne asks the further provocative questions: "What is to be made of this mass of nonsense? How can all this have a meaning, a motivation, a function, or at least a structure? The question of whether myths have an authentic content can never be put in positive terms' (1988: 2). These are questions we should never stop asking as long as we claim to analyse religious attitudes. What is meant by somebody holding a belief? Does it mean that people believe some fellow human beings can transform themselves and perform evil deeds in a temporary guise? Or were characters like this only metaphors and images for evil possibilities? Myths are one way of formulating valid, but not necessarily realistic, accounts of fundamental human conditions. Although I might appear to digress here from the given Goddess-theme, I would like to take the opportunity to discuss a darker side of Norse mythology and Scandinavian folklore: the supernatural as it was found in some women who knew more than other people and knew how to make use of their knowledge.

The mythological universe of the Norsemen, preserved in the lays of the *Poetic Edda* and through Snorri's writings, was inhabited by gods, goddesses, giants, dwarfs, elves, gnomes and other groups of creatures. Despite these several assemblies and their functions in the texts, a basic conflict appears between the structured Miðgarð, the home of gods and men, in sharp contrast to the chaotic Útgarð the world of demonic giants of different races. This fundamental strife is most thoroughly described in Snorri's *Edda*, but the oppositions are relevant for all Norse literature. Kirsten Hastrup has noted how the mythological universe mirrors the life of man: 'concepts of cosmology and of society were mutually-enforcing realizations of what seems to have been a basic conceptual structure' (1981: 63). And it must be remembered that the sources for our knowledge of Norse mythology are, to a considerable extent, poetry and art, not religious documents.

THE QUESTION OF BELIEF

While analysing texts on conceptions of the *mara*, the night-riding hag in Scandinavian folk-belief, I came across various early Nordic texts on shape-shifting. These made me realize that the cause of the metamorphosis was the core of many texts, not the *mara* herself. In all the disparate kinds of Norse texts, transformation is used as a plausible explanation for mishaps, illness and pain. The *mara* is certainly no goddess, nor a mythological being in the strict sense; she is, rather, spoken of as a temporarily transformed human being – more of a witch than a demon. Nevertheless, the legends and stories of her do connect with some of the mythological conflicts.

In the realistic Icelandic family sagas, people are said to perform deeds out of their bodies, without anything especially remarkable being made of this. In *Eyrbyggja saga* 16 a woman is taken to court accused of being a *mara* and in nightly guise having almost killed a young man. His relatives 'served a summons on Geirrid for being a night-witch and causing Gunnlaug bodily harm' (Pálsson and Edwards 1989). This incident has been called the first Scandinavian witch-trial and it demonstrates a pattern of social and erotic struggle combined with calumny, suspicion, frustration and insults found throughout the next thousand years in Scandinavian texts relating to shape-shifting. The district court summons is mentioned as something common, and clearly the accusation of shape-shifting was the ordinary solution. Under later Norwegian Christian laws it was also decreed that people who caused harm to men or cattle as night-riders should be fined. The reality of witchcraft was not questioned by the Church for several hundred years; rather, to the contrary, transformation was seen as one of many cunning ways of the Devil.

The problem of belief has puzzled many scholars within the field of Scandinavian studies, confronted with amazing episodes in sagas and myths, and the subject has been discussed from various points of view. Norse mythology is by no means a map of a concrete world, rather it is a guide to a mental universe. Hastrup sensibly states that in writing on Icelandic history, '"beliefs" are not an empirical category, because at the empirical level belief cannot be separated from knowledge' (1990: 197). Telling of shape-shifters was one way of expressing knowledge about the conditions of human existence.

Further, Hilda Ellis Davidson has pointed to some of the problems in interpreting texts on shape-shifting, and she views the transformers in the sagas more as literary characters:

> It would seem that on the whole the tales of shape-changers in the sagas are not told 'for true'. Their background may be realistic, but the tales themselves are not: they serve an artistic purpose, bringing a touch of fantasy, excitement, humour or horror into the saga according to the desire of the teller. They must, however, have their roots in popular tradition.
>
> (1978: 141)

Whether or not 'belief' can be traced, the question itself can be a treacherous one, and perhaps 'expressions of belief' is the limit for any interpretation.

The discussion on the concept of belief by the British anthropologist, Rodney Needham emanates from Wittgenstein's aphoristic question 'Ist der Glaube eine Erfahrung?' (Is belief an experience?). After a long exposition, Needham concludes that there might after all be something we can call 'belief':

> Perhaps, then, there is really some kind of inner state or process corresponding to the word 'belief', only one that we apprehend intuitively and which (like many sensations, emotions, and impulses) is recalcitrant to definition ... Statements of belief are the only evidence for the phenomenon; but the phenomenon itself appears to be no more than the custom of making statements.
>
> (1972: 106ff.).

Therefore, the praxis and the discourse are left for analysis.

Texts like myths and legends of course reflect reality, but they also create reality. In Norse texts shape-shifting is told of as if true and as though it serves to explain important things such as health, amorous capability, and strength. It is possible that there was more to the telling of the stories than amusement or a narrative purpose; why else would there be regulations against night-riding hags? Today, we are still confronted with contemporary fieldwork reports from Africa which tell not only of belief in shape-shifting but also of the experience of actual transformation.

ALTERATIONS IN GUISE

When reading Norse mythology and texts of Scandinavian folk-beliefs one encounters not only a shifting of guise but also abrupt disappearances, a sudden ability to fly, and different ways of expressing unique mental powers which imply specific conceptions of the human soul. Enigmatic emotions or a strong will, to take two examples, could take temporal form in a powerful guise. The *mara* texts had certain narrative advantages, since a shape-changer can disappear quickly, move across great distances in little time, or penetrate walls and locks where no one else can go. There are also psychological advantages, since the descriptions of the *mara* are broad enough to embrace personal experiences of nightmares and anxiety attacks.

Indices and catalogues of Nordic folklore archives link the *mara* and the werewolf in one section under the heading 'Transformed'. This connection arises from a solely southern Scandinavian tradition in which the two creatures appear in the same legend about the mother-to-be who tries to avoid delivery pains by magical means, and is in no way representative of the rest of Scandinavia:

> Those became *maras* and werewolves whose mothers were afraid of pains at childbirth and tried to evade them. If this was done the children were punished because in the Bible we read that a woman cannot give birth without pain. They may rid themselves of delivery pains by taking the foetal caul from a horse who has foaled and creeping through it, but the child they give birth to will be a werewolf if a boy and a *mara* if a girl.
>
> (NM EU 488, 12–13)[1]

This legend emphasizes the *mara* and the werewolf as involuntary victims of the mother's act; the compulsion towards transformation is a punishment and not an act of will. The heading 'Transformed' and the linking-together of the *mara* and the werewolf show that a distorted representation of *mara* traditions also needs to be considered. In most *mara* texts (legends, spells, apotropaic means, etc.) the motive for transformation is envy; malevolent thoughts are intentionally transferred into tangible form, and envy must be considered a factor of essential importance to the concepts of witchcraft and transformation (see Sehmsdorf 1988). The following story from Swedish Lappland is an evident example of how will and desire are used for destructive purposes:

> Old Stina was a dangerous woman. She came to my grandmother's cow barn once to help her with one of the cows which was calving. Stina wanted that calf but she did not get it. A few weeks later the calf died and so too the cow soon after. My grandmother was sure that Stina had killed them both with her envy.
>
> (Kvideland and Sehmsdorf 1988: 52)

Like many *mara* texts, the target of the old woman's desire is cattle and therefore has vast economic consequences. The acts are by no means emotional only; in this text envy is a very tangible experience.

The choice of terminology concerning alteration of appearance may cause some difficulties, since many alternative terms have been used: transformation, metamorphosis, shape-shifting and shape-changing. I use shape-shifting and shape-changing synonymously, and transformation as the wider concept of changing and shifting guise. Metamorphosis is more of a literary term to me, not applicable to mythology and folk-belief.

In *The Encyclopedia of Religion* James P. Carse gives an extensive definition of shape-shifting which reads: 'The alteration in form or substance of any inanimate object . . . can be caused either by the object changed or by an external force; it can occur for good or for ill and for reasons simple or profound' (1987: 225). This definition applies very well to the traditions of shape-shifters in Scandinavia from ancient to later centuries of folk-belief. The shape-shifters are said to be able to change in form or substance; they could appear in human form, or as animals, as objects, or just as a feeling of anxiety and horror. The *mara* could be a woman whose evil thoughts were given material form, or she could be the victim of a curse. However, the change always occurs for ill, the reasons for which may seem simple at one level, but are complex at another (as discussed below). Carse lists different types of shape-shifting: 'strategic deception', 'escape', 'punishment', 'liberation', 'immortalization', 'borderline and confused identities', and 'revelation'. Under 'borderline and confused identities' he writes of werewolves: 'some human beings could periodically pass into the form of a wolf' (1987: 228). Apparently he would regard the *mara* as a shape-shifter as well, but he makes no further comments on these kinds of sudden transformation.

The problem with Carse's definition is not that it is too wide, although he discusses such different subjects as the incarnations of Vishnu, Christ's resurrection and Ovid's metamorphoses in his article; but the fact that he makes no distinction between texts where changing guise is solely for narrative purposes, and those where the transformation is part of a system of plausible explanations and beliefs, can cause confusion. The lack of discussion of function is frustrating because it avoids a discussion of the meaning of the transformations. 'Borderline and confused identities', is a significant heading for shape-shifters in connection with witchcraft. They can appear in human shape, as objects or, by no means the least important, as strong and frightening emotions. In sharp contrast to mythological beings, many shape-shifters are told of as the people next door:

> In the old days there was a witch called Elin living at Västbo, and she was so skilled in magic she could milk any cow she chose, simply by hanging her garter from the roof.
>
> (Simpson 1988: 149)

This social interaction between neighbours forms the 'social correlate' with cosmology, as observed by Hastrup (1981). Shape-shifting is, in many Norse texts and other sources, closely connected with witchcraft and the special knowledge and gifts of certain persons. Writing on witchcraft beliefs, Mary Douglas describes some general characteristics which also throw light on the problems of shape-changing:

> to accuse of witchcraft is to accuse of evil practice on a cosmic scale. The witch is no ordinary thief, adulterer, or even common traitor. He is accused of a perverted nature, or of alliance with the enemies of human kind; in Europe with the Devil, on other continents with carnivorous predators. He is associated symbolically with the reverse of the way that a normal human lives, with night taking the place of day. His powers are abnormal, he can fly, be in two places at once, change his shape.
>
> (1992: 113).

I think it is reasonable to say that the realization of these perverted abnormal features is also a form of shape-changing; the *mara* texts tell of fellow human beings completely overtaken by irresistible desires. Three elements repeatedly appear in the apotropaic acts against the *mara*: warding-off, revealing the true identity, and, by no means least, punishment (Raudvere 1994). In this way, visible rituals confirm an invisible reality. Texts about witches, *mara*s, milk-stealers, Devils and other transformers connect social relations with fundamental conceptions of human life and the universe. In the end witchcraft and shape-shifting are questions of a fundamental ontological character.

The Devil played a vital part in European conceptions of witchcraft and shape-shifting. In scholastic theology, which had an immense influence on witch-hunters and demonologists over hundreds of years, the Devil was closer to matter than was God, who was perfect and complete above alteration. When closer to the material world the Devil constantly changed his form. Theological speculations regarding the Devil's multitude of disguises influenced and interacted with popular views. The general medieval image of the Devil was more of a comic fool than of a spiritual power, and in folk narrative he was in the end always cheated by the hero (Russell 1981; 1984). This figure played an important part in popular drama, story and legend. In Scandinavia the Devil grew more dangerous in popular opinion after the Reformation, although he still retained some of his old jocular traits. Since Old Nick was both amusing and evil, story-tellers and playwrights made use of the Devil's ability to change shape, and these ideas influenced the conceptions of other shape-shifters in folk-belief, on which theology also had a profound impact. In folk-belief all over Europe, supernatural beings including *mara* were supposed to have fallen like rain over the world as the Devil fell from Paradise. Like him, they were omnipresent and constantly threatening people.

NORSE SHAPE-SHIFTERS

Human shape-shifters are frequent in various kinds of Norse texts. There are different situations, mainly violent or amorous, and the shape-shifters' actions are predominantly evil. There are no moral judgements, no declaration that shape-shifting is either good or evil. It is the purpose of the act that determines which, although most act for personal gain. Not only humans change their shapes, but also the gods, notably Óðinn and Loki. Their temporary guises play an important role in the myths of the gods.

Special attention could be paid to female shape-shifters. By contrast to many of the male characters with the same abilities, the women act almost exclusively out of greed, envy, depravity, corruption and unrequited love. The stories of female shape-shifters are almost always connected with sexuality and witchcraft. This is clearly visible in the Icelandic family sagas, where many sequences fuse love and greed or envy.

A clear example can be found in *Kormáks saga* 18, where, out of envy, the wise-woman Torveig breaks up a young couple. As Kormák still rejects Torveig she pursues him to the sea, and approaches his ship in the shape of a walrus, but she is recognized by her eyes. While the sailors force the animal under the water, Torveig at home is at the same time said to be on her death-bed. People around her later conclude that her death was caused by the events at sea: the link between the two bodies, symbolized by Kormák's recognition of her eyes, is so strong that the human body cannot ward off the injuries inflicted upon the walrus. An analogous state prevails between the woman and the animal – a recurring theme in many texts about shape-shifting. More than Torveig's act of witchcraft itself, Kormák's counteraction forms the core of the text. He makes use of the knowledge of shape-shifting and the analogous link, and the original evil action turns out to be the victim's eventual salvation. This is a deeply essential point where literary descriptions connect with ritual practice. Apotropaic moves against evil-minded shape-shifters, returning dead, or assaulting demons are all based on the acceptance of such an analogous link. Strategies of this kind are also apparent in the obvious structural continuities. In apotropaic rituals, where unfamiliar objects close to livestock are cut, torn or broken while waiting for an unveiling, they also cause damage in the neighbourhood. A short legend from the Swedish west coast serves as an example of the sometimes unexpected result:

A shoemaker was working late at night when a cat came in. He took the last and hit the cat and broke her leg. In the morning one of his daughters had a broken leg.

(VFF 1650: 3)

47

'THE MAN WHO COULD TURN INTO AN ELEPHANT' VERSUS 'THE WOMAN WHO COULD TURN INTO A *MARA*'

Astonishingly, not many studies have been written on shape-shifting. When I came across Michael Jackson's article on Sierra Leone it was the first time I had read about transformation as an experience. In the article he tells of his encounters with a man who claimed that he could turn into an elephant. Jackson's questions and methods inspired me to try his approach on Scandinavian texts. His ideas are stimulating, but it must be remembered that there are considerable differences between today's Africa and ancient rural Scandinavia.

Jackson bases his analysis on fieldwork among the Kuranko and mainly on interviews with the man who experienced shape-shifting himself. In Scandinavia there are no such accounts of individual experiences, no narratives of personal experience of any alteration of bodily form, and no legends which deal with transformation itself. The Scandinavian sources are primarily documents from folklore archives, and all references to the context are constructions from historical sources. No fieldwork, therefore, can be done to corroborate the assumptions related to the Scandinavian texts.

In spite of these important differences between Jackson's sources and mine, there are also clear similarities in the conceptions of shape-shifting. In both, the conceptions are linked to 'tradition'; to the special knowledge of the wise, to the practice of ethno-medicine and acceptable explanations for things which happen. In both areas the connections with witchcraft for use and abuse are of great importance. And both are founded in oral tradition: 'hearsay evidence' as Jackson puts it (1990: 60), the strong authority of traditional knowledge. In Scandinavia, in the large corpus of extant texts dealing with shape-shifting, there are many narratives on personal experiences of meeting and seeing the *mara*, but none on being a *mara*, whereas elements of transformation appear frequently in the Kuranko myths and stories, where they are accepted as sensible truths. Jackson soon experienced how untenable it was to deny the phenomenon of transformation: 'Such scepticism has its place in academic discourse; among the Kuranko its social value is minimal' (1990: 63).

HOW PEOPLE COME TO BELIEVE IN SHAPE-SHIFTERS

Jackson's basic questions are: What are the grounds on which ideas of shape-shifters are accepted as true? What is their ontological status? There must be a world-view into which the transformation fits. In Scandinavian tradition the following assumptions are vital to understanding the veracity of shape-shifting: the soul can leave the body and assume a new and different shape; thoughts and feelings can take tangible form; and several different beings are associated with these conceptions, among them: *mara*, *häxa* (witch) *bjära* (milk-stealing witch), *manbjörn* (man–bear) etc. (Lindow 1978: 147ff.; Kvideland and Sehmsdorf 1988: 43ff.; Simpson 1988: 119ff.). The corpus of related texts tells us that within rural society it was not improbable for your neighbour's envy of your fine cattle to take the form of a *mara*. Yet, there are no reasons to believe that the world-views of rural populations in pre-industrial Scandinavia were less complex than our own, and one of the great advantages of Jackson's study is his use of proper philosophical terms instead of a misleading discussion based on true and false. Jackson tries in four different ways to meet questions about 'the connections under which the notion of shape-shifting could be entertained as reasonable and made intelligible and, most important, realized . . . as a sensible truth' (1990: 63).

When in search of the ontology of shape-shifting Jackson begins with the conception of personhood among the Kuranko and 'the ontological priority of social relationships over individual identity' (ibid.). The *mara* is not just the night-hag but, equally important, a human person in the close vicinity. If the *mara* is not defined as both the night-hag and the daytime woman there is a risk of obscuring the connections with witchcraft, and the purposes for alteration which I believe are a vital part of the *mara* traditions: a discussion of shape-shifting cannot be complete without questioning the components of personhood. A Swedish legend illustrates the problem. This relates how a farmer's horse was badly troubled by a *mara*. The farmer was so anxious about the horse that one night he tied sharpened scythe blades to the horse's back to protect it. The next morning he found his neighbour (either male or female) lying dead across the horse's back cut by the scythe blades. This legend describes a conflict between neighbours and a violent solution. It is a combination which connects the legend closely to other witchcraft texts; brutal force against the threat shows how real was the experience of the danger of witchcraft. The gravity with which the problem was regarded, the violence of the action, and the absolute link between the *mara* and the neighbour also connect the *mara* traditions with the wider concept of witchcraft.

Jackson makes an important remark on the belief that shape-shifting is grounded in 'ontology and world-view and does not derive its plausibility solely or directly from first-hand experience or hearsay accounts' (1990: 65). This is certainly also true about *mara* texts. The legends give not personal accounts but, rather, advice on how to protect against the *mara*'s assaults and other threats from witchcraft; these texts contain the most elaborate Scandinavian accounts of shape-shifting:

Witchcraft in rural Scandinavia was a system which defined man versus nature, social relations, man's relations with supernatural beings and powers, and related it to the every-day world. In all folklore recordings we can see a dynamic striving between the common ontological assumptions and individual experiences.

(Hastrup 1990: 212)

Encounters with the *mara* were, primarily, individual experiences of night-terrors and anxieties, and the conceptions behind this night-hag were part of a complex belief-system. The variety of expressions in the *mara* traditions shows how 'different individuals experience and construe the beliefs in different ways' (Jackson 1990: 65). The *mara* illustrates how common concepts of envy and witchcraft could be expressed in individual experiences, always within a local context but founded in a common worldview shared within society. Jackson states that there must always be a purpose behind shape-shifting (ibid.: 68), and legends of the *mara* always give a hint of malevolence:

On a farm both the cows and the horses were ridden by a nightmare. The owner of the animals was advised to keep watch so that nothing would enter the barn, but no matter, it was of no use. It was suggested that he clean everything so carefully that nothing remained inside with the animals. And so he did.

Then one night – it was a Saturday – he saw a piece of straw in the stall with a mare, and that piece of straw, he was quite sure, had not been there when he had cleaned everything up. So he took the piece of straw and set fire to it, putting out the fire while there was still something left of the straw. And on Sunday morning half the bedding of his daughter was found to be burned. Then she said that she never knew she had been the nightmare, but she had always felt tired and sick and had believed that she had been sleepwalking.

(Lindow 1978: 180–1)

Jackson's second approach to analysing transformation is through the critical context of belief; he discusses how beliefs in different situations and for different individuals have a very dissimilar veracity. In particular he mentions marginality and the social use of shape-shifting. Most legends appear within a context of conflict of power in which authority is executed with austere methods. Envy can be important in a society with limited resources, and we know that people regarded as witches were often in one way or another marginalized people, perhaps odd or peculiar, not fitting into the local definition of a 'normal' existence: people who, the rest of that society might believe, envied the rest: 'Envy is powerful. Some people once asked a witch whether she believed that there was magic. "No, I don't

believe so", she said, "but envy, envy! Envy will corrode even a stone"'
(Kvideland and Sehmsdorf 1988: 53).

Jackson also stresses shape-shifters as part of a historical context. There
are stories of them in the earliest recorded texts in Scandinavia. Myths in
the *Poetic Edda* and Snorri's *Edda*, as well as episodes in the sagas, deal
with various people's ability to change guise and appear in a new *hamr*
(skin) (see Davidson 1978). Personhood was expressed through a tangible
outside as well as an inner dimension, and a person who could practise
shape-shifting was *hamrammr*, with a special capacity, a strong *hamr*. *Hugr*,
the human mind, is a much more complex concept than the Christian view
of the soul; it refers to the totality of all human mental assets (thought,
will, feelings, desire, personhood), and, most importantly here, the *hugr*
could assume tangible form outside the body. Humans were shape-shifters
as well as the gods, particularly Óðinn and Loki, who could even change
sex; Loki disguised himself as an old woman when he tried to prevent
Baldr's return from the realm of the dead. Óðinn was the foremost *hamh-
leypa*, a being who leaves the body in a temporal *hamr*. Snorri tells in
Ynglinga saga how Óðinn lay as if dead or asleep while his *hugr* executed
various deeds for himself or for others in the shape of a bird, an animal,
a fish or a serpent. However, it should be noted that, in common with the
stories of humans, his regular body was left behind: only his soul assumed
the temporary shapes. This is prevalent in the Norse stories; there is never
any transformation with a complete disappearance of the ordinary body –
some part of it is always left behind.

There is an interesting stanza in *Hávamál* relating to Óðinn's ability to
hinder the souls of some night-hags (*túnriðor*) to get back to their regular
bodies. In Hollander's translation the lines read:

> ... if night-hags sporting
> I scan aloft in the sky:
> I scare them with spells   so they scatter abroad,
>   heedless of their hides,
>   heedless of their haunts.

This passage has received much attention, and in his commentary
Hollander writes of the 'hides' (*hamr*) in the fourth line: 'That is, of their
own "skins", or forms, which they leave behind on their rides. The incan-
tations cause the witches to forget both their original forms and their homes'
(Hollander 1962: 39).

The stanza is cryptic, as is the whole of *Hávamál*, but we can perceive
Óðinn's supreme power over the hags by means of spells, the spoken word.
A further description of shape-shifting can be found in the introductory
prose of *Vǫlundarkviða*, another poem from the *Poetic Edda*, where
Vǫlundr and his two brothers steal the swan-skins from three women said
to be Valkyries. These mythological females mostly serve Óðinn in Valhalla,

and in this text their inclusion is probably a way of saying that these were not ordinary women; nothing more is said about them or their origin, but they are forced to remain in human shape and marry the brothers. The motif is known from several fairy-tales from several continents, as well as from Scandinavian legends.

Jackson's last approach to the shape-shifters is the psychological and cross-cultural context. A common theme within shape-shifting texts is some kind of strong conflict and how to solve it. The *mara* was said to cause anxiety, pain and loss of breath on her nocturnal visits. She was an image of horror and danger in folk-literature; her assaults were always connected with feelings of solicitude and suffocation. The conflicts in the *mara* texts concern witchcraft, envy, greed – issues which can be described in social as well as cosmological terms – but there is also an explicit gender-conflict in the texts. Women especially are considered night-hags, connected with witchcraft, magic and milk-stealing. It is notable how violent are the operations executed against these female supernatural beings, in most cases by men. The question of gender in connection with witchcraft and shape-shifting is an intriguing matter. As Hastrup and others have shown, it was by no means only women who were accused of witchcraft, but the connection between women, sexuality and witchcraft appears to be a globally observed pattern.

GODS OF THE PAGANS, DEMONS OF THE CHURCH

Many continental pre-Christian gods became demons in Christian theology. Powers and abilities such as shape-shifting became unambiguously evil when treated by demonologists, and Scandinavia followed the rest of Europe in this process. João de Pina-Cabral writes: 'Those forces which had been the very basis of symbolic construction of the social order ... now became the enemies of the new order. A phantasmagoric anti-order was constructed, and upon its ruins the true order was raised' (1992: 45–6). And although the mythology and values of the old world were turned upside-down, a continuity in ritual praxis is apparent.

In the Middle Ages, theological systems were constructed to explain and unravel the demons' place in creation, and one central issue was whether witches and demons together formed a single one of the Devil's many ways to bring man to sin. If so, were demons to be regarded as actually existing, or were they merely a kind of superstition left from pagan times which made people fall away from the Christian faith? The changes in attitude towards these issues were complex during the Middle Ages and the Renaissance. Not least did beings like *incubus* and *succubus* attract the attention of the demonologists. Like the Scandinavian *mara*, they are described as sexually active and with the ability to change shape. The *incubus* was the male demon seducing women, while the *succubus*, (more properly *succuba*) was the female counterpart.

Discussions on the various categories of demons varied widely, from pious expositions on the intrusion of evil into the world, to detailed and coarse stories of the deeds of the demons. Many scholars, both traditionalists and modernists, have observed parallels between the demons of antiquity and the Scandinavian spirits of the night. Those most commonly mentioned are the Greek Ephialtes, who pressed upon and tormented humans during sleep; Hecate with her attendants and followers, who scourged the night; the Greek seducer, Pan, and his Roman equivalent, Silvanus; and the female demons of Semitic mythology, such as Lilith. These indeed show many similarities with the tradition of the *mara* in their character and actions.

Demonology and theories about angels and spirits were most important to theological education. Continental demonology began from a long scholastic discussion about non-human beings: whether they existed; if they did, whence they came; their status and independence in relation to the Devil. These are questions close to the problem of theodicy: why is evil in the world, in what ways do evil powers afflict people, and how can man resist them? It would lead too far into digression to try to account here for the question of demons and their origin in the history of ideas, but I wish to emphasize that even the learned elite, who affected the dogmatic development of the Church and the education of clerics, viewed supernatural beings as truly existing, with the potential to affect everyday life. One example is the question whether demons can beget children by humans, originating from an interpretation of Genesis 6:1-4, which ends:

> The Nephilim were on the earth in those days, and also afterward, when the sons of God came in to the daughters of men, and they bore children to them. These were the mighty men that were of old, the men of renown.

The question of the nature of such offspring and their relationship to angels was discussed in detail by the Fathers of the Church. The view of Augustine that demons, hags and their equivalents could be begotten in this way maintained a strong position among Catholics and subsequently Protestants alike – and was commonly referred to, not least by Lutheran orthodoxy (Cohn 1975: 175, 210–11, 234).

In the countryside parish clergymen were often themselves farmers' sons and, both before and after the Reformation, lived in a society where theologians discussed whether demons could breed offspring by humans, including the popular tradition of the *mara*, Elfwomen and Merwomen seducing men. From being a power able either to protect or to assault human beings, the shape-shifters became subject matter for a witch-crazed bureaucracy.

In the pre-Christian texts there are no moral judgements, no declaration that shape-shifting in general is either good or evil; it is the purpose of the act that determines which, although, as already said, most shape-shifters act for personal gain.

SOME FINAL REMARKS

By focusing on categories other than those commonly discussed as mythology in Scandinavian tradition I hope to have brought to attention the connection between mythology and cosmology on one hand, and between social and ritual praxis on the other. As Davidson writes in her article on the different names of were-animals:

> The use of these terms indicates that magic powers and powers beyond the ordinary were associated in some way with a change of form and possibly with the taking on of the animal shape, but it is not easy to know how far this is a metaphorical use of language and how far belief in an actual change of appearance is involved.
>
> (1978: 126)

We can never give any finite answer to the question whether the stories of the shape-shifters were believed in or not. But the texts, of widely varying origins, are the sources from which we can construct a world-view where shape-shifting gods and humans were a reasonable truth. The existence of shape-shifters cannot be reduced to questions about belief. There were other dimensions. The *mara* was an experience of anxiety, a cause of illness and misfortune, a conduit for social frustration, and an image for basic conceptions of cosmology and anthropology: i.e. the hag's ability to leave the body. Telling of the *mara* could, therefore, when part of a living oral tradition, serve several functions at the same time.

> To turn to Paul Veyne again, writing about the modalities of belief: 'But suppose that, instead of a cause, corrected by contingency, we have elasticity and a polygon with an indefinite number of sides (for often the sides will be counted in the retrospective light of the event). The resulting event is active. Like a gas, it occupies all the space left free between the causes, and it occupies them rather than not occupying them. History expends itself for nothing and fails to meet its own needs.
>
> (1988: 38)

NOTES

1   Translations are by the author unless otherwise stated.

REFERENCES

Manuscripts

NM EU   Nordiska museet, Stockholm.
VFF   Dialekt-och folkminessamlingen, Göteborg.

Books

Carse, J.P. 1987. 'Shape Shifting', in *Encyclopedia of Religion* 13, 225–9. New York.
Cohn, N. 1975. *Europe's Inner Demons*. London.
Davidson, H.E. 1978: 'Shape-Changing in Old Norse Sagas', in J.P. Porter & W. Russell (eds), *Animals in Folklore*. London. 126–42.
Douglas, M. 1992. *Risk and Blame*. London.
Eyrbyggja saga, trans. H. Pálsson and P. Edwards 1989. London.
Hastrup, K. 1981: 'Cosmology and Society in Medieval Iceland', *Ethnologia Scandinavica* 11, 63–78.
—— 1990. *Nature and Policy in Iceland 1400–1800*. Oxford.
Jackson, M. 1990. 'The Man Who Could Turn into an Elephant: Shape-Shifting among the Kuranko of Sierra Leone', in *Personhood and Agency*. Uppsala Studies in Cultural Anthropology 14. Uppsala. 59–78.
Kormáks saga, ed. Einer Ól. Sveinsson 1939. Íslenzk fornrit 8. Reykjavík.
Kvideland, R., & H.K. Sehmsdorf 1988. *Scandinavian Folk-Belief and Legend*. Minneapolis, Minn.
Lindow, J. 1978. *Swedish Legends and Folktales*. Berkeley, Calif.
Needham, R. 1972. *Belief, Language and Experiences*. Oxford.
Pina-Cabral, J de 1992. 'The Gods of the Gentiles', in K. Hastrup (ed.), *Other Histories*, London. 45–61.
Poetic Edda, The, trans. And ed. L.M. Hollander 1962. Austin, Tx.
Raudvere, C. 1993. *Föreställningar om maran i nordisk folktro*. Lund Studies in History of Religions 1. Lund.
—— 1994. 'Analogy Narratives and Fictive Rituals: some Legends of the *Mara* in Scandinavian Folk-Belief' *ARV* 50, 91–115.
Russell, J. 1981. *Satan*. Ithaca, NY.
—— 1984. *Lucifer*. Ithaca, NY.
Sehmsdorff, H.K. 1988. 'Envy and Fear in Scandinavian Folk Tradition', *Ethnologia Scandinavica* 18, 34–42.
Simpson, J. 1988. *Scandinavian Folktales*. London.
Snorri Sturlusson, ed. B. Aðalbjarnarson 1941. *Heimskringla: 'Ynglinga saga'*. Íslensk fornrit 26. Reykjavik.
Veyne, P. 1988. *Did the Greeks Believe in their Myths?* Chicago, Ill.

CHAPTER FOUR

FREYJA AND FRIGG

——— .•. ———

Stephan Grundy

Although most of Scandinavia's myths focus on the deeds of those two great gods Óðinn and Þórr, nevertheless there are at least two female figures who play a fairly prominent role in the Eddas: Freyja and Frigg. The two of them seem to have little in common: Frigg appears as Óðinn's wife, patroness of the home, and a relative model of social virtue. It might be somewhat rash to state that Frigg is the Mother Goddess of the north, but she is certainly a maternal figure in the myth in which she plays the most active part – the story of Balder's death, where she tries to protect him from all harm. The kenning Friggjar niðjar (descendants of Frigg) is used for the gods in general in Egill Skalla-Grímsson's *Sonatorrek* – written in the mid- to late tenth century – so her maternal character is clear (Jónsson 1967–73: B I, 34). Freyja, on the other hand, is sexually very free and active. Many of her activities, such as the practice of *seiðr* (magic), put her firmly outside the sphere of normal society; she might be called the 'wild woman' of Northern myth.

However, Frigg and Freyja share certain characteristics which cast doubt on the original distinction between them. Both of them have falcon cloaks, which each of them lends to Loki in a time of need, and both are possessors of jewellery obtained by unchastity. Frigg is well documented as Óðinn's wife, not only in the Old Norse materials, but also in the *Origio gentis Langobardorum* (Waitz 1873: 2–3), while Snorri describes Freyja as the wife of Óðr, who often wandered on long journeys and left her weeping to search for him. Snorri does not identify Óðr with Óðinn but, as pointed out by Jan de Vries among others, there is little doubt that the two were originally the same: a similar doublet appears with the names of the gods Ullr and Ullin (1956: II, 104). The name Óðinn is simply an adjectival form of Óðr (see Britt Mari Näsström, p. 69 below), suggesting, as de Vries stated, that Óðr was most probably the elder form (1931: 33). This in turn suggests that Snorri's account may have unknowingly preserved an older myth of Freyja as the wife of Óðr, or that Snorri, in his desire to present a coherent and systematic mythology, used the two forms to emphasize the distinction between Frigg, the wife of Óðinn, and Freyja, the wife of someone else.

The problem of whether Frigg and Freyja may have been a single goddess originally is a difficult one, made more so by the scantiness of pre-Viking Age references to Germanic goddesses, and the diverse quality of the sources. The best that can be done is to survey the arguments for and against their identity, and to see how well each can be supported.

The most telling similarity between Frigg and Freyja lies in the tales of them bartering their bodies for jewellery. In *Sǫrla þáttr*, Freyja is Óðinn's faithless mistress, who sold her body to four dwarves for a remarkable necklace, which Loki then steals at Óðinn's command (*Flateyjarbók* 1860: I, 275–6). In Saxo's *Gesta Danorum*, Frigga suffers the embraces of a servant so that he will take the gold from the statue of Othinus (Óðinn) for her own jewellery, whereupon the god departs in anger at the double insult to his image and his bed (Saxo/Olrik 1931: XXV). It seems clear that either a single myth has been duplicated for Óðinn's two women, or else Óðinn's original wife has been separated into two goddesses, both of whom retain the attribute of the necklace and its associated infidelity with a person or persons of lower social status – a particularly obnoxious act.

Although both versions were written down by antiquarians, and neither can be considered totally reliable, some elements of the *Sǫrla þáttr* version of the story can be verified as stemming from the heathen period. In the ninth-century poem *Haustlöng*, Þjóðólfr ór Hvini calls Loki 'thief of Brísingamen' (Finnur Jónsson 1967–73: 16) and in *Húsdrápa*, Úlfr Úggason describes Heimdallr battling with Loki over a jewel, which Snorri claims is Brísingamen (ibid.: 128). Snorri also mentions that Heimdallr can be called 'recoverer of Freyja's necklace', though he does not cite a particular skald's usage (1966: 1, 264). The *Sǫrla þáttr* account ends differently from the tale described by Snorri; the necklace incident is related as a prelude to the tale of the Everlasting Battle on Hoy, which Freyja instigates at Óðinn's command to recover her necklace. Since this version appears nowhere else, and the relative antiquity of the alternative version is attested, it seems probable that the *Sǫrla þáttr* composer instigated the battle as a penance to bridge these two ancient stories. Certainly, in the oldest account of this battle – that of the ninth-century *Bragi inn gamli* – there is no reference to godly intervention (Jónsson 1967–73: BI, 1–4). However, there is no reason to doubt the basic tale of the winning and theft of the necklace; and since the Brísingamen is attributed to Freyja wherever it is mentioned, the authenticity of the myth as a story of Freyja is difficult to doubt.

By contrast, whatever tale of the Norse gods lay behind Saxo's version of the infidelity story, it must have undergone considerable alteration to appear in the form in which he presented it. Certainly there are no other instances of gods despoiling one another's shrines anywhere else in the Norse corpus, and this seems a wholly unlikely element of authentic myth. It may also be noted that Saxo does not seem to have known of the existence of Freyja, although he mentions her male twin, Freyr, a number of times. Given his tendency to moralize at every turn, it seems unlikely that he would have left such a fruitful field as Freyja's sexuality unploughed had he known of her; whereas it is probable that the author of *Sǫrla þáttr*, who does not mention Frigg, did at least know the antiquarian pantheon as presented by Snorri. He certainly does not say at any point that Freyja is Óðinn's wife; only that Óðinn 'loved Freyja greatly because she was fairest of all women at that time' (*Flateyjarbók* 1860: II, ch. 228, p. 275). In fact, Saxo is by no means a reliable source for Norse myth, although his source-material was extremely wide-ranging and in some instances, such as the story of Balder, seems to have preserved valid alternative accounts of the myths known from Iceland. Such elements of authenticity as survived in his work did so in spite of the process of transmission and his extremely heavy editorial hand. Thus, although the possibility that Saxo's account of Frigg's infidelity was based on a genuine heathen legend cannot be altogether rejected, it cannot be considered as substantiative evidence in and of itself.

Snorri, writing some two hundred years after the conversion of Iceland, has no doubt that Frigg and Freyja are two different goddesses, but matches them as equals in oddly ambiguous terms: 'Frigg is the most excellent ... Freyja is the most glorious together with Frigg; she was wedded to that man who is called Óðr (Snorri 1966: I, 114). Since Snorri is often suspected of giving to the myths of his heathen ancestors a structure and specificity which they may have originally lacked, he might also be suspected of clarifying a previously opaque division between the two chief goddesses (or names or aspects of a single goddess) of the Northern folk. However, the mid-twelfth-century skald Einarr Skúlason referred to Freyja as 'Óðs beðvina' (Óðinn's bed-friend) in his *Øxarflokkr* (Jónsson 1967–73: BI, 449); and 'Óðs mær' (Óðinn's maid) is given to the giants in *Vǫluspá* 25 (Neckel and Kühn 1962: 6) a description also found for Freyja in Snorri's account of the building of the walls of Asgarðr and in þrymskviða. This suggests that the distinction between 'wife of Óðr' and 'wife of Óðinn' existed at least as early as the conversion of Iceland, if the general opinion that *Vǫluspá* dates from roughly 1000 CE is correct. Further, the name Óðr is nowhere identified as a by-name of Óðinn; it does not appear in the *þulur* (lists of poetic names), nor anywhere else apart from the connection with Freyja. The absence from the *þulur* and related materials such as the list of Óðinn-names in *Grímnismál* might be explained by the obvious relationship with Óðinn; however, the name Óðinn itself is listed among the rest of Óðinns *heiti* (by-names) as are other doublets such as Herjan and Herjafǫðr, or Sigfǫðr and Siggautr. The absence of the name Óðinn from kennings except in the context of Freyja at least suggests that Óðr was not a common name for Óðinn. It is conceivable that Óðr might have been invented as a separate figure in the Christian period; but this is implausible since the independent Wod also survives in Wild Hunt folklore as far south as Switzerland. This evidence thus seems to suggest that the distinction between the 'wife of Óðr' and the 'wife of Óðinn' may be archaic: that is, pre-dating the Viking Age.

One of the chief arguments against a single identity for Frigg and Freyja is that of their pedigrees: Frigg is the daughter of Fjörgynn, a god whose precise nature is unknown: de Vries suggests the probability that this name was a masculine doublet of the feminine Fjörgyn – a name given to Þórr's mother, Earth. Alternatively it could have been the name of an earlier, perhaps pre-Germanic, thunder-god (de Vries 1956: II, 275). Frigg is always counted among the Æsir, never among the Vanir, who are carefully noted as a quite different race of gods. Freyja, however, is firmly classed among the Vanir; she is the twin sister of Freyr, born of Njörðr and Njörðr's unnamed sister according to *Lokasenna* 36 (Neckel and Kühn 1962: 101). This firmly rooted distinction of race between Freyja and Frigg would seem to establish them as basically different in kind as well as in person. However, the identification of Frigg's father as Fjörgynn when a feminine Fjörgyn, who seems to be the personified earth, also exists, raises some suspicion when Freyja's parents are considered. The Old Norse Njörðr is a regular development from the name Nerthus, whom Tacitus in the first century CE described in *Germania* 40 as Terra Mater (Tacitus/Hutton 1980: 196). Much has been made of this apparent change in sex; however, given the well-documented existence of the twins Freyr and Freyja, as well as several other male/female pairs (see below) and the reference to Njörðr getting children on his sister, it is plausible that Njörðr and Nerthus could have represented another such pair. If that is so, and if we accept Tacitus' description of Nerthus as Mother Earth, then it requires little ingenuity to see the pair Fjörgyn/Fjörgynn as possible alternatives for Nerthus/Njörðr, and thus to identify Frigg with Freyja. This cannot stand alone as proof that Frigg is of Vanic origin, and there are other difficulties with this association which I will discuss later on; but it does present a substantial hindrance to the use of the As/Van distinction alone in differentiating the two goddesses.

The second major argument against their original identity is that of the two goddesses' distinctive characterization and functions in the Norse myths. Frigg is a virtual paradigm of wife and mother. Except in Saxo's tale, she appears to be chaste; no discussion of her lovers or scandalous behaviour has come down to us, although in *Lokasenna* 26 Loki says to Frigg that she 'has ever been greedy for men' (Neckel and Kühn 1962: 101) and accuses her of having slept with Óðinn's brothers, Vili and Vé. Snorri's account, however, may clarify this accusation: in *Ynglinga saga* 3, he tells us that Óðinn's brothers ruled in the god's absence while he was journeying, and shared Frigg between them, but that Óðinn took his wife back when he returned (Snorri/Finnur 1923). In this case the possession of Frigg seems to be part and parcel of the possession of the realm; therefore she can hardly be blamed for unchastity. Frigg appears as a protective wife in *Vafþrúðnismál*, which begins with Óðinn asking Frigg's advice about visiting the giant Vafþrúðnir; she replies that she would rather have him at home, but blesses him when he insists on going (Neckel and Kühn 1962: 45). One of Frigg's by-names is Hlín, the Protector and, as discussed earlier, she appears as the protector of her doomed son, Balder. As seen in the prose to *Grímnismál*, Frigg may act as a patronness to a chosen human, but her role is a maternal one again – she is Agnarr's foster-mother. Frigg appears specifically as a goddess of maternity in *Völsunga saga,* where Rerir and his wife call on her for a child. In German folklore, Friday, though otherwise unlucky, is thought the best day for marriages, which de Vries attributes to the influence of Frija (1956: II, 306).

By contrast to Frigg, Freyja is a goddess of considerable and free sexuality: in *Lokasenna* 30, Loki says of her that she has slept with 'all gods and elves' in the hall (Neckel and Kühn 1962: 102). The tale of her selling her affections to four dwarves for the Brísingamen has already been mentioned, and when she appears in *Hyndluljóð* as the patron goddess of the hero Óttarr, she is not his foster-mother, but his lover (Neckel and Kühn). Her patronage is also apparently, like Óðinn's, as dangerous as it is protective: Hyndla accuses her of riding Óttarr (whom she transformed into a boar) on his *valsinni*, a journey to be slain. Only once, in *Oddrúnargrátr*, does she appear as a patroness of childbirth; a prayer to help in giving birth calls on 'kind wights / Frigg and Freyja / and many gods' (Neckel and Kühn: 235). This poem, however, is often thought to be among the youngest of the Eddic lays. Jónas Kristjánsson perceives the general influence of Christianity in its lack of power and drama (1988: 64), while Hollander comments that the invocation of 'Frigg and Freyja' in it is probably a deliberate archaism introduced to give the poem a heathen flavour (1962: 279), so that this instance of Freyja as a birth-goddess must be regarded as somewhat spurious. Another of the clearest distinctions between Frigg and Freyja, in their mythic function, is Freyja's role as the object of attention from giants: according to Snorri, she is part of the price asked by the giant who rebuilds the walls of Asgarðr (1966), and in *þrymskviða*, the giant Ðrymr, who has stolen Ðórr's hammer, will return it only if he is given Freyja in return (Neckel and Kühn: 112). The implication of these myths is that Freyja is available; Frigg, by contrast, is apparently secure in the position of Óðinn's wife.

Freyja is also associated with magic in a way that Frigg is not. In *Vǫluspá*, a mysterious witch called Gullveig (possibly meaning the intoxication of gold) brings trouble among the Æsir; later she travels under the name of Heiðr, practising *seiðr*. In *Ynglinga saga* 4, Snorri says specifically that Freyja first taught this art to the Æsir (ed. Finnur 1923). Whether he had more information than we have or was simply extrapolating from *Vǫluspá* we do not know, but little serious argument, if any, has been raised for the identification of Gullveig/Heiðr with Freyja. Frigg, by contrast, may have the prophetic capabilities which distinguished Germanic women of rank – according to *Lokasenna* 29 she 'knows all fates . . . though she does not herself speak' (Neckel and Kühn: 102) – but she never practises magic in the Old Norse sources.

Freyja is certainly a goddess of wealth: most skaldic references to her are based on her association with treasure. Gold is Freyja's tears; a precious object is referred to as her daughter. Einarr Skulason says in *Øxaflokkr* that 'Freyr's niece [either Hnoss or Gersimi] bears her mother's eyelash-rain' (Finnur 1967–73: B I, 450) which means 'there is gold on the precious object'. In ordinary usage both names, Hnoss and Gersimi, Freyja's daughters according to Snorri's *Edda*, meant treasure. This makes it not only possible, but likely, that the identification of these as Freyja's daughters was a simple product of poetic convention in which Freyja was recognized as the source of treasure: perhaps as the weeper of golden tears, perhaps as a goddess ruling over wealth. The role of a deity of riches is something which Freyja has in common with Óðinn; he possesses the arm-ring Draupnir, which drips eight gold rings of weight equal to its own every ninth night, and Freyja herself mentions in *Hyndluljóð* 2 that he is a giver of gold (Neckel and Kühn: 288); but there are no such tales in relation to Frigg.

In several ways Freyja seems much more like a feminine counterpart of Óðinn than does Frigg: both Freyja and Óðinn generate gold and magicians, both are wanderers and free with their personal favours. Further, Freyja also appears to function as a battle-goddess and goddess of death, which Frigg apparently does not. The name of Freyja's hall, Fólkvangr, means 'Army-Plain'; it is, in fact, a battlefield, and *Grímnismál* 14 tells us that Freyja chooses half the slain every day, while Óðinn has the other half (Neckel and Kühn). Freyja's particular interest in collecting warriors does seem to imply a role as battle-goddess, as other references to the Norse afterlife imply that the dead go where they are best suited – either to join their kin, or to the hall of the god who corresponds to their social and personal status. The fact that Freyja and Óðinn share a function as apparent equals lends some plausibility to the theory that Freyja might originally have been seen as the wife of Óðinn. However, it must also be noted that the Norse gods often duplicate functions, particularly between the Vanir and the Æsir: for instance, Njörðr and Þórr are both called on for good winds at sea; Freyr and Óðinn are both closely associated with kingship and both are battle-gods. Thus the account of Freyja and Óðinn sharing out the slain could also be interpreted as reflecting a function common to both the Vanic and the Æsic pantheons.

Regarding the opposite argument, possible support for the close identity of Frigg and Freyja may be found in the fact that they appear together in only two Eddic poems, *Oddrúnagrátr* (discussed above) and *Lokasenna*

(Neckel and Kühn). The age of *Lokasenna* is more open to debate than that of *Oddrúnagrátr*: on the one hand it has been argued that the satirical treatment of the gods suggests a Christian author; on the other, the language and meter suggest an early date (Kristjánsson/Foote 1988: 39), and Gurevich puts forward the theory that this mockery 'should be interpreted not as a sign of the "twilight" of paganism, but as a mark of its strength' (1992: 167). In either case the poem seems to have preserved a quantity of ancient lore, and cannot be dismissed too lightly. Though the names of the two goddesses are not mentioned together in *Grímnismál* or *Vǫluspá*, these poems do seem to contain references to both deities. In *Grímnismál*'s extensive categories of gods and their dwellings only Freyja is named directly; but Sága, who drinks with Óðinn in Sökkvabekkr, may be a by-form of Frigg used for alliterative purposes (though Frigg's own name is used to alliterate with that of her hall, Fensalir, in *Vǫluspá*). Hollander suggests that the names of the two halls, Sunken-benches and Fen-Halls, may be compared (1962: 55), and the verse itself suggests a close permanent relationship between Sága and Óðinn: 'Sökkvabekkr hight the fourth . . . where Óðinn and Sága drink through all days, glad, out of golden cups' (*Grímnismál* verse 7, Neckel and Kühn: 58)). In *Vǫluspá*, only Frigg is mentioned by name, but the giving of 'Óðr's maid' to the giants is also described, as is the mysterious witch Gullveig/Heiðr. Snorri recounts the former story with Freyja as the prize; and, as previously mentioned, there is little dispute regarding the theory that Gullveig/Heiðr is also a form of Freyja. The question of the religious orientation of *Vǫluspá*'s author is generally considered to be mixed; either he was a heathen affected by Christian millenarian theology, or a Christian still steeped in ancestral lore. This and the poem's probable date have raised numerous questions regarding its accuracy as a reflection of heathen eschatological belief, but the veracity of the earlier half is seldom called into question.

In skaldic poetry Freyja and Frigg are portrayed as decidedly different persons. Óðinn is *Friggs faðmbyggvi* (dweller in Frigg's embrace) in one of the earliest surviving skaldic poems, the early tenth-century *Haraldskvæði*. And I have already mentioned the late tenth-century kenning, 'descendants of Frigg', for the gods. Although both Freyja and Frigg are used as parts of kenning for 'woman', the same can be said of all the goddesses and valkyries. Other than that, they do not overlap: Frigg is referred to in terms of her family relationships such as Óðinn's wife, Baldr's mother, and mother of the gods; clearly distinct from Freyja, 'Óðr's maid', Njörðr's daughter and Freyr's sister. In fact, according to Snorri, Freyja's Vanic origin is strongly emphasized by such descriptives as 'Van-Bride' and 'Vanað's'; and Freyja's most common appearance in skaldic poetry is in kennings for gold, as discussed earlier, whereas Frigg has no such connections.

Therefore, as far as the surviving Old Norse literary materials are concerned, it seems quite clear that Freyja and Frigg were firmly differentiated in antiquarians' accounts and probably also in the Viking Age. However, this could have been a property of the myth-making process: a tale requires a definite subject, and myth is by no means guaranteed to reflect with total accuracy either common belief or cultic practice. It remains plausible that poets and story-tellers might have exaggerated the distinction between two aspects of Óðinn's wife to suit their narrative purposes – the more so in those sources I have referred to, which probably stem from the post-heathen period, when the narrative value of the tales in question was more important than the description of actual religious belief. Compounds of Frigg as place-names are relatively few, while there are a great many that appear to be compounds of Freyja. (The difficulty of distinguishing between the name-elements Freyja and Freyr confuses the issue considerably, since we know that Freyr was one of the more popular gods.) At least it can be said that there is no significant regional distinction between Frigg, and Freyja/Freyr compounded place-names, which would otherwise have argued for a common identity between Frigg and Freyja.

One major and seldom-discussed point is that raised by Adam of Bremen's account of the heathen temple at Uppsala. According to him, the three great god-images in it were those of Þórr, with his sceptre; Wodan, armed for battle, and Fricco, distributing peace and pleasure among men, whose idol is fashioned with a gigantic "priapus". 'If plague and famine threaten, a libation is poured to the idol Þórr; if war, to Wotan; if marriages are to be celebrated, to Fricco' (Tschan 1959: 207–8). For several reasons the last is generally identified with Freyr. Firstly, Þórr, Óðinn and Freyr seem to have been the most popular gods of the Viking Age, both in myth and cult. Freyr is especially associated with Sweden – Uppsala in particular; it is, therefore, natural to assume that his statue would hold one of the three high places at the great temple there. Further, Snorri tells us, in his *Edda* and in *Ynglinga saga*, that Freyr is the god to call upon 'for prosperity and peace', and that he rules over 'rain and sunshine, and thus ... the produce of the earth' (1966: I, 96). However, it is impossible to derive the name Fricco from Freyr, for, as Paul Bibire has pointed out to me, Fricco is a regular Latin derivation of what would have been the weak masculine form of Frigg. This raises the possibility that Adam of Bremen, or one of his informants, knew of an Old Norse god called *Friggi. If this god were identical with Freyr, there would be fairly conclusive evidence for an original sole identity for Frigg and Freyja, as it seems extremely unlikely that a goddess would share a name with a god to whom she bore no relationship; or that a single god would be the masculine half of two distinct male/female doublets. As the root word had already ceased to be productive, it is impossible that *Friggi could be a title: it must have been either a personal name, preserved for some centuries, or a secondary formation from the name Frigg. The presence of the doublet relationship is not in itself sufficient proof that *Friggi/Frigg is identical with Freyr/Freyja; there are other examples, both from the Vanic cult (the probable doublets of Njörðr with Nerthus and Fjörgyn with Fjörgynn) and among the Æsir, where a goddess Zisa – etymological double of Tyr or Ziw – appears to have been worshipped in the area of Augsburg (Grimm/Stallybrass 1966: I, 291–9). As with his translation of Óðinn as Wodan, Adam would have used German forms when he knew them. Further, he did not attempt to Latinize either Þórr or Wodan; therefore it is reasonable to accept his lack of Latinization of *Friggi. However, since the Friccotype names not only appear in Old High German and were not particularly rare (see *Zweite Merseburger Zaubersprach*: Braune 1979: 89), there is a degree of uncertainty as to whether Adam actually knew a form *Friggi or whether he used Fricco as a German form, from a confused knowledge of the pantheon.

One of the chief arguments in favour of the theory that the name Freyja was a later development of Frigg is the fact that Freyja's name is not attested anywhere outside Scandinavia, whereas Frigg's appears in the *Origio gentis Langobardorum* (see above), in the Old High German *Zweite Merseburger Zauberspruch* (Braune 1979) and in the Old English Frig-dæg (Friday). It is also possible, though not proven, that the influence recurs in the place-names Freefolk, Frethern, Frobury, Froyle and Friden (Wilson 1992: 21). The spread certainly implies that a common Germanic goddess *Frijjo was known. Although it is always dangerous to argue from silence, we can say that there is no evidence for a common Germanic goddess *Fraujon. If Freyja were an ordinary sort of name, or even descriptive, as for example Wodan the furious, and Frija the beloved, this might be taken as suggesting that she was a different figure. However, since the name is a distinct title, the Lady, it is possible that, originally, Freyja had another personal name. From the evidence of the names it is entirely plausible that Óðinn's wife could have been given the title (and possibly taboo-name) Freyja in Scandinavia. The survival of the feminine form of Freyja as the ordinary title *frau* until the modern period suggests that the process in Scandinavia did not happen on the continent, and also that an independent goddess Freyja was not known there. (By contrast, *fro*, and probably the Gothic equivalent, *frauja*, were almost certainly used not as a specific god's taboo name but with a definite connotation of religious, as well as secular, authority in the native culture, the former surviving only in certain formulaic expressions and as a plural adjective (Green 1965). In Scandinavia, of course, the titles Freyr and Freyja must have dropped from ordinary use at quite an early date, as they do not appear in a human context (with the sole exception of the half-kenning title *húsfreyja*, for housewife).

The main difficulty in evaluating the absence of Freyja from most of the Germanic world where Frigg was known is the matching absence of evidence for any of the other deities from her family of gods, the Vanir, in the same areas. The origin of the distinction between the Æsir and the Vanir is uncertain; but whether they are pre-Indo-European deities or Indo-European fertility gods, the tribal division is likely to be ancient, as is the name, which is difficult to analyse etymologically. Finding the Vanic gods themselves outside Scandinavia is problematical. Nerthus, the Terra Mater of the North Sea Germans, whose name or its masculine equivalent developed into ON Njörðr, father of Freyja and Freyr, does not appear south of the North Sea; but the question of whether the god who was given the title, Freyr, in Scandinavia was known elsewhere in the Germanic world is somewhat more thorny. If he is the same god as Ing or *Ingwaz (for which there is a reasonable, though disputed, amount of evidence), he was then known to the Goths – a runic name Enguz appears in the Salzburg–Wiener MS. This name, if not the letter for which it was used, corresponds to that of the Anglo-Saxon rune Ing; and the 'Rune Poems' verse for it describes what may be a ritual procession of the sort Tacitus associates with Nerthus, and the *Gunnars þáttr Helmings* attributes to Freyr (*Flateyjarbók* 1860). Much ink has been spilled over whether the 'Phol' of the *Zweite Merseburger Zauberspruch* might not also be the same deity as the Old Norse Freyr, but the evidence is too scant to permit a plausible hypothesis. It is also worth noting that, while forms of the word *Ansuz (singular of Æsir) are found in all branches of the Germanic tongue, Vanr appears, as far as we can tell, only in Old Norse.

If the Vanir were known only to the Scandinavians and North Sea Germans (and perhaps to the Goths) it becomes much less likely that the common Germanic *Frijjo was originally one of their number. Further, Freyja and Freyr are difficult to separate: they share a holy animal, the swine (both of them ride a boar called 'gold-bristled'), and some of their functions, such as the provision of wealth and pleasure are also common to the two of them. And, according to Loki, the attraction that Freyja unwillingly holds for male giants has an opposite parallel in the courtships between the male Vanir and female giants. Freyja is defined by her association with the Vanir, whereas the primary importance of Frigg seems to be through her association with Wodan. This is so in the Old Norse and on the continent, where Frija never appears independently of her husband, and it is a reasonable guess that the cult of Frigg spread with that of Wodan. It is not impossible that the wife of *Wodhanaz had originally been one of the Vanir, and, if so, the process of migration could have separated her from her kin in the beliefs of those tribes which wandered, while leaving the relationship intact in Scandinavia. However, if the separation between Frigg and Freyja were a product of the Germanic migrations, it seems unlikely that the wandering Frigg-persona should then have returned to take over the position of Óðinn's chief wife in the north. Alternatively, if theories that the cult of Wodan sprang up first in the south and later came to Scandinavia were correct, there would be a strong argument for completely different origins for Frigg and Freyja.

Finally, it must be noted that the Norse Frigg's characteristics are very closely reflected in the scanty materials we have concerning this goddess on the continent. These are seen in the similarities between the Frea of the *Origio gentis Langobardorum*, who tricks Godan into betraying his favourites to grant victory to hers, and the Frigg of the prologue to *Grímnismál*, who tricks Óðinn into destroying his foster-son, who had been the rival of hers. Also, in the *Zweite Merseburger Zauberspruch*, Frija has a sister whose name, Volla, is identical to that of the Norse goddess, Fulla, whom Snorri describes as Frigg's handmaiden (1966). Though somewhat more Old Norse material concerning Freyja has survived, she has nothing in common, so far as we can tell, with the continental Frija, except a certain knowledge of magic, which was shared by many of the Germanic deities.

It may never be definitely proved that Frigg and Freyja were originally different goddesses, but I believe that a stronger case can be made for this argument than for its converse; and if it is true, we are then left with the question of explaining the relationship between Freyja and Óðr, which has been one of the strongest points for a sole identity for Frigg and Freyja. It is often forgotten, however, that the early Germanic people occasionally practised polygamy: in *Germania* 18, Tacitus comments that 'the very few exceptions [to Germanic monogamy] . . . consist of those with whom polygamous marriage is eagerly sought for the sake of high birth' (1980: 157). Polygynous marriages are known to have taken place among the Merovingian and Carolingian families; the only Germanic law-code where such relationships were expressly forbidden was that of the Visigoths. In Scandinavia polygyny was likewise rare, but Haraldr inn Hárfagrir, for instance, was married to several wives simultaneously. As the activities of the gods tend to reflect the social norms of their worshippers, it is by no means inconceivable that in the earlier period Óðinn could have rejoiced in Freyja and Frigg simultaneously, and that, as this form of marriage became less common through the Viking Age and after the Christianization of the North, it was therefore less easily recognized among the gods.

REFERENCES

Adam of Bremen, trans. and ed. F.T. Tschan 1959. *History of the Archbishops of Hamburg–Bremen*. New York.
Bostock, J.K., K.C. King, and D.R. McLintock eds 1976. *A Handbook of Old High German Literature*, 2nd edn. Oxford.
Braune, W. ed. 1979. *Althochdeutsches Lesebuch*. Tübingen.
Davidson, H.R. Ellis 1964. *Gods and Myths of Northern Europe*. Harmondsworth.
de Vries, J. 1931. *Contributions to the Study of Othin, especially in his Relation to Agricultural Practices in Modern Popular Lore*, FF Communications 94. Helsinki.

—— 1956. *Altgermanische Religionsgeschichte*, 2 vols. Berlin.

—— 1962. *Altnordisches etymologisches Wörterbuch*, 2nd edn. Leiden.

Dumézil, G. 1973. *Gods of the Ancient Northmen*, trans. and ed. E. Haugen. Berkeley, Calif.

Green, D. 1965: *The Carolingian Lord*. Cambridge.

Grimm, J. 1966. *Teutonic Mythology*, trans. J.S. Stallybrass. 4 vols. New York.

Flateyjarbók 1860, 3 vols. Christiania.

Förstemann, E. 1900, 1913–16: *Altdeutsches Namenbuch*, 1: *Personennamen*, 2nd edn; 2 and 3: *Orts- und sonstige geographische Namen*, 3rd edn, ed. H. Jellinghaus. Bonn.

Gurevich, A. 1992: 'Heroes, Things, Gods and Laughter', in J. Howlett (ed.) *Historical Anthropology of the Middle Ages*. Cambridge.

Helm, K. 1937: *Altergermanische Religionsgeschichte*. 2 vols. Heidelberg.

Jónsson, Finnur 1966. *Lexicon poeticum*. Copenhagen.

—— ed. 1967–73. *Den Norsk–Islandske Skjaldedigtning*. Copenhagen.

Kristjánsson, J. 1988. *Eddas and Sagas* trans P. Foote. Reykjavík.

Neckel, G., and H. Kühn eds 1962. *Edda*, 3rd edn. Heidelberg.

Olson, M., ed. 1906–8: *Völsunga saga ok Ragnars saga Loðbrókar*. Copenhagen.

Poetic Edda, The trans. and ed. L.M. Hollander 1962. Austin, Tx.

Saxo Grammaticus, ed. J. Olrik and H. Ræder 1931. *Saxonis Gesta Danorum*, 2 vols. Copenhagen.

Shippey, T.A. ed. 1976. *Poems of Wisdom and Learning in Old English*. Cambridge.

Snorri Sturluson, 1966. *Edda Snorri Sturlusonar*, 3 vols. Osnabrück.

Snorri Sturluson, ed. F. Jónsson 1923. *Heimskringla*. Copenhagen.

Tacitus, trans. E.M. Hutton, ed. E.H. Warmington 1980. *Germania*. Cambridge.

Turville-Petre, E.O.G. 1964. *Myth and Religion of the North*. London.

Waitz, G. ed. 1878. *Monumenta Germaniae historica: Scriptores rerum Langobardicae et Italicarum*. Hanover.

Wemple, S.F. 1981. *Women in Frankish Society*. Philadelphia, Pa.

Wilson, D. 1992. *Anglo-Saxon Paganism*. London.

CHAPTER FIVE

FREYJA – A GODDESS WITH MANY NAMES

---•*•---

Britt-Mari Näsström

Grét ok at Óði
gulli Freyja.
Heiti eru hennar
Hǫrn ok þrungva,
Sýr, Skjalf och Gefn
ok hít sama Mardǫll

Freyja cried (tears of) gold for Óðr. Her names are Hǫrn and þrungva, Sýr, Skjalf and Gefn and also Mardǫll.

This enumeration belongs to the supplement of *Skáldskaparmál*, usually called *þulur*, which had the purpose of supplying poets with appropriate synonyms for the gods (Snorri/Jónsson 1926: 199). Snorri further explains these names in *Gylfaginning*, where he says that Freyja is married to a certain Óðr. When her husband went away on long and dangerous journeys Freyja cried tears of red gold for him. She did not, however, sit inactively mourning her husband, but searched for him among many people, and therefore she wore a lot of names (Snorri/Lorenz 1984: 34).

Óðr is described as Freyja's husband not only in Snorri´s text, but also in *Skáldskaparmál* (1926: 120) and in *Vǫluspá* as *Óðs mey* (*Eddadikte*/Helgason 1971: I, 7), while in skaldic poetry we find the kenning *augna regn Óðs bedvinu* (rain from the eye of Óðr's wife), which again alludes to Freyja's tears of pure gold (Egilsson 1966: 39).

In other contexts such as *Sǫrla þáttr* and *Sólarljóð* we find Freyja connected with Óðinn, which is sometimes understood as a late phase of the religious development when she took over the position of Frigg. The difference between the two goddesses is, however, blurred in the myths, where we find that both are given the quality of licentiousness[1], especially combined with greediness for gold and precious jewellery. Today, there are also more concrete associations between them, like the name of the flower *Galium verum*, which was variously called *Freyja gräs* and still is named *Friggjar gras* in modern Icelandic; and the constellation Orion's belt, known originally as *Frigge-rocken* or *Freyja-rocken* respectively, i.e. the spinning-wheel of the goddesses.

There is, though, less doubt that Óðinn and Óðr were originally one and the same person. The names derive from the noun *óðr*, with various meanings such as 'agitation', 'skill in poetry', 'poetry', 'intellect' and 'ecstasy'. By contrast, the adjective *óðr*, means 'furious', 'mad', 'terrible', even 'mentally disordered'. To sum up, the word conveys an extraordinary mental condition, strongly deviating from normal or everyday behaviour, in either a favourable or a pejorative sense.

This is obvious in *Hyndluljóð*(*Eddadikte*/Helgason 1971: II, 88) where the variant *æði* was emended by Bugge to Óði and in the same strophe also *eðlvina* to Óðs *vina* (Bugge 1883: 264). These emendations thus gave two other examples of Óðr as Freyja's husband. However, what Bugge reads as a *lectio difficilior*, *æði* and *eðlvina*, should in my opinion be interpreted in their original form, *æði*, *œði* meaning raging; here in the special sense of oestrous, which would agree with the following line about the goat Heiðrún in heat. The strophe should, accordingly, be interpreted as:

Rant at æði, ey þreyandi, skutuz þér fleiri und fyrirskyrtu, hleypr þú, eðlvina, úti á náttum sem meðhǫfrum Heiðrún fari.

You ran ever yearning in lechery, under the front of your shirt still others have crept. You ran in heat, my lustful friend, as Heiðrún with the he-goats in the night.

Perhaps the philologists of the nineteenth century were misled by their romantic intentions, when they put forward the existence of Óðr in the poem.[2]

Before leaving the problem of Óðr–Óðinn, which is closely connected with Freyja and her many names, we must ask why Snorri used the short form Óðr, thus inventing a husband for Freyja. Among many explanations, L. M. Hollander draws a parallel with the story of Cupid and Psyche, where he argued that their roles had become inverted in the Nordic interpretation: i.e. *óðr* (soul) represented the male, whereas Freyja, or rather Frîja – deriving from *fría* (to love) – was the female (Hollander 1950: 304–8). His argument that the motifs of Freyja's longing and tears were too sentimental to have risen from the Nordic temperament and therefore must be a borrowing from classical mythology is not convincing. Although we know that Snorri was influenced by the twelfth-century Latin Platonists, especially concerning the myths (Dronke & Dronke 1977: 171–6; Ross 1987: 14), it seems a little hazardous to presume some philosophical speculation concerning 'soul' and 'love' in his brief notices about Óðr and Freyja. It is more likely that he and earlier mythographers separated Óðinn from Freyja, leaving the short-form Óðr as her partner.[3]

In this case, as in that of Freyja's many different names, we are dealing with the problem of the difference between mythology as a learned construction, and the cult as it was experienced by the people. From other religions we know that the same god or goddess could appear under different names, usually owing to the fact that he or she once had a by-name, which related to a cult-place or a specific function. The Greek god Apollo, originating from Asia Minor, had many such by-names – as, for example, Epikouros (the Helper), which later appears as an independent god. The reverse development is found in the personification of the healing-hymn, the Paian, a god in the Greek-ruled Knossos, who appears as such in the *Iliad* but was later identical with Apollo (Burkert 1985: 145). The great goddesses of the eastern Mediterranean in particular carried many different names in different areas – as, for example, the Phrygian Kybele, who appeared under the names of Artemis and Rhea in the major cities of the west coast of Asia Minor, while the Romans called her Magna Mater, and the Gauls Berecynthia, among other names (Näsström 1990: 40–5). In many cases it is fruitless to search for the original name behind specific variants; we are only able to call attention to the fact that one god or goddess could appear under different names in different places, whereas their function and attributes are the same.

Freyja's name Mardǫll/Marþǫll appears in *kenningar* for gold: for example, *Mardallar tár* (Mardǫll's tears); *þárs Mardallar, Mardallar grátr* (Mardǫll's weeping); *Mardallar hvarma fagrregn* (the fair rain of Mardǫll's eyelids) (Egilsson 1966: 393). The name has been interpreted as a compound of *marr-* (sea) and *-dǫll* or *-þǫll*, where -dǫll is probably a feminine form of *-dallr*, meaning 'the shining' (Snorri/Lorenz 1984: 440; Turville-Petre 1964: 153). 'The One shining over the sea' could imply a connection with a certain star like Stella Maris used as a by-name of Isis (Giebel 1990: 167) and later of the Virgin Mary. Another possible interpretation of 'the shining' is that it is an allusion to Brísingamen (the shining adornment), which was Freyja's principal possession. Brísingamen was, according to an older hypothesis a symbol for the sun, and the name Mardǫll, was connected with the sunrise and the sunset in the sea. These attempts to explain obscure myths or myth-elements as meteorological or cosmological phenomena have their obvious weakness, and the question about the origin of the name Mardǫll must therefore remain open.

A connection between Mardǫll/Freyja and Brísingamen and, on the other hand, Heimdallr, is possible. Heimdallr was the one who fought with Loki about Brísingamen. It is told in Úlfr Úggason's *Húsdrápa*:

Ráðgegninn bregðr ragna rein at Singasteini frægr vid firna slœgium farbata magr vári ; módaflugr rædr átta mœðra ok einnar mǫgr áðr fǫgru hafnýra.

The wise powerful guardian [= Heimdallr] of the way of the gods [= Bifrost] travelled together with the very cunning son of Farbaute to

Singastein; the brave son of one and eight mothers managed first to reach the beautiful sea-kidney.

(Úlfr/Jónsson 1967: 136)

The episode is related by Snorri in *Skáldskaparmál*, where he describes Heimdallr: 'He is also the visitor of Vågaskär and Singastein – where he and Loki fought about the Brísingamen ... they appeared in the form of seals' (Snorri/Jónsson 1926: 83). An emendation of the name Singastein gives *signastein* (magic stone), which creates an analogy with *hafnýra* (sea-kidney) in the next strophe. *Hafnýra*, a brown or red stone, was used in folk-medicine to facilitate deliveries and in Iceland was called *lausnarstein* (delivery stone). It is possible to associate this colour with 'fire' (Müllendorf 1886: 217–18), which is the literary translation of the word *brísing*, and which makes Brísingamen identical with the 'holy stone' and the 'sea-kidney'. The adornment would then rather refer to Freyja's function as helper in childbirth (Pering 1941: 222; see Grundy: 60). It is possible that the allusion is to the stanza in *Lokasenna* where Loki accuses Gefjon of having intercourse with the white young man, *sveinn inn hvíta*, who gave her the adornment (*Eddadikte*/Helgason 1971: II, 50). This white young man could then be an allusion to Heimdallr, who in *Gylfaginning* is called *hvíti-áss* (Snorri/Jónsson 1926: 30). Gefjon is, as we shall see, another aspect of Freyja. The fertility aspect which Heimdallr shares with Freyja is also appropriate here. But, instead of Mother Goddess, it is the father-god, Ríg-Heimdallr, who begets the three social classes during his journey on earth. However, the names of Mardǫll and Heimdallr contain further correspondences to Freyja; Heimdallr translates as 'the One shining over the world', and Mardǫll as 'the One shining over the sea'.

Hǫrn/*Härn is probably derived from *hǫrr*, meaning 'flax' or 'linen', and survives in many place-names, such as Härnevi (Brink 1990: 50). We know that cultivation of flax arrived early in Scandinavia and was surrounded by many magical perceptions: it protected against evil and gave fertility to mankind (Tillhagen 1986: 16–19). The flax itself was connected with women, even being called the 'seed of the woman', and some records show that it had be sown on a Friday and that women dressed in their best clothes took part in the sowing on the day hallowed to the great goddess of the North (Tillhagen 1986: 24–8). The spinning of flax was connected with her in folklore, and the product, linen, was the dress of the bride. Freyja, the protectress of love between man and woman, was the natural protectress of weddings, and for the bride the phrase *ganga und líni* meant the wedding.

Gefn means 'the giving', alluding to the fertility aspect of the goddess, and comparable with Gabiæ and Aligabiæ, names of the so-called Matres or Matronæ (de Vries 1970: II, 293). The name is, as mentioned earlier, another form of Gefjon, who appears in the Eddic poetry and in Snorri's mythology as an independent goddess. Gefjon is unique in the Nordic pantheon since she is not married. Snorri calls her *mær* (maiden) and adds *henne þióna þær er meyjar andaz* (those who die as maidens serve her) (Snorri/Jónsson 1926: 35).[4] On the other hand, Gefjon also carries the qualities of a fertility-goddess, as in her *skemtan* (liaison) with King Gylfi and the creation of Sjælland, or the above-mentioned episode with the white young man. In the late *Breta-sǫgur* three gods appear, Saturnus, Jupiter and Gefjon, behind whom we recognize Óðinn, Þórr and – to complete the Dumézilian triad – Gefjon–Freyja (*Hauksbók*/Det Konglige Nordiske Oldskriftsselskab 1892–6: 240–1).

Sýr is usually interpreted as 'the sow', alluding to a coarse symbol of the fertility-goddess, or, in obsolete explanations, as a form of totemism, where the goddess appears in the shape of an animal (Phillpotts 1920: 169). The most appealing etymology, however, derives from the IE stem **s(w)er-*, meaning 'to protect', 'to shield'. During the course of time the word lost its original meaning and became interpreted as the homonymous 'sow' (Schrodt 1979: 114–19). However, the double meaning of the word was used in *Ólávs saga helga*, where Óláv's foster-father, Sigurþ, carries the by-name Sýr (Snorri/Aðalbjarnarson 1951: 7). It is hard to believe that a man in his position would accept being called 'the sow' by his subjects. But, in *Hreiðars þáttr* we find the other meaning of the name, when his enemies make a pun of it and present him with an amulet in the form of a silver pig, which raised his anger (*Hreiðars þáttr*/Sigfúson 1945: 254). The pun is thus the evidence of the fact that *sýr* carried two meanings, especially as we also find the name in kennings like *sarlaxa Sýr* and *Folk Sýr*, used in positive senses (Egilsson 1966: 557). Likewise, when a goddess like Freyja is called Sýr it is preferable to choose the archaic alternative. However, there is an affinity between the boar and the twin couple Freyr and Freyja, in relation to their warlike characters rather than to the aspect of fertility (Davidson 1964: 98–9).

Þrungva appears only in this enumeration and was probably derived from *þrá* (pining) (de Vries 1970: 618), and alluding to the love-goddess longing for her partner. Under the name Menglǫð (the One, who is gladdened by adornment) Freyja here appears again as the loving and yearning woman. This Eddic poem, in literary form close to folk-song, relates the meeting between Menglǫð–Freyja and her beloved:

> My wish have I won: welcome be thou
> with a kiss I clasp thee now;
> the loved one's sight is sweet to her
> who has lived in longing for him
>
> Full long sat I on Lyfiaberg,
> bided thee day after day;
> now has happened what I hoped for long
> that, hero, thou art come in my hall.

Heart-sick was I, to have thee I yearned,
whilst thou didst long for my love.
Of a truth I know: we two shall live
our life together.

This is an invitation from the goddess to her partner to unite with her in a holy wedding, which in its deepest sense is a manifestation of the creation and the cosmic order. The cosmic perception is expressed in myths and is performed in a ritual where the union between them is demonstrated through symbolic forms.

Discussions about cultic weddings have attracted great interest among other toponymic scholars, who have seen a connection in the existence of male and female place-names close to each other. This could mean that gods like Ullr and Þórr were united in a cultic wedding with the fertility-goddess under the names Njärð, Hǫrn and Freyja, which were reflected in place-names like Ullvi-Härnvi in Bro, Uppland, and Torstuna-Härnvi in Västmanland (Hellberg 1986: 49; Brink 1990: 50). This is sometimes considered highly speculative, yet there is nothing that disproves this theory if one compares with other religions. Apart from those with a monotheistic and unisexual perspective, most celebrate holy weddings in the form of processions, leading a god to his divine bride, or vice versa. These constitute a regular element in the festival calendar. The implicit meaning of such a ceremony is, in many cases, not only direct symbolic coitus to strengthen fertility in people, beasts and soil, but also a token of agreement, economical exchange, etc., which united one village with another. Holy weddings could take place between the king and the goddess or between the king and the queen, who represented the god and the goddess. Moreover, a discrepancy between the myth and the ritual is rather common in these examples. A well-known example is the *hieros gamos* on Samos between Zeus and Hera, which was expressed in myth and ritual, but which only existed as ritual in Athens, whereas the myth is explicitly told in *Iliad* 14, 295 (Widengren 1969: 117ff., 155ff., 253ff., 390).

The literary sources, such as that of Menglǫð's greeting, as well as the story about Freyr and Gerðr in *Skírnismál* (*Eddadikte*/Helgason 1971: II, 30), are further expressions of the phenomenon, but cultic weddings between a male and a female deity from different villages are not attested in them. The closest to such a wedding appears in the short passage about Freyr, his priestess and the cunning Gunnar Helming in *Flateyjarbók*, which relates how a woman played the role of Freyr's wife during his travels in the kingdom of Svear (*Flateyjarbók* I/Vigfúson & Unger 1860: 337–9). The place-name theory, however, presupposes a wedding between two gods.

Skjalf appears in *Ynglingatal* 10 as a Lappish/Finnish princess (*Ynglingtal*/Noreen 1925: 201) abducted by King Agni, together with her brother Logi, from their father, Frosti – as Snorri tells us – whereas

Figure 5.1   Nineteenth-century expression of the goddess Freyja.

Ynglingatal mentions Skalf with the kenning *loga dís*.[5] These two versions of the course of events, and a third in *Historia Norwegiae*, agree in that fact the Skjalf hanged her husband (when he was drunk, according to Snorri, who is obviously delighted by such explanations). Skjalf could be the mother of the dynasty of Skilfingar, the name of the Ynglinga dynasty after Agni; this is also mentioned in *Beowulf* (*Beowulf*/Swanton 1978: 36). As an eponymous heroine of a royal clan she provides a female parallel to Freyr and the Ynglinga dynasty. (For the interpretations and etymologies of Skjalf, see Gade 1985: 59–71.)

Hanging is usually connected with the cult of Óðinn, and, according to Dumézil's tripartite theory, belongs to the first function, that of the priest-king (Dumézil 1973: 127–54). Nevertheless, according to the *Historia*

Norwegiae there was another royal victim, Dómaldi, hanged in sacrifice to the goddess Ceres – probably Freyja – in the dynasty of Ynglingar. When Adam of Bremen discusses the hanged male victims in the holy grove of Uppsala, he does not mention to whom these sacrifices were performed. Scholars prefer Óðinn in this connection, but there is nothing to contradict the possibility of another god or goddess. There is also a possibility that this sacrifice coincided with the *dísablót* in Uppsala before the Christianization process, since this *blót* was moved back a month in order not to coincide with the Christian Easter. Adam relates that the great *blót* took place in the vernal equinox, which should be identical with the original time of the *dísablót*. His note that the *svear* sang 'many indecent songs' during the festival could suggest a fertility rite (Adam av Bremen/Svenberg 1984: 225). There is a close relationship between Freyja and the anonymous collective of goddesses called *dísir* regarding their functions. They received sacrifice in the Dísarsal, which literally means 'the hall of the (great) dís'. It is probably the identity of Freyja that is concealed behind the single *dís* representing the collective as a *pars pro toto*. Therefore, was it Freyja herself who received the male sacrifices in the grove near the temple? The suggestion is indeed, at this point, conjecture only, but it is as credible as the statement that the recipient was Óðinn.

And, finally, Freyja is also called Vanadís (Sturlason/Jónsson 1926: 90), which is a kenning composed of *Vanir* and *dís* (the woman of the Vanir, 35) and equivalent to *Vana goð/gyðja* in the same passage. Her many names would, in my opinion, reflect the manifold functions which belong to her, and although the fragile sources might leave us little information regarding their origin, yet we can interpret them and compare them with different myths in order to deepen and elucidate our understanding of the image of Freyja, the great goddess of the North (Figure 5.1).

NOTES

1 See Grundy (pp. 57–8 above) for the possibility that this attribution to Frigg was a later addition by Saxo.
2 However, the word *eðlvina* is difficult to interpret and there are other suggestions: see Mundal 1992: 246 n. 3.
3 For the problem Óðinn–Óðr, see de Vries 1970: II, 87–9; Turville-Petre 1964: 176; Ström and Biezais 1975: 151.
4 Holtsmark suggests that this phrase displays Snorri's tendency to show the perversion of the pagan gods. The word *þjóna* belongs to the sermon of the Virgin Mary, but Snorri uses it in a context which is the opposite to that of the Virgin Mary (Holtsmark 1964: 1; see Nässtrom 1992: 197 for Gefjon as the chaste goddess.)
5 This is a disputed kenning. According to Noreen, *log* derives from *liugan* (marriage); consequently, *Loga dís* means 'the *dís* of marriage', i.e. the wife (Noreen 1925: 226). Gro Steinsland considers Skjalf to be a giantess (according

to her hypothesis regarding the holy marriage) and interprets *loga dís* as an allusion to the flames that surrounded the giant's world (Steinsland 1991: 387–9, with reference to Gade 1985: 59–71).

REFERENCES

Abbreviations

AnEWb *Altnordisches etymologisches Wörterbuch*, ed. J. de Vries. Leiden.
ANF *Arkiv för Nordisk filologi*, Lund.
ÍF Íslenzk Fornrit, 1932–, Reykjavík.

Adam av Bremen, trans. E. Svenberg. 1984. *Gesta Hammaburgensis ecclesia pontificum*. Stockholm.
—— trans. and comm. A.A. Lund 1978. *Gesta Hammaburgensis ecclesia pontificum, Beskrivelse af øerna i Norden*. Højberg.
Beowulf, ed. M. Swanton 1978. Manchester.
Brink, S. 1990. *Sockenbildning och sockennamn*. Uppsala.
Bugge, S. 1883. 'Bem'rkninger til norrøne dikter 1', in *Hyndluljoð*, ANF 1, 249–65.
Burkert, W. 1985. *Greek Religion*. Cambridge, Mass.
Davidson, H.R. Ellis 1964. *Gods and Myths of Northern Europe*. Harmondsworth.
de Vries, J. 1970. *Altgermanische Religionsgeschichte* I–II. Berlin.
—— ed. 1962. *Altnordisches etymologisches Wörterbuch*. Leiden.
Dronke, P. and U. 1977. 'The Prologue of the Prose Edda: Explorations of a Latin Background', in Einar G. Petúrsson and Jónas Kristjánsson (eds.) *Sjøtíu Ritgerðir helgaðar Jacobi Benediktsyni*. Reykjavík. 153–76.
Dumézil, G. 1973. *From Myth to Fiction*, trans. D. Coltman. Chicago and London.
Eddadikte I–II, ed. Jón Helgason 1971. Copenhagen, Oslo and Stockholm.
Egilsson, S. ed. 1966. *Lexicon poeticum*. Copenhagen.
Flateyjarbók I, ed. Guðbrandr Vigfúson & C.R. Unger 1860. Christiania.
Gade, K.E. 1985. 'Skjalf', *ANF* 100, 59–71.
Giebel, M. 1990. *Das Geheimnis der Mysterien*. Zurich.
Hauksbók, ed. Det Konglige Nordiske Oldskriftsselskab 1892–6. Copenhagen.
Hellberg, L. 1986: 'Hedendomens spår i uppländska ortnamn, in *Ortnamnsällskapets i Uppsala årsskrift*, ed. T. Andersson. Uppsala.
Hollander, L.M. 1950. 'The Old Norse God Odr', *Journal of English and Germanic Philology*, 49, 304–8.
Holtsmark, A. 1964: *Studier i Snorres mytologi*. Oslo.
Hreiðars þáttr, ed. Björn Sigfúson. 1945, in *Ljósvetninga saga*, Í F. Reykjavík.
Müllendorf, K. 1886: 'Frija und der Halsbandsmythos', *Zeitschrift für deutsche Altertum* 30, 217–59.
Mundal, E. 1992: 'Heiðrún: den mjødmjølkande geita på Valhalls tak', in *Eyvindarbók*, ed. F. Høgnebo et al. Oslo. 240–7.
Näsström, B-M. 1990. *O Mother of the Gods and Men: Some Aspects of Emperor Julian's Discourse on the Mother of the Gods*. Lund.
—— 1992. 'The Goddesses of Gylfaginning', in *Snorrastefna*, ed. Úlfar Bragason. Reykjavík. 193–203.
Noreen, A. ed. 1925. *Tjoðolf ar Hvin*. Stockholm.
Norges historia, ed. A. Salvesen 1969. Oslo.
Ólavs saga helga, ed. Bjarni Aðalbjarnarson 1945, in *Heimskringla* II, IF. Reykjavík. 1–481.

Pering, B. 1941. *Heimdall.* Lund.
Phillpotts, B. 1920. *The Elder Edda and Ancient Scandinavian Drama.* Cambridge.
Ross, M. Clunies 1987. *Skáldskaparmál.* Odense.
Schrodt, R. 1979. 'Der altnordische Beiname Sýr', *ANF* 94. Lund.
Snorri Sturluson, ed. B. Aðalbjarnarson 1951. *Heimskringla* I. Reykjavík.
—— ed. F. Jónsson 1926. *Edda* . Copenhagen.
—— ed. G. Lorenz 1984. *Edda.* Darmstadt.
Steinsland, G. 1991. *Det hellige bryllup og norrøn kongeideologi.* Oslo.
Ström, Å.V., and H. Biezais. 1975. *Germanische und baltische Religion.* Stuttgart.
Ström, F. 1961. *Nordisk Hedendom.* Göteborg.
'Sörla þáttr', ed. Guðbraudr Vigfúson and C.R. Unger 1860, in *Flateyjarbók,*
    Christiana. 277–82.
Tillhagen, C.H. 1986. *Vävskrock.* Borås.
Turville-Petre, G. 1964. *Myth and Religion of the North.* London.
Úlfr Úggason, ed. Finnur Jónsson 1912. *Húsdrápa* 2, in *Den Norsk–Isländska*
    Skaldediktningen. Copenhagen.
Widengren, G. 1969. *Religionsphänomenologie.* Berlin.
Ynglingatal, ed. A. Noreen 1925, in *Kungliga Vitterhets historie-och Antikvitetes*
    Akademiens Handlingar 28, Stockholm. 195–254.

CHAPTER SIX

MEG AND HER DAUGHTERS: SOME TRACES OF GODDESS-BELIEFS IN MEGALITHIC FOLKLORE?

——— •◆• ———

Samuel Pyeatt Menefee

INTRODUCTION

The scholar seeking beliefs in supernatural women in megalithic folklore has much from which to choose. Kit's Coty, a megalithic chamber tomb in Kent, for example, was said to be raised by three witches, with the capstone added by a fourth (Grinsell 1976: 124; Evans 1946), while Spinsters' Rock in Devon was similarly erected by three spinsters – before breakfast (Menefee 1971: div. 5/2/3). Both Mitchell's Fold and *Preseb y Fuwch Frech* (The Speckled Cow's Crib) stone circles in Shropshire and in Clwyd, served as shelters for a cow who gave milk to all comers until a witch milked her into a sieve (Grinsell 1976: 155–6, 244; 1982). Ireland has several monuments called Bheara's House or Aynia's Cove (Menefee 1971: div. 5/9/4), and in western France and the Channel Isles some standing stones are identified as having been carried by a fairy while she knit (see Menefee 1971: div. 5/2/0), or as having been spindles of the Virgin Mary. Another group of traditions concern fairies, *cailleachs*, Guinevere or other supernatural women alleged to have carried or dropped stones forming various monuments; hence the *Tombeau de la Groac'h Rouge* near Prat in Côtes du Nord, carried by a red fairy in her apron, the *Clios des Très Pierres* in Jersey, carried by three fairies in their aprons to frighten the Turks (Menefee 1971: div. 5/2/0) and *Barclodiad-y-Gowres* (Apronful of the Giantess), the Auld Wife's Apronful of Stones and the Skirtful of Stones. In addition, this tradition is also localized in Ireland, where Swift has described how one *cailleach*:

> Determined now her tomb to build,
> Her ample skirt with stones she filled,
> And dropped a heap on Carron-more;
> Then stepped one thousand yeards to Loar,
> And dropped another goodly heap;
> And then with one prodigious leap,

Gained carron-beg; and on its height
Displayed the wonders of her might.

(Grinsell 1976: 43–4)

Some of these traditions will be touched on elsewhere (see Davidson, p. 101 below), while others, although interesting, will be left for subsequent discussions. This study will concentrate on one isolated tradition, which, although not obviously related to the topic, may at second glance repay scrutiny and offer evidence of surviving traces of a hitherto unarticulated goddess-tradition.

LONG MEG: THE FOLK-TRADITION

At Little Salkeld in Cumbria stand two megalithic monuments, the first a circle known as Long Meg and her Daughters and the other – the retaining wall of a Bronze Age cairn – as Little Meg. The latter is not associated with any particular stories, but the circle is rich in traditional lore.

This site is made up of seventy-seven stones, each about ten feet in length, with a single large megalith at its entrance: 'this the common people call Long Meg, and the rest her Daughters' (Hardy 1892: 166). The name and tradition have been associated with this monument since about 1600, when Reginald Bainbridge, 'scole mister of Applebie', reported to Camden: 'They are commonlie called meg with hir daughters. They are huge great stones, long meg standes above the ground in sight xv fote long and tre fathoms about' (Rowling 1976: 77). Similarly, in 1634, three Norwich soldiers who visited the area refered to 'Stony Meg and her 77 daughters as hard-hearted as herselfe' (Hardy 1892: 166; Grinsell 1976: 164, 288; Legg 1904). Other tales surrounding the megaliths are of particular interest. Celia Fiennes, the diarist, writing circa 1703, refers to the site as Long Meg and her *Lovers*. 'The story is that these soliciting her to an Unlawfull Love by an Enchantment are turned w^t her into stone; the stone in the middle wch is called Meg is much bigger and have some fforme Like a statue or ffigure of a body, but the Rest are but Soe many Cragg stones' (Grinsell 1976: 165). Grinsell reports a similar story recorded by Stukeley in 1743, 'and a variant stating that they were witches turned into stone', noted by Hutchison in his 1794 *History of Cumberland*. Further, some said that '[i]f a piece be broken off Long Meg, she would bleed' (ibid.).

WHO WAS LONG MEG? A QUEST FOR IDENTITY

To the question 'Who was Long Meg?', there appear to be at least three possible answers. First, in Old Scots, the term meg means a wench. Lindsay, for example, refers to the 'muirland MEG, that milkes the yowis, Claggit with clay aboune the howis' (Farmer and Henley 1937: 299). Meg and her Daughters are not the only Cumbrian monument bearing this epithet; the existence of Little Meg has already been noted, while there is also a Meg's Cairn near Ously, on the Maiden Way (Grinsell 1976: 167, 165). Coates similarly reports the association of four hills with Meg or Mag in the vicinity of the Wandlebury chalk figures in Cambridgeshire (Coates 1978: 77).

A second possibility is one offered by Leslie Grinsell that 'Meg may ... have been Meg of Meldon, reputed to have been an early seventeenth-century witch' (Grinsell 1976: 164). This appears to be unlikely as Bainbridge's mention to Camden shows that the name of the stone was in existence as early as 1600.

Finally, Meg has been identified with Long Meg of Westminster, heroine of several ballads and chapbooks dating from the sixteenth century. Charles Hindley mentions an edition of *The Life and Pranks of Long Meg of Westminster*, printed in 1582 by William How for Abraham Veale, at Paul's Churchyard at the sign of the Lambe (Hindley 1872: iii; cf. Ashton 1882: 323; Partridge 1982: 516; Halliwell 1848: 1). Hindley questions the date because of a manuscript title-page, and notes that the piece must be earlier than the 1632 edition. C.C. Mish claims this to be spurious (Mish 1968: 82). Whether or not this is the case (and Hindley quotes from the alleged book) there is no question that two ballads about this hoyden were registered during the 1590s – 'long Meg of Westminster' in 1590, and 'the madd merry pranks of Long megg of Westminster' five years later (Rollins 1967: 133, 140). In addition to several literary allusions, one of the earliest being by John Lyly in 1589 (Hindley 1872: xxiii), there is a play, recorded in Henslow's diary in 1594, which ran for eighteen performances (Ashton 1882: 324). There are versions of the *Life and Pranks* from 1635 and 1636. The former is reproduced in Hindley (1872: xxxi–xxxvi, [1]–47) and Mish (1968: 83–113), and in later chapbook versions reprinted in Hindley (1872: iv–xxi) and in Ashton (1882: 325–6). One of these is mentioned by Grose as 'a small penny history, well known to school-boys of the lesser sort' (Grose 1811, in Hindley 1872: xxviii).

A selective examination of the 1635 text is necessary to shed light on the Cumberland tradition. The dedication notes that 'to please your fantasies many men have made pleasant gigs, as the jests of Robin Hood and Bevis of Southampton':

> When I was idle I bethought me of Long Meg of Westminster and her merry pranks, as pleasant as the merriest jest that ever passed the press. A woman she was of late memory and well beloved, spoken on of all and known of many; therefore there is hope of the better

acceptance . . . I hope you will use Long Meg as a whetstone to mirth after your serious business. And if she have any gross faults, bear with them the more patiently for that she was a woman . . .

(Mish 1968: 83)

Not surprisingly, this was addressed 'To the Gentlemen Readers'. According to the story, Long Meg was born in Lancashire during the reign of Henry VIII, came to London at the age of 18, sometime prior to 1529 (her mistress is depicted as drinking with Dr Skelton, who died in that year: see Ashton 1882: 323), and was in the city in the 1550s, during the reign of Queen Mary, when the last episode of the story occurs. She is described beating up a grasping carrier, a Spaniard, a vicar, a bailiff, a cozening trencherman, a nobleman (and the watch), two thieves, a constable, (several) Frenchmen, a miller, a waterman, a 'roaring boy' and a friar, although, interestingly enough, she is extremely submissive to her husband. Additionally, there are hints that Meg may not have had the most moral of reputations. Arriving in London, she cheers the other girls brought up by the carrier:

here at London may we win gold and wear gold, and here are not so many maids before us but what we may find husbands as well as the rest. All is not broken stuff the carrier brings, and if it were, what then? That the eye sees not, the heart rues not.

(Mish 1968: 84).

Appraising her, Will Summers the jester advises 'that she shall be kept for breed[ing]; for if the king would marry her to Long Sanders of the court, they would bring forth none but soldiers' (ibid.: 87).

There is, further, the cryptic comment that many resorted to the house where Meg was resident 'for whatsoever she got of the rich (as her gettings were great) she bestowed it liberally on them that had need' (ibid.: 92). Two thieves are made to swear on the skirt of Meg's smock that they will 'never hurt women, nor company that any woman is in' (ibid.: 101–2), and she subsequently accompanies the king's troops to France as a laundress (ibid.: 103–4). Thereafter Meg keeps a house for lodgings and victuals at Islington, one of her rules being that

whatever gentleman or yeoman came into her house, and had any charge about him, and made it privy to her or any of her house, if he lost it by any default she would repay it ere he passed; but if he did not reveal it, and after said he was robbed, he should have ten bastinadoes with a cudgel and be turned out of doors.

(ibid.: 107–8)

Friar Oliver upbraids Meg as 'a lewd woman, a swearer, a ruffler, a fighter, and a brawler', a particularly nettlesome statement to the sick heroine as the friar himself is not the holiest of individuals. The churchman and Meg's female neighbours 'began to be merry. Friar Oliver he was blithe and gamesome with the young wives, and showed fruits of his life in his outward actions, for a more bawdy friar there was not in England and that knew Meg well enough' (ibid.: 111–12). It is perhaps not surprising that, before administering one of her famous drubbings, she accuses the priest of living 'not as holy men of the Church should, for thou art a whoremaster, frequenting the company of light and lascivious women, given to covetousness, and sitting all day bibbing at the ale-house' (ibid.: 112).

The association of Meg with immorality is strengthened by some of the period references previously mentioned. John Lyly, writing in 1589, asks, 'doost remember howe that bastard Junior complaines of brothelis, and talkes of Long Meg of Westminster?' (quoted Hindley 1872: xxiii) Perhaps more telling is the statement in Vaughan's *Golden Grove* of 1608 that 'Long Meg of Westminster kept alwaies twenty courtezans in her house, whom, by their pictures, she sold to all comers' (Rimbault 1850: 131), or the reference in *Holland's Leaguer* (1632) to a house in Southampton which 'at the first foundation . . . was renowned for nothing as much as for the memory of that famous amazon *Longa Margarita*, who had there for many yeeres kept a famous *infamous* house of open hospitality' (ibid.: 131).

All this suggests a link with the 'Unlawfull Love' of the Cumbrian circle, but several factors make it appear unlikely that the megalithic tradition derived from Meg of Westminster. The London heroine is described as hailing from Lancashire, not Cumbria, and even assuming the validity of the 1582 edition, this does not give much opportunity for an oral tradition to have established itself independently of some other source. A further complication in determining origins is the existence of a stone – in fact a slab of blue and black marble – known as 'Long Meg of Westminster' in the southern cloister of Westminster Abbey.

LONG MEG OF WESTMINSTER: THE STONE

The tradition associated with this monument dates from at least 1654, when it appears in a poem 'Long Meg of Westminster to Dulcinea of Toboso' in Gayton's *Festivous Notes on the History of the renowned Don Quixote*:

> I, Long Meg, once the wonder of the spinsters,
> Was laid, as was my right, i' the best of minsters,
> Nor here the wardens ventur'd all this whiles

To lay, except myself, one in those iles.
Indeed, untill this time, ne'r any one
Was worthy to be Meg's companion.

(Hindley 1872: xxiv–xxv)

That the tradition was widely reported by the mid-seventeenth century is suggested by the discussion in Fuller's *Worthies*:

That such a *gyant-woman* ever was in Westminster, cannot be proved by any good witness (I pass not for a late lying *pamphlet* [presumably the 1634 or 1635 text]), though some in proving there of produce her gravestone on the *south-side* of the *cloisters*, which (I confess) is as long, and large, and entire *marble* as ever I beheld. But be it known, that no *woman* in that age was interred in the *cloisters*, appropriated to the sepultures of the *abbot* and his *monkes*.

(Fuller 1662: 236; quoted Rimbault 1852: 133)

Similarly, Henry Keefe, in *Monumenta Westmonasteriensis* (1652) notes the existence of the tradition, but identifies the burial as that of Gervasius de Blois, an abbot of the monastery (Rimbault 1852: 131). Rimbault, writing on the problem, states that he will 'not enter into the question as to whether any "tall woman" of "bad repute" was or was not buried in the cloisters of Westminster, as it is very likely to turn out that the *original* "long Meg" was a "great gun", and not a creature of flesh and blood' (ibid.: 133). To understand this association with the 'Meg mythos', it is necessary to examine other large guns known as 'long Meg', the most famous of which, 'Mons Meg', or 'Roaring Meg', is now situated at Edinburgh Castle.

LONG MEG, MONS MEG, ROARING MEG: THE GUN(S)

Fuller's *Worthies* (1662) notes the proverb 'As long as Megg of Westminster', stating that it 'is applyed to persons very tall, especially if they have *hop-pole-height*, wanting *breadth* proportionable thereunto' (Fuller 1662: 236; quoted Rimbault 1852: 133). After discussing the alleged tombstone of Meg in Westminster Abbey, Fuller concludes:

If there be any truth in the proverb, it rather relateth to a great gun, lying in the tower, commonly call'd *Long Megg*; and in troublesome times (perchance upon *ill* may day in the reign of King *Henry* the eighth), brought to *Westminster*, where for a good time it continued. But this *Nut* (perchance) deserves not the cracking.

(Fuller 1662: 236; Rimbault 1852: 133)

Grose notes, in relation to the same proverb: 'Some think it alludes to a long gun, called Megg, in troublesome times brought from the tower to Westminster, where it long remained' (Grose 1811: 207; quoted Rimbault 1852: 133). Fuller's 'nut' is indeed hard to crack, particularly since this Westminster cannon does not appear to be the same as the better-known Mons Meg of Edinburgh. A quick summation of the Scottish cannon's history will not only provide evidence for the separate existence of several pieces of ordnance bearing this name but will suggest further connections with the Cumbrian circle and the London virago.

Sir Daniel Wilson, in speaking of the Edinburgh gun, notes 'the usually received traditions as to its history, which derived the name from its supposed construction at Mons in Flanders. The name, however, is probably of local origin and simply signified "Big Meg"' (Wilson 1891: 169–70). Both Hogg and Rogers, however, appear to suggest a foreign origin, concerning the accident which killed James II. His mortal injury was caused by an explosion from a breech-loading bombard. The accident involving a breech-loading cannon may have resulted in the production of Mons Meg as a muzzle-loader (Hogg 1963: 11; 1970: 211; Rogers 1975: 21–2). The gun itself is 13' long, with a bore width of 2' 3½", and is constructed of iron staves and hoops (Wilson 1891: 169; Grant 1881: 74). Grant discounts a Mons origin for the piece, giving instead this story of its founding:

> she was formed by Scottish artisans, by order of James II, when he besieged the rebellious Douglases in the castle of Thrieve, in Galloway, during 1455. He posted his artillery at the Three Thorns of the Carlinwark ... but their fire proving ineffective, a smith named M'Kim, and his sons, offered to construct a more efficient piece of ordnance. Towards this the inhabitants of the vicinity contributed each a *gaud*, or iron bar. Tradition, which never varied, indicated the place where it was forged, a mound near the Three Thorns, and when the road was formed here, that mound was discovered to be a mass of cinders and the iron debris of a great forge. To this hour the place where the great gun was posted is named *Knock-cannon* ... To reward M'Kim James bestowed upon him the forfeited lands of Mollance. The smith is said to have named the gun after his wife; and the contraction of the name from Mollance to *Monce*, or *Mons* Meg, was quite natural to the Scots, who sink the l's in all similar words.
>
> (Grant 1881: 74–5. Cf. W.W.E.T. 1852: 105 –
> questioning the date of casting)

In 1489 the gun was used at the siege of Dumbarton; while Wilson notes its movement between Edinburgh Castle and the abbey of Holyrood during the reign of James IV at times of festivity: 'Some of the entries on the occasion are curious, such as – "to the menstrallis that playit befoir *Mons* down the gait, fourteen shillings; eight elle of claith, to the *Mons* a claith to cover her, nine shillings and fourpence" etc' (Wilson 1891: 170). In 1497 the gun was employed in James's invasion of England in support of pretender Perkin Warbeck; it was fired to celebrate the retrieval of the cannon-ball from Weirdie Mure and its return to the Castle), and Grant reports: 'It was frequently used during the civil war in 1671 and two men died of their exertion in dragging it from the Blackfriars Yard to the castle. On that occasion payment was made to a person through whose roof one of the bullets had fallen in mistake' (Grant 1881: 75; Wilson 1891: 170). In most, if not all, of these early mentions, the gun appears to have been referred to as 'Mons', but by 1650, when Parliament captured the castle, it is listed as 'the great iron murderer, Muckle Meg' (*Provincial Antiquities*, quoted Wilson 1891: 170; Hogg 1963: 228). Ray, in his *Observations* (*c.* 1661) refers to the 'great old iron gun which they call *Mounts Meg*, and some "Meg of Berwick"' and Andrew Symson, writing *c.* 1700, also notes *Mounts Meg* as the name (Grant 1881: 75). The gun 'burst in 1682, in firing a royal salute to the Duke of York, afterwards James VII, a circumstance that did not fail to be noted at the time as an evil omen' (Wilson 1891: 170). It was removed to the Tower of London as unserviceable in the 1750s and did not return to Edinburgh until 1829 (ibid.; Grant 1881: 75). Grant further notes that 'a demibastion near the Scottish gate ... [in Berwick] bears, or bore the name of *Megs Mount*, which in those days was the term for a battery. Another, in Stirling, bore the same name; hence we may infer that the gun has been in both places' (1881: 75).

While the Westminster gun is believed to have been brought there in the time of Henry VIII and was in London in 1662, the Edinburgh cannon was present in Scotland at the time of Mary Queen of Scots' first marriage, and was also in 'Auld Reekie' in 1650 in *c.* 1661. This strongly suggests the existence of separate guns with the same or similar appellations. An argument might be made that the Edinburgh name derived from the London cannon in the mid-seventeenth century, but this ignores the existence of other Megs. A 'Roaring Meg' was 'presented by the Fishmongers' Company of London to the City of Londonderry in 1642' (W.W.E.T. 1852: 105, citing Simpson 1847: 41), while a demi-cannon of the same name was applied by the Cavaliers with dire effect on the Roundheads at Hopton Heath on 19 March 1643 (Hogg 1963: 223). On the Continent a further bombard, forged for the city of Oudenarde in 1382, and now in Ghent, was variously known as 'Dulle Griete', 'Mad Margery', or 'Mad Meg' (Rimbault 1850: 133; 'Northman' 1852: 260; Hogg 1970: 210). Rogers gives the date of the gun as 1430 (1975: 21). Hogg, an authority in the field, notes that some have derived the word *gun*, which 'first appeared in low Latin as *gunna* about 1370 ... from *Gunna*, the pet form of the old Scandinavian name *Gunnhilda* for a woman, and meaning battle and war. The fact that female appellations were occasionally bestowed on well-known pieces of ordnance, as for example *Mons Meg*, does lend some support to this view' (Hogg 1963: 3; 1970: 22). Whatever view is taken about this alleged connection, there is little doubt that the cannon of old England boasted several folk-epithets: in addition to the well-known 'Twelve Apostles' (Hogg 1963: 18; 1970: 51–2), there was 'Gog' and 'Magog' (ibid.: 223), while 'Queen Elizabeth's Pocket Pistol', over 23 feet in length (Hogg 1970: 74–5) and the 'Queen's Pocket Pistols', weighing 5790 lbs. (Hogg 1963: 224), are reminiscent of objects with local heroic associations such as Hickathrift's Candlesticks, called after the giant of that name (Porter 1969: 189). An 1852 correspondent to *Notes and Queries*, indeed, desired to know 'the origin of calling any huge piece of ordnance 'a roaring Meg' (W.W.E.T. 1852: 105).

There are other potential associations linking these guns, particularly the Edinburgh bombard, with Long Meg and with Meg of Westminster. The sexual cant meaning of 'Mons Meg' (see Farmer and Henley 1987: 345; Partridge 1982: 530) appears to date only from the nineteenth century, but John Taylor, the Water Poet, gives a 1618 tradition associated with the Edinburgh cannon in *The Pennyles Pilgrimage*, which matches surprisingly well with the 'unlawful love' of the Cumbrian Meg, and the courtesans associated with her London counterpart. On his journey to Edinburgh, Taylor visited the castle:

> Amongst many memorable things which I was shewed there, I noted especially a great piece of ordnance of iron . . . it is not for batterie, but it will serve to defend a breach, or to tosse balles of wilde-fire against any that should assaile or assault the castle; it lyes now dismounted, and it is so great within, that it is told me that a childe was once gotten there: but I, to make tryall crept into it, lying on my backe, and I am sure there was roome enough and spare for a greater than my selfe.
>
> (Taylor 1618; quoted Daiches 1986: 64–5).

'UNLAWFUL LOVE' AND WITCHCRAFT: FURTHER PARALLELS

The connection of megalithic monuments with sexual activity is common in many parts of Europe. Grinsell notes the existence of several stories in Sardinia and Corsica 'of standing stones and other stones said to have been a friar and a nun turned into stone for having an affair contrary to their religious vow' or individuals who practised 'free love' (Carrington and Grinsell 1982: 64; Menefee 1971: div 4/0/0). Elsewhere the menhir at Poligny, Jura, is a giant petrified for his attempted rape of a local girl – the stone is still used by young women to promote their fertility. All of this is directly parallel to the 'unlawful love' of the Long Meg circle in Cumbria. The existence of petrified weddings in western France and south England and of 'wanton dancers' similarly treated at St Buryan in Cornwall (Menefee 1974: 23, 24–5, 35, 39–42) provide indirect support for a connection, as do the Irish traditions of tombs being the beds of Diarmid and Grainne during the year-and-a-day period of their elopement. Some sixty–five monuments so named exist (Grinsell 1976: 42) about one–third of which are located in County Clare (Menefee 1971: div. 2/6/5). Handfast marriages were made through holed stones at Douglas in Co. Antrim and in Orkney, at Callendish, and in Sutherland and Argyll (Grinsell 1976: 15). As late as 1880 liaisons at the menhir of Kherderf in Morbihan were believed to guarantee pregnancy (Menefee 1971: div. 2/6/5), and similar activities connected with French monuments could be added. In Wessex

> [t]he sexual aspect of the ... Cerne Abbas hill figure is emphasized by the local tradition that barrenness in women may be cured if the woman sits on the right part of the giant's figure, though some say that it is necessary to have sexual intercourse on the giant to ensure success. Modern tradition still warns young girls not to picnic in the area. A nineteenth-century vicar stopped the scourings, as the festivities accompanying them tended to demonstrate too much the traditional view that the giant was a fertility god.
>
> (Palmer 1973: 119)

And the testimony of Wood-Martin indicates that traditions of 'runaway couples and aphrodisiac customs' were still associated with Irish monuments in the nineteenth century. Particularly interesting is the experience of one traveller, named Dutton:

> when he was trying to visit the BallyCasheen Bed of Dermot and Grania (Co. Clare). He asked a group of girls where the monument could be found and was given a laugh when he asked one to show him the way. After consultation in Gaelic with an older girl, and apparently a good deal of persuasion, she agreed to guide him if she made certain that if he were a stranger, she know [sic] his name. As it was growing late, he became impatient and rode away. A few miles down the road he asked a herdsman's wife the location of the bed and mentioned the girls' strange reaction to his request. She replied, No wonder for them, for it was the custom that if she went with a stranger to Darby and Crane's bed, she was certain to grant him everything he asked.
>
> (Menefee 1971: div. 2/6/5)

Borlase felt 'that such a reputation is still attached to these monuments from anecdotes he heard, as well as covert jokes in Gaelic between the people who accompanied him to these beds' and 'reports a similar belief connected with some Welsh dolmens, associated with illicit and clandestine meetings' (Menefee 1971: div. 2/6/5). Also to be noted as a possible analogue or parallel are the Rolandsöule of northern Germany, stones depicting a knight in armour which Arthur Evans suggests may have derived from Christianized idols. Women of ill-repute had their hair shorn before the stone at Halle as late as the eighteenth century, while Evans quotes Olaus Magnus to the effect that there was formerly a similar effigy, 'Long Thor', at Skeninge in east Gothland, before which 'evil-doers, notably adulterers, were brought . . . for punishment or execution' (Evans 1895: 41–2, 42 n. 1).

Other stories associated with Long Meg, while not showing the diversity of the traditions of 'unlawful love', have links with other megalithic beliefs. The tale that the circle's stones were petrified witches finds parallels in the story of druidesses petrified by St Revan at Plouzone, Finistère (Menefee 1971: div. 4/0/0); of the witch Medgel or Litchell, who milked the cow into a sieve at Mitchell's Fold and was turned to stone; and perhaps too of the *Leac nan Galileacha Dubha*, the Stones of the Black Hags, on north Uist who some claim were similarly treated for milking cows not their own (Grinsell 1976: 54–6, 155–6, 194). The witch at the Rollright Stones was not petrified but became an elder-tree and, like her Cumbrian counterpart, could be 'bled' (ibid.: 148), a tradition shared with a standing stone at Staunton, Gloucestershire, which reacted similarly if pricked with a pin at midnight (Crawford 1925: 199). The 'Niobe motif', in which Meg's daughters are petrified along with their mother, can be paralleled by the Children of the Mermaid at Inishcrone – seven offspring of a mortal–mermaid union, who were petrified by their mother when she returned to the sea (Menefee 1974: 28). The Seven Sisters in Kerry may have had a similar story attached (ibid.: 58), and other sibling traditions involving multiples of seven could, of course, be cited.

LONG MEG: THE SHORT OF IT

The search for Meg and her Daughters has come full circle. An unidentifiable female may or may not have been petrified with her daughters or with her lovers, as a sexual libertine or as a witch. In turn, she has been a megalith, a chapbook heroine, a real-life bawd, a gravestone in Westminster Abbey, and half the ancient ordnance of Britain. Whether these transformations make her a goddess is unclear. Yet the very protean nature of this Cumbrian monolith and its traditions makes it of interest; while 'the Rest are but Soe many Cragg stones', the view of Celia Fiennes can certainly be seconded: 'Meg is much bigger and have some fforme Like a statue or figure of a body.

REFERENCES

Ashton, J. 1882. *Chap-Books of the Eighteenth Century with Facsimiles, Notes, and Introduction.* London.

Carrington, D., and L.V. Grinsell 1982. The Folklore of Some Archaeological Sites in Corsica, *Folklore*, 93, 61–9.

Coates, R. 1978. The Linguistic Status of the Wandlebury Giants, *Folklore*, 89, 75–8.

Crawford, O.G.S. 1925. *Long Barrows of the Cotswolds.* Gloucester.

Daiches, D. ed. 1986. *Edinburgh: A Travellers Companion.* London.

Evans, A.J. 1895. The Rollright Stones and their Folklore, *Folk-Lore* 6, 6–51.

Evans, J.H. 1946. Notes on the Folklore and Legends Associated with the Kentish Megaliths, *Folk-Lore* 57, 36–43.

Farmer, J.S., and W.E. Henley 1937. *A Dictionary of Slang: An Alphabetical History of Colloquial, Unorthodox, Underground and Vulgar English*, Book 2. Ware.

Fuller, T. 1662. *Worthies.* London.

Grant, J. 1881. *Cassells Old and New Edinburgh: Its History, its People, and its Places* I. New York.

Grinsell, L.V. 1976. *Folklore of Prehistoric Sites in Britain.* Newton Abbot.

— 1982: *Mitchell's Fold Stone Circle and its Folklore.* Guernsey.

Grose, F. 1811. *Provincial Glossary.* London.

Halliwell, J.O. 1848. *Descriptive Notices of Popular English Histories.* London.

Hardy, J. ed. 1892. *The Denham Tracts: A Collection of Folklore by Michael Aislatte Denham and Reprinted from the Original Tracts and Publications Printed by Mr. Denham between 1846 and 1859* I. London.

Hindley, C. ed. 1872. *The Old Book Collector's Miscellany: or, A Collection of Readable Reprints of Literary Rarities, Illustrative of the History, Literature, Manners and Biography of the English Nation during the Sixteenth and Seventeenth Centuries* II. London.

Hogg, O.F.G. 1963. *English Artillery 1326–1716: Being the History of Artillery in this Country Prior to the Formation of the Royal Regiment of Artillery.* London

— 1970. *Artillery: Its Origin, Heyday and Decline.* London.

Legg, L.G.W. 1904. *Relation of a Short Survey of 26 Counties observed in a seven week journey begun on August 11, 1634 ... by a Captain, a Lieutenant and an Ancient.* Stuart Series 7. London.

Lyly, J. 1589. *Pappe with an hatchet, alias A figge for my God sonne. Or Cracke me this nut.* London.

Menefee, S.P. 1971. Megalithic Folklore, 6 vols. Unpublished.

— 1974. The 'Merry Maidens' and the 'Noces de Pierre' *Folklore* 85, 23–42.

Mish, C.C. ed. 1968. *Short Fiction of the Seventeenth Century.* New York.

'Northman' 1852. A Roaring Meg, *Notes and Queries*, 13 March, 260.

Palmer, K. 1973. *Oral Folk-Tales of Wessex.* Newton Abbot.

Partridge, E. 1982. *A Dictionary of Slang and Unconventional English: Colloquialisms and Catch-phrases Solecisms and Catachreses Nicknames Vulgarisms and Such Americanisms as have been Naturalized.* London, Melbourne and Henley.

Porter, E. 1969. *Cambridgeshire Customs and Folklore.* London.

Rimbault, E.F. 1850. Long Meg of Westminster, *Notes and Queries*, 27 July, 131.

— 1852. Long Meg of Westminster, *Notes and Queries*, 7 Feb., 133.

Rogers, H.C.B. 1975. *A History of Artillery.* Secaucus.

Rollins, H.E. 1967. *An Analytical Index to the Ballad-Entries (1557–1769) in the Registers of the Company of Stationers of London.* Hatboro, Pa.

Rowling, M. 1976. *The Folklore of the Lake District.* London.

Simpson, R. 1847. *Annals of Derry*. Londonderry.
W.W.E.T. (1852) A Roaring Meg, *Notes and Queries*, 31 Jan., 105.
Taylor, J. (1618) *The Pennyles Pilgrimage: or, The money-less perambulation of John Taylor from London to Edenborough*. London.
Wilson, D. (1891) *Memorials of Edinburgh in the Olden Time* I. Edinburgh and London.

CHAPTER SEVEN

MILK AND THE NORTHERN GODDESS[1]

—— .◆. ——

Hilda Ellis Davidson

Links between milk and the goddess go back to very early times. In Ancient Egypt Hathor appears as a cow-goddess protecting the Pharaoh, and when depicted in human form as a sky-goddess, she wears on her head a sun-disk flanked by cow's horns. The sky itself might be imagined as a great cow with its belly speckled with stars, which every morning produced a bull-calf, the rising sun (Clark 1959: 87; Bleeker 1973: 31ff.). Milk was drunk in Egypt and had associations with the Otherworld; milk offerings were made to deities, princes were represented being suckled by goddesses, and the dead Pharaoh as receiving new life from Hathor's milk on his journey to the nether world (Darby 1977: 87, 760). One of the chief Mesopotamian goddesses, Ninhursag, protected the animals of the wild, and also domestic herds (Jacobsen 1976: 104ff.); sacred cattle and sheep were kept at her temple at Lagash, and milk from the sacred dairy given to the royal children (Levy 1948: 97).

In India the reasons why the cow is a sacred animal have provoked much debate, but its importance as provider of milk evidently goes back to early times, probably to the period before the coming of the Aryans (Ferro-Luzzi 1987: 109). In the earliest literary texts, the Vedas, the cow is associated with the goddess Aditi (Lodrick 1981: 6), while one of the most popular goddesses of recent times, Śrī-Laksmi, was said in some sources to have come into being when the primeval Ocean of Milk was churned by gods and demons (Kinsley 1989: 61), and she became linked with Vishnu, the dominant god who caused the churning to take place. Goddesses in India are frequently described as cows, and milk and milk-products offered to them and to the gods. Milk is seen as a life-giving drink, symbol of whiteness and purity as well as of bounty and fertility, and the pressing-out of milk from breast or udder has become the symbol for any kind of giving-forth (O'Flaherty 1980: 28).

Such concepts encourage a search for links between milk and the Northern goddess, although the subject has received little attention up to now. One peculiarity about milk as a drink is that in some parts of the world adults are unable to digest the lactose because the lactase enzyme fails to work. This is common among peoples of central Africa, the Chinese and Japanese, Inuyt and North American Indians (Darby 1977: 770). A different reason for not using milk as part of the diet in Southern Europe was that there were good supplies of wine and oil, and grazing for cattle was limited (Freyn 1979: 41). Sheep's milk was drunk on farms, and cheese made from this was a popular food, but milk was difficult to transport in the hot summer, and Romans in the cities regarded it as a drink fit only for infants and invalids. 'Why', asked Clement of Alexandria, arguing for the necessity for changes in ways of thinking, 'do we not go on using our first food, milk, to which ... our nurses accustomed us from birth?' (Perowne 1969: 129).

However, in northern Europe the herding of cattle, sheep and goats, animals whose milk can be drunk or made into butter or cheese, has gone on since the Bronze Age. Milk and milk-products have formed an essential part of the diet from early times in Scandinavia and the British Isles (Weinhold 1856: 114, 152). The importance of milk and butter in Norway has been made clear by Svale Solheim in his detailed study of life on the *sæter*, the high pastures to which the cattle were moved in spring (Solheim 1952), and in Ireland by A.T. Lucas (1960–2; 1989). While milk was obtained not only from cows but also from ewes and she-goats and from deer, according to legend it is the cow that is most clearly linked with goddesses, and I intend to concentrate on this.

Solheim has collected evidence for an enormous wealth of rites, customs, spells, prayers and beliefs in Norway concerned with the protection of cows, and their well-being during the summer season. Herders and milkers working to produce a good supply of butter and cheese to see them through the winter knew themselves to be threatened by bad weather, pestilence, accidents to the animals, or inefficiency in the dairy. There were constant appeals to supernatural powers for assistance, from the time when the farm people prepared to set out for the mountain pastures to their return at the end of summer. In Ireland, Patricia Lysaght has shown how on 1 May each year there was constant endeavour up to very recent times to protect potential supplies of cream and butter from neighbours who might try to steal them by magic rites (Lysaght 1992: 31ff.). Similar uncertainties and dread of failure must have troubled workers in the dairy in pre-Christian times, so that there must have been continual appeals to supernatural powers on a matter of such importance to the community. The churning of milk in the old stand-churn was notoriously unpredictable, and inexplicable failures would be blamed on hostile magic.

Although in general the herding and stable-work was done by men, milking and dairywork were a matter for the women, and therefore it seems probable that the dairy was one of the regions over which a goddess would preside. Yet this possibility has gone almost unrecognized in work done on carved stones of the Roman period in Britain showing goddesses associated with plenty. In other parts of Europe Mother Goddesses of this type were usually shown with horns of plenty, baskets of fruit, possibly eggs or loaves. In Britain, however, they are sometimes provided with different objects, and it seems possible that some of these are associated with the dairy.

The objects to look for are those used up to the last century on isolated farms in Yorkshire or the Lake District (Hartley and Ingilby 1981: 33, 36), and the most likely would seem to be the churn of the old upright type, known as the stand-, dash- or plunger-churn (Figures 7.1 and 7.2). One Celtic goddess is shown on a number of carved stones on Hadrian's Wall and in the Cotswolds with just such an object. The assumption that this is Rosmerta, whose name is thought to mean 'Great Provider', and who is shown on stones on the Continent in company with Mercury, is not fully accepted but seems plausible (Webster 1986: 59ff.). Various unconvincing explanations have been given for her 'tub', such as a magic tub, a dyeing vat, a vessel for making wine, and even a washer-woman's tub, and Webster asks doubtfully: 'How could a wooden tub be seen as a symbol of plenty?' (ibid.: 61). But this attribute closely resembles the old stand-churn, bound with metal hoops and worked from the top, especially on a stone from Corbridge, where the goddess is apparently stirring it with a long-handled implement (Figure 7.3). The churn would be a very appropriate symbol for plenty, worked by a bountiful goddess. On a stone from Gloucester, the goddess, here shown with Mercury (Figure 7.4), is pouring into her tub from a dish something which could well be cream, and the tub appears again on stones from Bath, Wellow and Newcastle upon Tyne (Webster 1986: plates 6–10). It seems possible that the object, like a spoon with a long handle, held by the goddess on some stones could be the plunger or churn-dash rather than a clumsy attempt at a cornucopia or a copy of Mercury's caduceus, as has been suggested.

Another possible goddess connected with the dairy is a little wooden figure found at Winchester in 1971 (Ross 1975: 335). She holds what is plainly a key in one hand, and what seems to be a folded cloth in the other (Figure 7.5). I find it hard to accept Anne Ross's explanation of this as a representation of Epona or a priestess of her cult, on the grounds that the cloth is the *mappa* held up by the emperor to start a chariot race. Epona is normally shown with one or more horses, riding or feeding them. A cloth was important in the dairy, as liquid was strained through it in cheese-making, but another possibility is suggested by the use of the *brat* or mantle of St Brigid on many farms in Ireland to ensure a good milk-supply and to lay on sick animals or those which were calving. It might be preserved on a farm for years, since the longer it was kept, the greater its potency was thought to be (Danaher 1972: 31ff.), and it consisted of a ribbon, scarf or piece of material left out to be blessed by the saint on her visit to the farm on the eve of her festival. There might also be an explanation for the

Figure 7.1 Standchurn from North Yorkshire, hooped with iron girths, and plunger.

Figure 7.2 Stand-churn in use. (Drawings by Eileen Aldworth; based on illustrations in Hartley and Ongilby, *Life and Tradition in the Yorkshire Dales,* 1989.)

Figure 7.3 Goddess (Rosmerta?) with her tub. (From Corbridge Museum.)

key other than that by Ross, who thought it was the symbol of the power of the goddess to conduct the dead to the next world. From a purely practical point of view, the key of dairy or store-room was of great importance and was kept by the mistress of the house. When St Brigid was staying in a strange house and wanted to find food for some hungry guests, she is said to have asked a dumb boy to tell her where to find the key, and he received the power of speech in order to do so (Stokes 1890: 191). But the key of a goddess might also protect animals from harm. Solheim (1952: 248) records a Norwegian charm in which the Virgin Mary goes to the

Figure 7.4 Stone, depicting Mercury and Rosmerta, from Shakespeare Inn, Gloucester. (Now in Gloucester City Museum; drawing by Eileen Aldworth.)

wood with her nine hanging keys, and locks in all wild creatures such as wolverine and bear which might harm cattle, 'all but the good farm dog'. Another charm, quoted in the transcript of a trial in Norway in 1722, refers to the Virgin's keys as a means of helping women in childbirth:

> Virgin Mary, gentle mother,
>
> loan your keys to me,
>
> to open my limbs
>
> and my members.
>
> (Kvideland and Sehmsdorf 1988: 147)

The use of this formula was apparently forbidden in some parts of Scandinavia after the Reformation. Solheim also quotes an appeal by the herdsmen to St Olaf to use his key against predators in the same way. Thus there are other possibilities for interpreting the symbol of a key in the hand of a goddess than have been previously considered.

Symbols in the dairy might serve as another possible link with the pre-Christian cult of a goddess. Lily Weiser-Aal (1947: 117ff.) has done a careful study of the carved wooden vessels used in dairies in Norwegian museums, and noted symbols not part of the original ornament carved on the base, or added elsewhere. These are presumably protective signs to drive away evil influences or increase the butter yield, and some seem to be symbols associated with the sun, such as concentric circles, whirling discs and circled stars. Similar signs may be noticed beside the goddess from Corbridge with

Figure 7.5   Wooden figure of goddess, from Winchester.
(Drawing by Eileen
Aldworth)

97

her possible churn. They have been noted too on buckets from the Oseberg ship-burial, a ninth-century grave in southern Norway in which a woman of high rank, possibly a priestess of the goddess, was buried (Davidson 1989b: 117). Solheim gives more designs on wooden dairy vessels and butter stamps which suggest a link with traditional sun symbols (Solheim 1952: 146ff.), resembling those noted by Miranda Green on pipe-clay figures of Venus from Roman Britain (Green 1984: 25ff.).

Certain rites connected with milking may also be relevent. In Norway on the Feast of the Annunciation, Our Lady's Day (25 March), the girls doing the milking were encouraged to go out early, so that if the day was clear the rising sun might shine on the vessels in which the milk was carried; this was to ensure that they would not fall behindhand with their work that summer (Solheim 1952: 7). Again, on St John's Eve at Midsummer, when milking was done three times a day for the first time, those going out in the evening should finish milking before the sun went down, so that it could shine on their vessels (ibid.: 512).

Other customs possibly influenced by pre-Christian rites in Ireland are those associated with St Brigid. Her feast-day on 1 February replaced one of the four festivals dividing up the year in pre-Christian times. It was the day on which spring sowing was due to begin, but its old name, *Imbolg*, is thought to mean parturition and it may originally have been associated with the birth of farm animals (Ó hÓgain 1990: 60). Among St Brigid's powers was that of increasing the herds of cattle, sheep and pigs, thus ensuring good supplies of milk, butter, cheese and bacon. Her 'mantle' (*brat*), already mentioned, was the cloth left on windowsill or step or on the latch of the door on the night before, so that she would touch it when visiting the house. If the length had increased in the damp night, this was a good omen for crops and cattle and the well-being of the family, while the *brat* was used for healing sick animals, helping them to bear their young, and making sure there would be plenty of milk for calves, lambs and foals (Danaher 1972: 33). On St Brigid's Eve a figure representing her might be made from the churn-dash wrapped in hay or straw (ibid.: 27); fresh butter formed part of the meal on that day, while farmers made gifts of milk and butter to poorer neighbours. A cake or a dish of milky porridge might be left for the saint's visit during the night, set on the flat end of the churn-dash with its handle stuck into the ground.

The historic existence of an abbess of Kildare named Brigid is in doubt (Ó Cathasaigh 1982: 82ff.), but there are many legends about her. In the seventh-century Life by Cogitosis we are told that in her youth she churned butter and guarded her father's herds as well as helping with the harvest The story of her birth in the Irish *Life* in the *Book of Lismore* (Stokes 1890) is of especial interest. She is said to be the daughter of a bondmaid made pregnant by her master, Dubhthaig, and to have been born when her mother was going out at sunrise one morning with a vessel of milk and stepping across the threshold, symbolizing the liminal position of Brigid between the human and supernatural worlds. The baby was washed in milk from her mother's pail, a custom which may go back to pre-Christian times, since a secular rite of washing the newborn in milk is mentioned in records of a Church council at Cashel in 1171 (Lucas 1989: 5). The infant Brigid was also nourished on the milk of a special cow, since ordinary cow's milk made her sick, and this was a white animal with red ears, procured from the Otherworld by her foster-father. Her cow was said to accompany her on visits to the farms, and a sheaf of hay might be left out for it (Danaher 1972: 15).

Another white, red-eared cow was possessed by the *Cailleach Bhearra*, the Hag of Beare, who appears to have been a powerful goddess; her foster-child, Calc, used to be bathed in the sea on its back each morning, according to a tale of the tenth or eleventh century (Ó hÓgain 1990: 119). The Irish battle-goddess, the Mórrígan, claimed to be able to take on such a shape, leading a herd of a hundred other white, red-eared cows in the *Táin Bó Regamna*, and references to such cows appear in many early Lives of the Irish saints.

As for the Celtic goddess, Brigid, from whom it is assumed that many of the traditions about the saint have been transferred, she is said, in the *Lebor Gabala*, to have owned two oxen, after which two plains in Cardow and Tipperary were named, and these could give her warning of any rapine committed in Ireland (Ó hÓgain 1990: 60). Another case of a goddess with oxen is in the Icelandic legend of Gefion, told in the *Heimskringla* of Snorri Sturluson (*Ynglinga saga* 5). She used four oxen, said to be her sons, to plough out a tract of land in Sweden where there is now a lake and to drag this to Denmark to become the island of Sjælland; Snorri quotes a verse from a ninth-century poet as his source. Again, from Wales we have the legend of the fairy wife of Llyn y Fan Fach in Carmarthenshire, as recorded in 1861, the most famous of the legends of a supernatural woman from beneath a lake who becomes the wife of a farmer, bringing a herd of cattle with her (Wood 1992). When her husband unwittingly breaks the contract made with her, she calls her animals together and returns with them to the lake, and her calling song, mentioning various animals by name, is given in the version quoted by Sir John Rhys (1901/1980: 10). Finally, she summons four grey oxen ploughing in a field, and they move six miles to the lake, dragging the plough with them and making a well-marked furrow over the land, said to be still visible. The importance of the oxen in local tradition is indicated by the statement in 1881 of an old woman, who claimed to remember crowds gathering on the first Sunday or Monday in August, when the lake waters were said to boil up as a sign that the Lake Lady and her oxen would appear.

Evidence for a wealth of tradition concerning Otherworld cattle from both Germanic and Celtic sources is too plentiful for me to do justice to it here. Solheim has made a special study of tales from Norway of such cattle said to have been seen by the grandmother of some other older relative of the informant, and occasionally by the teller herself. It seems almost always to be women who claim to have heard or seen them and to have met their owners, also women, belonging to the *underjordisk* (underearth or mound-dwelling) folk, or to the *huldre* (fairy) people. Similar traditions from Sweden are given by Tone Dahlstedt (1991). The colour and appearance of these animals are usually stressed; they are fine, well-nourished creatures with large udders, and, while occasionally said to be white, can also be a variety of colours, with grey or red markings, or brindled. Solheim thought the choice of colour, which varied in different parts of Norway, might be due to the introduction of new breeds into certain areas (Solheim 1952: 419).

The white cattle with red ears mentioned in early Irish literature (Lucas 1989: 240ff.) are a breed known to have existed in Britain from Roman times onwards. A considerable number survived into the last century, and one herd has been preserved at Chillingham in Northumberland. In his detailed study of these cattle, Kenneth Whitehead (1953) supports the theory that they were brought to England by the Romans to be used in ritual processions and for sacrifice, since the native British cattle were black. If correct, this might help to account for the association of this type of animal with the Otherworld in early literature. The supernatural cows are also said sometimes to be hornless, grey-brown animals, and this may be the group to which the famous Brown Bull of the *Táin* was thought to belong (Lucas 1989: 239).

While in Scandinavia the cattle are thought to dwell under the earth, they are under the water in the Welsh tales, and in Denmark there are legends of cattle which belong to the merfolk and come up out of the sea to graze on land (Simpson 1988: 235). The idea of cows and dairywork down below the earth and the surface of the water was strengthened by traditions of certain wells in Wales which at times produced milk instead of water. One example, from a chronicle of Margam Abbey, is a claim, said to be supported by witnesses, that in the year 1185 a stream of milk flowed from St Illtud's Well on Gower, and what seemed to be curds and 'a certain fatty substance floating about, such as is collected from milk, so that butter can be made from it' was to be seen around the edge of the well (*Archaeologia Cambrensis*, 1st series, 3 (1848): 264; Bord and Bord 1985: 105).

In Scandinavian tales of Otherworld cows, a milkmaid is sometimes asked by a strange woman if she will milk her herd for her, so that she can leave to attend a funeral or go to a feast (Kvideland and Sehmsdorf 1988: 299; Solheim 1952: 452ff.). The girl asks in surprise where this herd can be found, and is told that they are close to her own cows and that milking-vessels will be provided. As a reward for her help, she may receive

one of these splendid animals as a gift, to become a treasured family possession. Should she refuse to take the cow, however, the animal will be called
back by its owner, who in some tales sings a verse summoning it by name.
Calling-songs naming a number of cows are recorded from both Norway
and Sweden and are said to have been sung by the supernatural women
(Solheim 1952: 459; Dahlstedt 1991: 22). There is a striking resemblance
here to the calling-song of the lady of Llyn y Fan Fach when she took her
cattle into the lake and to another in a tale from Glamorganshire (Rhys
1901/1980: 24, 26). The names given to the cows are mostly descriptive
ones: Yellow One, Speckled One, and so on. Juliette Wood points out that
the verses do not appear to be old (Wood 1992: 71 n. 34), and such songs
in both Wales and Scandinavia may be modelled on later songs known to
the story-tellers. In Scandinavia such songs are not linked to the fairy-bride
motif, or to the calling-back of animals after they have been in human
possession for some years.

Another way of acquiring Otherworld cattle was by throwing steel over
them. In one Norwegian tale a man throws a scythe (Kvideland and
Sehmsdorf 1988: 232) and is able to keep one of the cows, and there is a
Swedish tale of a milkmaid who tried to drive a strange cow away by
throwing her sowing at it. Because there was a steel needle in the cloth,
the supernatural woman who owned the cow could not take it back, even
when the girl urged her to do so (Dahlstedt 1991: 13). Occasionally an
exchange is made; in one case a cow is given in return for four goats, and
in another for an axe (Solheim 1952: 461).

A different motif linked with supernatural cows in England is that of
the bountiful cow which supplied generous amounts of milk to all who
came. The legend of the White Cow of Mitchell's Folk in Shropshire was
recorded by Charlotte Burne (1883/1973: 93), who found that it was well
known in the district. In a time of famine, a pure white fairy cow appeared
on a hill every morning and evening, and anyone might come to milk her
so long as only one vessel was brought by each comer; this was always
filled, whatever the size. However, one day a mean old witch came with a
sieve and milked the cow dry, as shown in a carving in the church at
Middleton-in-Chirbury done by the vicar in 1879 (Westwood 1985: 259).
In some versions of the tale the cow is said to have died of grief, as at
Preston in Lancashire, where its huge bones were said to have been
found on Cow Hill (Burne 1883: 41), or to have stamped its foot in
rage, leaving a mark on the rock before it vanished, as at South Lopham,
Norfolk (Westwood 1985: 257-9). In Warwickshire there was a tradition
that it turned into the monstrous Dun Cow, slain by Guy of Warwick
(ibid.: 22).

An interesting study of the self-milking cow, a symbol of bounty and
divine revelation, has been made in India by Gabrielle Ferro-Luzzi (1987).
She collected well over four hundred variants of the tale of a mysterious

cow which regularly emptied its udder over an anthill or cairn, beneath which was discovered a sacred lingam or image of a god, whereupon the local rajah built a temple to house the sacred symbol. The author's purpose was to show the various ways in which a tale might develop, but her work also provides evidence of the concept of the cow as a bountiful figure, revealing something hidden. Few parallels are given from Europe, and the Stith Thompson motif index is not very helpful here. There is, however, an interesting body of the boy-king St Kenelm, as told in a poem of the *South English Legendary* (Bennett and Smithers 1966: 103). The body of the child, murdered through the malice of his sister, remained for a long time undiscovered, but a white cow belonging to a widow began to spend the whole day in the valley where he was buried, away from the rest of the herd. Although the animal went without food, it remained 'fair and round' and gave more milk than all the others. In this thirteenth-century version, the body is not discovered solely through the behaviour of the cow, although it is stated that the local people noticed and wondered at it. A letter is brought down from heaven by a white dove and given to the Pope, who sends messengers to enquire into the matter, but this seems likely to be a later elaboration. It is perhaps also worth noting that in Norway the bell-cow, the leader of the herd, was sometimes milked on the ground when the cattle arrived at the summer pastures, as an offering to the local spirit thought to dwell under the earth (Solheim 1952: 77).

In the field of mythology there is a tradition recorded by Snorri Sturluson in his *Edda* of a primeval cow called Audhumla existing before the gods along with the giant Ymir, who was nourished by four streams of milk which flowed from her teats. The cow licked the salty ice-blocks until a handsome being called Buri emerged, and his son Bor was the father of Óðinn and his two brothers, who slew the giant Ymir and created the world from his body (*Gylfaginning* 5). Snorri was writing in the thirteenth century, and his source for this myth is not known; some, like Bruce Lincoln (1987: 69ff.), want to derive it from an Indo-European origin myth. The name, Audhumla, means something like 'rich hornless cow' (Turville-Petre 1964: 319 n. 4), and hornless cows are sometimes included among Otherworld cattle (Lucas 1989: 240). There is a folk-tradition, recorded in East Yorkshire in the eighteenth century, that the giant Wade and his wife were nourished by a cow called Bel (Charlton 1779: 40). Wade was known to the Anglo-Saxons as a giant (Davidson 1958: 136) and, although later Bel was given as the name of his wife (Rushton 1986: 136), the earlier form of the legend may have been one of a single giant and his cow, as in Snorri's account.

There are numerous examples from the British Isles of offerings of milk to helpful spirits who protected the herds and helped in the dairy, taking some of the cream in return. On Welsh farms a dish of fresh creamy milk with a slice of wheaten bread might be set out for the brownie each evening, and Rhys records the tale of a mischievous servant girl who once substituted a dish of urine and rough barley bread; she got a severe beating from invisible hands next morning, and the helpful spirit departed, never to return. In the Highlands of Scotland, cold whey might be left for the Maiden who protected the cattle, and one night on a farm in Lismore a new maid left hot whey in the pail, after which the maiden was never seen again (MacDougall 1978: 50). On another farm, a pail of milk used to be left for the Maiden, and if this was not done it was feared that the calves might get loose and suck the cows dry (ibid.: 52). Sometimes milk-offerings were poured into a hole in a stone, as on the island of Colonsay, to guard against the possibility of the cows going astray and falling over the cliff (MacGregor 1937: 45-6). Butter too might be thrown into a lake, as at Loughkeeran, Ireland (Macneill 1962: I, 232), and cheeses are said to have been given to a Lake Lady in Wales (Sikes 1880/1991: 14i); many centuries earlier, cheeses were included among offerings thrown into a lake by Gregory of Tours (Hagberg 1967: II, 67).

In Tudor times both male and female spirits were said to frequent the dairy, and Ben Jonson in a masque of 1603 refers to Mab, the 'mistris-Faerie', who robbed the dairy each night and could 'hurt or helpe the churnin' (Jonson/Herford and Simpson 1947–52: lines ll. 53–6). I have suggested elsewhere that the little hooded figures, the *cucullati*, represented on carved stones on Hadrian's Wall and in the Cotswolds in the Roman period, were the forerunners of later brownies and other house-spirits (Davidson 1989a). These little men were evidently linked with goddesses, since a group of three of them is sometimes shown with a female figure resembling a Mother Goddess. Scandinavian traditions indicate a similar link between the main fertility deities, such as Freyr and Freyja, and the humbler land-spirits who helped Icelandic farmers with their sheep and goats.

It seems likely that more may be learned about these elusive goddesses by the study of rites and customs connected with women's crafts and mysteries, such as dairywork, brewing, baking, spinning, healing and midwifery in early times. The importance of the seasonality of milk, for example, was brought home to me by an article by Charles Phythian-Adams (1983) on May customs in Stuart and Hanoverian London. He points out that in early spring the cows still depended on winter fodder, and no milk could be taken from them until their calves were weaned. But in May, when they were out in the pastures, milk-production reached its peak, and those who had been short of protein during winter and spring could expect new supplies. On the eve of May Day, young men brought in greenery from the wood, while the girls collected flowers, associated with bridal garlands. The pairings-off in the woods which so horrified the Puritans had on the whole a beneficial effect in encouraging young people to marry, and often resulted in repectable betrothals, so that originally they appear to have had the backing of the community (Phythian-Adams 1983: 88).

On the morning of May Day the young folk visited farms on the outskirts of London to breakfast on such delights as milk laced with rum, syllabubs (for which the cow was milked directly into wine, port or sherry), sour milk and curds with sugar and cream, junkets and cream-cakes. It is hard for us to realize now the excitement of fresh cream and milk in Maytime, both a necessity for survival and a source of pleasure after the Lenten austerities. Phythian-Adams argues that, rather than being based on vague memories of prehistoric fertility ceremonies or the Roman rites of Flora, as was once thought, the Maytime customs depended on the close relationship between the community and the natural environment, something now largely lost. In the May rites of the seventeenth century we can recognize an appropriate setting for a goddess of bounty, and it is surely no accident that May was the month dedicated to the Virgin Mary. In the past there must have been many goddesses of Maytime in northern Europe, and these were surely closely linked with the cow, symbol of divine giving, a possible visitant from the Otherworld, and an animal close to the goddess, loved and tended by women.

NOTE

1 I am most grateful to those who have helped me to find evidence for this paper, and must especially acknowledge the generosity of Dr Reimund Kvideland, Dr Catharina Raudvere and Jennifer Westwood in sending me valuable material. My thanks are also due to Dr Hilary Belcher, Dr John Brockington, Dr Patricia Lysaght, Dr Audrey Meaney, Dr Jane Renfrew, Dr Joyce Reynolds and Dr Juliette Wood for answering queries and supplying references, and to Dr Tone Bringa for help in the interpretation of Norwegian records.

REFERENCES

Bennett, J.A.W., and G.V. Smithers eds 1966. *Early Middle English Verse and Prose.* Oxford.
Bleeker, C.K. 1973. *Hathor and Thoth: Two Key Figures of the Ancient Egyptian Religion.* Numen Supplement 26. Leiden.
Bord, C. and J. 1985. *Sacred Waters: Holy Wells and Water Lore in Britain and Ireland.* London.
Burne, C. 1883/1973. *Shropshire Folklore*, ed. from the collections of G.F. Jackson. London.
Charlton, L. 1779. *History of Whitby and of Whitby Abbey.* York.
Clark, R.T. Rundle 1959. *Myth and Symbol in Ancient Egypt.* London.
Dahlstedt, T. 1991. *Kvinnors Moten med Vittra*, Umea.
Danaher, K. 1972. *The Year in Ireland.* Cork and Dublin.
Darby, W.J., with P. Ghalioungi and L. Grivetti. 1977. *Food: The Gift of Osiris.*

Davidson, H.R.E. 1958. 'Weland the Smith', *Folklore* 69, 145–59.
—— 1989a. 'Hooded Men in Germanic and Celtic Tradition', in G. Davies (ed.), *Polytheistic Systems*, Cosmos 5. Edinburgh. 105–24.
—— 1989b. *Myths and Symbols in Northern Europe: Early Scandinavian and Celtic Religions*. Manchester.
Ferro-Luzzi, G.E. 1987. *The Self-milking Cow and the Bleeding Lingam: Criss-Cross of Motifs in Indian Temple Legends*. Wiesbaden.
Freyn, J.M. 1979. *Subsistence Farming in Roman Italy*. London.
Green M. 1984. 'Mother and Sun in Romano-Celtic Religion', *Antiquaries Journal* 64, 25–31.
Hagberg, U.E. 1967. *The Archaeology of Skedemosse* II. Stockholm.
Hartley M. and J. Ingilby 1981. *Life and Tradition in the Yorkshire Dales*. Lancaster.
Jacobsen, T. 1976. *The Treasures of Darkness: a History of Mesopotamian Religion*. New Haven and London.
Jonson, B. ed. C.H. Herford and P. Simpson 1947–52. Works, 2 vols. Oxford.
Kinsley, D. 1989. *The Goddesses' Mirror: Visions of the Divine from East and West*. New York.
Kvideland, R., and H.K. Sehmsdorf 1988. *Scandinavian Folk-Belief and Legend*. Minneapolis, Minn.
Levy, R. 1948. *The Gate of Horn*. London.
Lincoln, B. 1987. *Priests, Women and Cattle*. Berkeley and London.
Lodrick, D.D. 1981. *Sacred Cows, Sacred Places: Origins and Survivals of Animal Homes in India*. Berkeley, Los Angeles and London.
Lucas, A.T. 1960–2. 'Irish Food before the Potato', *Gwerin* 3, 8–40.
—— 1989. *Cattle in Ancient Ireland*. Rhine Lectures. Kilkenny.
Lysaght, P. 1992. 'Beltaine: Irish Maytime Customs and the Reaffirmation of Boundaries', in H.R.E. Davidson (ed.), *Boundaries and Thresholds*. Stroud. 28–53.
MacDougall, L. 1978. *Highland Fairy Legends*, with introduction and notes by A. Bruford. Ipswich.
MacGregor, A.A. 1937. *The Peatfire Flame: Folk-tales and Traditions of the Highlands and Islands*. Edinburgh and London.
MacNeill, M. 1962. *The Festival of Lughnasa: A study of the Survival of the Celtic Festival of the Beginning of Harvest*. Oxford.
Ó Cathasaigh T. 1982. 'The Cult of Brigid', in J. Preston (ed.) *Mother Worship*. Chapel Hill, NC.
O'Flaherty, W.D. 1980. *Women, Androgynes and Other Mythical Beings*. Chicago, Ill.
Ó hÓgain, D. 1990. *Myth, Legend and Romance: An Encyclopaedia of Irish Folk-Tradition*. London.
Perowne, S. 1969. *Roman Mythology*. London.
Phythian-Adams, C. 1983. 'Milk and Soot: The Changing Vocabulary of a Popular Ritual in Stuart and Hanoverian London', in D. Fraser and A. Sutcliffe (eds.), *The Pursuit of Urban History*. London.
Rhys, J. 1901/1980. *Celtic Folklore, Welsh and Manx*, 2 vols. Oxford.
Ross, A. 1975. 'A Wooden Statuette from *Venta Belgarium*', *Antiquaries Journal* 55, 335–6.
Rushton, J. 1986. *The Ryedale Story*. Yorkshire Countryside Handbook. Helmsley.
Sikes, W. 1880/1991. *British Goblins: The Realm of Faerie*. London.
Simpson, J. 1988. *Scandinavian Folktales*. Penguin Folklore Library. London.
Snorri Sturluson, ed. F. Jónsson. 1926. *The Prose Edda*. Copenhagen.
Solheim, S. 1952. *Norsk Saettertradisjon*. Inst. f. sammenlignende Kulturforsking 47. Oslo.

Stokes, W. 1890. *Lives of the Saints from the Book of Lismore*. Anecdota Oxoniensis, Medieval and Modern Series I, 5. Oxford.

Turville-Petre, E.O.G. 1964. *Myth and Religion of the North: The Religion of Ancient Scandinavia*. London.

Webster, G. 1986. *The British Celts and their Gods under Rome*. London.

Weinhold, K. 1856. *Altnordische Leben*. Berlin.

Weiser-Aal, L. 1947. 'Magiske tegn pa Norske trekar', *By og bygd; Arbok f. Norsk Folkemuseum* 5, 117–44.

Westwood, J. 1985. *Albion: A Guide to Legendary Britain*. London.

White K.D. 1970. *Roman Farming*. London.

Whitehead, K.D. 1953. *The Ancient White Cattle of Britain*. London.

Wood, J. 1992. 'The Fairy Bride Legend in Wales', *Folklore* 103, 56–72.

COVENTINA'S WELL

——— ·•· ———

Lindsay Allason-Jones

Coventina's Well is one of the best known of the smaller sites along Hadrian's Wall and, in some ways, the most enigmatic. The story of its excavation and subsequent interpretation can be described as a moral tale which reveals more about the nineteenth- and twentieth-century interpreters than the goddess they have tried to understand.[1]

The site is situated in a small valley immediately to the west of the fort of Carrawburgh (*Procolitia*). The valley, which contained several religious establishments during the Roman period, is often flooded by the streams which bubble from the ground, making it very difficult to visit any of the sites and, in particular, Coventina's Well. Despite the difficulty of access, the site was noticed as early as 1731, although it was not until October 1876 that John Clayton, local antiquary and owner of the site, began to excavate after the area had been disturbed by lead-miners. Under the foremanship of Mr Tailford, Clayton's archaeological assistant, a rectangular reservoir was uncovered which measured 8' 6" × 7' 9" internally and exceeded 7' in depth. It was noticed that the masonry rested on the natural gravel and enclosed a number of small springs: the term 'well' is, therefore, a misnomer. Further soundings revealed that the Well or reservoir was placed in the centre of a large rectangular enclosure, 40' × 38' internally with 3' thick walls and a west entrance which appeared to be merely a 18' wide gap with no obvious door fittings.

Richmond in 1955 suggested that the shrine was a variant on the Romano-Celtic type of temple, with the Well taking the place of the more common cella (Richmond 1955: 196). No other example of this type has been found in the military zone to date, and this appears to be the only Romano-Celtic temple in Britain with a west door. Lewis, in his volume on Romano-British temples, compares Coventina's Well with Temple 3 at Springhead in Kent, which also had a sacred reservoir open to the sky (Lewis 1966: 87). There is no reason to believe that either the parapet around the Well itself or the boundary wall was particularly high – very little stone robbing appears to have been perpetrated on the site. No examples of roofing material were found, which supports the suggestion that there was no roof, nor even a lean-to ambulatory. The neighbouring shrine of the Nymphs and *Genius Loci* has since been excavated and also shown to have been open to the sky (Smith 1962: 59–81). At the time of its excavation

Coventina's Well attracted much attention from the general public and academics alike, not just for its interest as a Romano-Celtic temple, or because of its significant relationship to the fort of Carrawburgh and the Vallum, but because of the contents of the Well, which included coins, sculpture, inscriptions, jewellery, bones and many other objects. This paper will not look in detail at the 16,000+ coins found in the Well, interesting though they are, but will concentrate on some of the other items to see if they can answer our questions about Coventina herself.

The name of the deity to whom the Well was dedicated was immediately revealed to the nineteenth-century excavators, as variations on the theme of the word Coventina were found on all but one of the inscribed stones and on one of the pottery thuribles:

COVENTINAE	[3],	[8]		
COVVENTINAE	[4],	[14]		
COVENTINE	[5],	[7],	[9],	[10]
CONVETINAE	[6]			
COVONTINE	[12]			
CONVENTINAE	[13]			
COVETINA	[142]			
COVETINE	[11][2]			

This open-minded attitude to the constraints of spelling is commonly seen on religious dedications in the military north, particularly as far as the names of Celtic deities are concerned. The deities Belatucadrus, Veteres and Antenociticus are obvious examples. It has been suggested that the diversity of spelling was due to the fact that the Celtic language was only spoken, not written down, so any attempt at transcribing Celtic words would invariably be a stab in the dark. There could be no approved spelling, and in the case of Veteres even the grammar appears to have been open to debate as it is unclear whether *veteres* refers to a god or a goddess, or even a group of deities. The different spellings of Veteres are undecided whether the word started with a *U* sound or an *H* sound, suggesting that the pronunciation produced a noise halfway between the two, far beyond the scope of the Latin alphabet. This sort of linguistic debate is, of course, of absorbing interest to archaeologists today but would have been of little concern to the Celtic or Roman worshippers. The gods knew who was meant, and it is doubtful if the newly Romanized population ever stopped to consider why Celtic deities should suddenly feel obliged to develop the ability to read inscriptions in foreign languages when they had managed without this skill for hundreds, possibly thousands, of years.

Despite the variations of spelling, it seems to be beyond dispute that in this instance we are dealing with one deity, whose name was Coventina or Conventina. Various theories have been put forward as to the meaning of this name. Dr Wake Smart suggested a derivation of *gover* meaning 'a rivulet' or 'head of a rivulet' (Clayton 1880: 21). The Reverend Dr Hoopell preferred to believe that *cov* meant 'memory' in the Celtic language, and *cofen* 'memorial', and deduced that the temple was in reality a cenotaph (Clayton 1880: 21). Charles Roach Smith at first thought that the word referred to the Convenae of Aquitaine – an area known for its springs – and he drew attention to the presence of the First Cohort of Aquitainians at Carrawburgh (Smith 1880: 115-35). He later changed his mind and divided the word into two parts: 'coven' or 'conven' for *convenio*, signi-fying a coming-together, and *tina*, which was Ptolemy's name for the River Tyne (Longstaffe 1880: 107). Unfortunately for this theory, the confluence of the North and South Tyne Rivers is some distance from Carrawburgh, but the theory had several supporters. W.H.D. Longstaffe went one stage further and divided Coventina into three parts: *con*, *went* and *tina*, and interpreted the relief of the three nymphs found in the Well as the goddess Tyne with her attendant streams or naiads, the Con and the Went [1] (ibid.: 88–107). Norah Joliffe, in 1941, put forward the idea that Coventina was the goddess of a *conventus* or community of German soldiers stationed at Carrawburgh (Joliffe 1941: 58). This theory has also had a number of supporters, but as a *conventus* is simply an administrative convenience, rather than an area with which people might have emotional ties, it seems unlikely that it would be blessed with a guardian deity. Even if such a deity existed, one would expect the deity's name to reflect the name of the locality rather than the rather arid word *conventus*.

Professor K.H. Jackson has suggested (in a personal comment) that the *co* part of the name looks very much like the Celtic preposition which is equated with the Latin *cum* meaning 'with'. The *in* part is a familiar Celtic noun- and adjective-forming suffix, while the *a* at the end is the same nomi-native singular feminine suffix as the 'a' of the Latin first declension. The *vent* part of the word has been described by Rivet and Smith, in their major work *The Place Names of Roman Britain*, as 'a well known problem' (Rivet and Smith 1979: 262–5). Often translated as 'market', *vent* has been shown by Rivet and Smith to have been a medieval re-Latinization of ver-nacular French *'vente'* meaning 'sale'. They agree with Jackson that no Indo-European roots are visible and point out that no derivations appear in Cornish or Breton, both useful languages for extracting Celtic meanings.

At the end of all this debate all that emerges is that the name Coventina has so far defied interpretation and is, at present, no help in explaining the goddess. All the combatants mentioned previously were happy that it was indeed a goddess who was concerned. Even if one is not convinced by learned discourse on feminine-singular suffixes, the stele of Titus Cosconianus [4] illustrates a clearly female form linked with an inscrip-tion referring to Coventina (Figure 8.1). However, in 1924 J.R. Harris propounded a theory that after the Roman period Coventina moved to

France and changed sex to become St. Quentin, a continental saint with aquatic connections (Harris 1924: 162–72).

Others have taken the relief found in the Well – which shows three reclining women, each holding a jar aloft whilst pouring liquid from a second jar (Figure 8.2) – as proof that Coventina was a group of three deities, although Wallis Budge preferred to see the relief as Coventina with two attendants (Budge 1907: 310). This is a particularly ambiguous relief – there is no inscription to prove that Coventina is involved at all, and the fact that the relief came out of the Well should not be taken as proof of

90 STONE STELE DEDICATED TO THE WATER·GODDESS [103]
COVENTINA BY TITUS DOMITIUS COSCONIANUS, THE PREFECT OF
THE FIRST COHORT OF THE BATAVIANS. ON THE UPPER PORTION OF
THE STELE, IN RELIEF, IS A FIGURE OF THE GODDESS, WHO HOLDS
A WATER-PLANT IN HER RIGHT HAND, AND A VESSEL FROM
[PROCOLITIA]   WHICH WATER FLOWS, IN HER LEFT.

Figure 8.1 Stele of Titus Coscanius, from Coventina's Well.

identity: the Well also produced an altar to Minerva [15] and a silver ring dedicated to the Matres [32]. When the shrine to the Nymphs and *Genius Loci* was discovered in 1957, it was suggested that this relief had originally come from that shrine, a suggestion supported by the earlier find of an inscribed base dedicated to the Nymphs found 'near' the Well (Collingwood and Wright 1965: no. 1547). Alternatively, it has been suggested that this is Venus with attendant nymphs, comparable with a relief from High Rochester with which this stone is often confused (Phillips 1977: no. 218).

At the time when Coventina's Well was excavated no other reference to the deity had been found. Since then two altars from the Lugo area of north-west Spain, and one from southern France, have been identified as possible dedications to the same deity:

Os Curvenos, Spain:
> CONVE/TENE/E.R.N

Santa Cruz de Loyo, Spain:
> CUHVETENAE/BERRAL/OGEGU/EX VOTO/FLAVIUS
> VALERIANUS

Narbonne, France:
> IVCUNDUS CO(N) /VERTINE F(ILLIUS) MACER(IAM)/
> CIRCUM ARAM VOLK(ANI/MAGIS)TERIO SUO
> (REIP/D)IENSIUM DONAVIT

THE WATER-GODDESS COVENTINA
AND TWO WATER-NYMPHS HOLDING VASES OF WATER AND
POURING OUT STREAMS OF WATER.
[PROCOLITIA]

Figure 8.2 Relief of three nymphs, from Coventina's Well

The first was found in a stream at Os Curvenos and at first sight looks convincing, but Monteagudo drew attention to the first *N* being in miniature and thus expanded the inscription to *cohors veteranus numen* etc. The 'E.R.N' has been variously interpreted as *ex reditu nostro, ex responsu Numini* or *ex ratione nostra* (Monteagudo 1947: 68–74).

The altar from Santa Cruz de Loyo appears to equate Coventina with Berralogegus, but the spelling of the name is bizarre, even by Coventina's standards, so a completely different deity cannot be altogether ruled out (Vives 1971).

The inscription from Narbonne is more complex. Monteagudo suggested that as the Seventh Legion Gemina despatched a vexillation of 1000 men to Britain in AD 119, it is possible that a veteran of the legion returned to Galicia, taking the cult of Coventina with him (Monteagudo 1947). Lambrino argued that the cult travelled the other way: that it was through the legion that the cult was brought to Carrawburgh (Lambrino 1953: 74–87). However, there is no evidence that the Seventh Legion Gemina was ever on Hadrian's Wall, and if the cult was of special significance to the legion, one would expect it to have introduced Coventina into Pannonia and Italy when on duty in those areas, but again no evidence has emerged so far.

Lambrino was loath to abandon this continental connection. He held that Coventina was the goddess Brigantia in another guise and made much of the facts that Coventene in north-west Spain is only a few miles from Corunna, the ancient Brigantium, and that Cunctius (now Briançon) was also called Brigantio. This would seem to add extra confusion to an already complex situation.

The distribution map reveals the scale of the difficulty: the shrine is at Carrawburgh in northern England; there are two altars in Spain and one in France, which may or may not be part of the cult; but all the worshippers who give their place of origin on the Carrawburgh altars come from the Low Countries – Frisiavonians, Batavians and Cubernians, as well as others who simply call themselves 'Germans'. Without more evidence one cannot put forward a theory as to the origins of the cult or even claim Carrawburgh as the centre of the cult. There can be no doubt that Coventina was regarded as an important deity: she is referred to on one of the thuribles as Augusta [142], the only non-Capitoline goddess to be so called in Britain, and as *sancta* on one of the altars [12] – again the only goddess so designated in Britain. This may argue against Clayton's contention that Coventina was of purely local concern.

As well as the inscriptions and reliefs, the Well was packed with objects of bronze, bone, pottery, glass, lead, leather, jet and shale, as well as animal bone, deerhorn and the 16,000 coins mentioned earlier. Again, there has been much debate as to how these objects found their way into the Well. There were two main theories: the first can be described as the 'invasion evasion' theory: that is, everything was thrown down the Well when, according to the *Daily Chronicle* for 23 October 1876, 'the garrison was hard pressed by the enemy'. The second theory was that the entire contents were devotional offerings. Clayton summed up this theory with the words: 'love-sick damsels cast into the Well their spare trinkets in the hope of obtaining the countenance of the goddess in their views. To these interesting ladies we are doubtless indebted for the brooches, rings and beads found in the Well' (Clayton 1880: 31). He does not include the altars or reliefs in this list – possibly he baulked at the picture of hefty wenches lifting large slabs of stone. He was, however, very worried by the offerings of money: 'the waste of current money, if thrown to any great extent into the water by way of offering, must have been most unsatisfactory to the Pagan priests'. He seems to have viewed the morals of this hypothetical priesthood with deep suspicion: 'the opening of the temple of the goddess Coventina would, no doubt, attract devotional offerings of money which might posssibly escape the grasp of the pagan priests' (ibid.). It should be remembered that Clayton was, by profession, a lawyer and town clerk of Newcastle, and by religious persuasion a Low Church Anglican, his brother Richard being a noted nineteenth-century Evangelist.

A combination of the two theories would seem a more satisfactory explanation: the smaller objects and the coins having been votive deposits, thrown in by individuals over the two centuries that the Well was in use, while the altars, reliefs and thuribles were placed in the Well at the end of its history, as a single act. The evidence of the coins indicates that nothing went into the Well after the period AD 378–88. This suggests a link with the Theodosian edicts against paganism. Theodosius became emperor in 379 and, despite his personal tolerance, the campaign against paganism gradually intensified until, in 391, sacrifice was declared illegal and all pagan temples were closed to the public. The following year another edict declared that there was to be no more domestic worship of the *lares* and *penates*, no incense was to be burned or garlands displayed, and the governor of a province and his *officium* were charged with executing this order. The excavation of Carrawburgh Mithræum shows evidence for two destructions, the second of which can be associated with the rise of Christianity (Richmond and Gillam 1951: 42–3). The large altar in the neighbouring shrine of the Nymphs and *Genius Loci* had also been subject to an attempt to move it off its pedestal in the fourth century (Smith 1962: 61). No doubt any imperial edicts would have been more zealously enforced in military areas than in the civilian sectors, particularly if the commanding officer was a Christian. With the risk of the shrine's destruction, whether real or imagined, the worshippers of Coventina may have placed the furnishings of the shrine, all the miniature altars and pottery which stood around the Well, into the water and covered it all over, rather than have it destroyed by profane hands. It is quite clear that the stone, pottery and glass objects had been lowered carefully into the water in order to avoid breakages, not thrown in, in a panic.

In comparing the material with that discovered in other pits or wells or at other shrines to Celtic or Roman deities, one becomes aware that, although the Well was packed with objects, there are certain categories of find that are noticeable by their absence. The nineteenth-century antiquaries refer to iron-work amongst the Well's contents. None of this now survives, unless it has been confused with the superb collection of ironwork on display in Chesters Museum, now labelled as coming from Chesters Fort (*Cilurnum*). However, there is no indication in the contemporary texts that the ironwork included the weapons one might expect if Coventina was a goddess of war as Coulston and Phillips have suggested (1988: no. 147). This can be compared with the deposits of weapons at Jordan Hill and Newstead (Ross 1968: 266–70). Coulston and Phillips based their theory on the decoration of Altar 7, which has a tree with knobbly foliage on the left side of the shaft and the figure of Victory holding a wreath and a palm branch on the right side.

There are no *ex votos*. By the end of the second century AD, *ex votos* were becoming less common than they had been in Republican times, but one might still expect them if Coventina had been a goddess with specifi-cally healing powers. On the evidence of the Lydney Temple and similar shrines, Anne Ross has suggested that a bronze statuette of a dog [38] (Figure 8.3) supports the cult's claim to a healing function (1967: 339–40). However, there is a lack of any mention of the dog in contemporary accounts until 1880, when it appears in Robert Blair's sketchbook labelled 'Cilurnum'. It was not until 1907 that Wallis Budge attributed the dog to Coventina's Well (Budge 1907: 71). Unfortunately, Budge was very unre-liable in providing accurate provenances for the objects in Clayton's collection. As it would seem improbable that the contemporary accounts, particularly that given in the *Illustrated London News*, would have failed to include such a charming object if it had been found with the rest of the material from the Well, it should be remembered in discussions of Coventina's role that the dog may not be relevant at all.

Sir Mortimer and Lady Wheeler put forward a theory, based on the discovery of 320 bone pins at Lydney, that the presence of pins indicated curative qualities. They supported this theory with the comment 'in Greece pins were a favourite form of votive offering made by women to their special divinities at the time of childbirth' (Wheeler and Wheeler 1932: 41–2). Unfortunately, only two bone pins are known to have come from the Well. The Wheelers also postulated that the discovery of 300 bracelets at Lydney again indicated a healing cult. 'It is a safe inference', they remarked, 'that any marked concentration of feminine offerings at an ancient sanctuary indicates that the presiding god or goddess dispensed relief in connection with childbirth and its attendant ills' (ibid.: 42). Only five bracelets come from the Well.

Figure 8.3 Statuette of a dog, thought (probably erroneously) to have come from Coventina's Well

Despite Clayton's fantasies about lovelorn damsels dropping their jewellery into the Well in order to gain Coventina's aid in matters of the heart, only ten brooches, fourteen finger-rings, two hairpins and five bracelets were found (Figure 8.4). Of these only the hairpins can be seen as unequivocally female. Brooches were worn by men to fasten cloaks; it is only the chained pairs of brooches that can be confidently claimed to be female, as only female clothing would require this form of fastening. The brooches found in the Well are all types that have been found on male skeletons of Roman date in Britain. Finger-rings were also worn by men, particularly signet-rings and religious rings. Even bracelets were worn by men of Celtic origin, although they tended to prefer somewhat more solid bracelets than the rather fine strands found in the Well.

The Well also produced a quantity of glass beads, but these may have all come from a single necklace, as they include twenty-four gold-in-glass beads of the Egyptian type [127]. All the inscriptions refer to male worshippers, but this may not be significant in itself as women rarely dedicated stonework to a deity on their own behalf, the ratio of female dedicators

Figure 8.4 Silver finger-ring dedicated to the Matres, from Coventina's Well.

to male in Roman Britain being about one to ten (Allason-Jones 1989). Possibly, the pieces of jewellery are the female equivalent of an altar dedicated by a man, but it is likely that items of jewellery were seen to be an appropriate offering with which to placate a female deity.

The artefacts which might be regarded as male are not particularly impressive: a strap-end, three studs, a seal-box, three belt-buckles and seven bell-shaped studs, none of which has a healing connection. Of these only the buckles could be regarded with any confidence as being exclusively male, on the grounds that articles of female clothing of Roman date requiring belts have not been discovered so far; but, that having been said, women may have had buckled satchels, boxes or horse-harness. The finds from the Well do not prove conclusively that there were female devotees of the cult, whether lovelorn or not.

The strongest argument for regarding Coventina as a healing goddess, whether for men or for women, is the spring itself. Hübner suggested that, as the three nymphs on the relief discussed earlier held up their vases, the water must have been taken internally (Hübner 1877: 269), but the water has no medicinal properties. It is not a sulphur or chalybeate spring; nor were any metal drinking-vessels found, as at the source of the Seine. There is a strong body of evidence for the association of flowing water and healing in the Celtic mind and, as Cunliffe has stated, 'since water came from the earth, it was appropriate for the deity of the source to be female reflecting one of the powers of the earth mother' (Cunliffe 1979: 89). As religious beliefs changed, springs and wells became Christianized, and nymphs and goddesses gave way to female saints. It is therefore arguable that, as a female deity associated with a spring and accorded the title 'nymph' on at least one of the inscriptions, Coventina can scarcely have avoided acting as a healer even if it was not her primary responsibility.

Ross has pointed out the seemingly fundamental association of the cult of the head with water (Ross 1967: 105–13). There is no way of knowing how part of a human skull found its way into the Well, but human heads are not unknown in such contexts. The lack of a jawbone and the lower part of the cranium suggests that the whole skull was not deposited, and this in turn argues against the ritual deposit of a severed head. The Roman

Figure 8.5 Face-pot found in Coventina's Well

authorities were completely averse to human sacrifice and it is unlikely that a cult practising such rites would have been allowed to continue to do so just outside the west gate of a fort. It is more probable that a worshipper, having discovered this fragment, felt that the Well was the right and proper place for it. Three small bronze masks [35-7] and the head of a male statue [2], as well as the heads on the front of one of the altars [8] and on the spout of a pottery jug [144], suggest, however, that the human head was not without significance to the cult (Figure 8.5).

Amongst the material which might first be assumed to be rubbish are a number of shoe-soles. There is no indication that the shoes were complete with uppers when they entered the Well. Shoes and boots are known from a number of other votive deposits and they appear to have had a funerary significance. They have been found in graves at Puckeridge, Curbridge, Petty Knowes and Lanchester, when no other grave goods were discovered to suggest that the corpses were clothed. Salway has surmised that the 'dead were felt to need a good pair of boots for their journey to the Underworld' (Salway 1981: 705). The excavation of a cemetery building at Cirencester revealed over 2000 hobnails, this giving rise to the idea that boots were made especially for the dead or that a handful of hobnails may have been thrown in as a symbolic gesture (Wilson 1975: 273).

Stripped of all the confusion and biased interpretation with which Coventina's Well has been overlaid since its discovery, the goddess and her offerings are as ambiguous now as they were when first unearthed. Without the new evidence that the discovery of another inscription or shrine would provide, we can go no further than to conclude that Coventina was an 'all-rounder', concerned with all aspects of her worshippers' lives, rather than a deity with specific responsibilities. The evidence available so far seems to argue against Coventina being a typical Celtic healing deity and, although called 'nymph', the epithets *sancta* and *augusta* suggest neither that she was a purely local goddess nor that Carrawburgh was the centre of her cult.

NOTES

1   This paper is based on the full report on the excavation and contents of the well, Allason-Jones and McKay 1985, published by the Trustees of the Clayton Collection, Chesters Museum.

2   Numbers given in square brackets throughout the text refer to the catalogue entries in the full report.

REFERENCES

Allason-Jones, L. 1989. *Women in Roman Britain*. London.

Allason-Jones, L., and B. McKay 1985. *Coventina's Well: A Shrine on Hadrian's Wall*. Chesters.

Budge, E.A.W. 1907. *An Account of the Roman Antiquities preserved in the Museum at Chesters*. Newcastle Upon Tyne.

Clayton, J. 1880. 'Continuation of Description of, and remarks on, the Temple of Coventina and its Contents', *Archaeologia Aeliana* 8, 20–39.

Collingwood, R.G., and R.P. Wright. 1965. *Roman Inscriptions of Britain*. Oxford.

Coulston, J.C., and E.J. Phillips. 1988. *Corpus signorum imperii Romani*, I, 6. Oxford.

Cunliffe, B. 1979. *The Celtic World*. New York.

Harris J.R. 1924. 'Coventina's Well', *Archaeologia Aeliana* 21, 162–72.

Hübner, E. 1877. 'Der Fund von Procolitia', *Hermes: Zeitschrift für Klassische Philologie* 12, 257–72.

Joliffe, N. 1941. 'Dea Brigantia', *Archaeological Journal* 98, 36–61.

Lambrino, S. 1953. 'La Deese Coventina de Parga (Galicie)', *Revista da Faculdade de Letras de Lisboa* 18, 74–87.

Lewis, M.J.T. 1966. *Temples in Roman Britain*. Cambridge.

Longstaffe, W.H.D. 1880. 'Coventina', *Archaeologia Aeliana* 8, 88–107.

Monteagudo, L. 1947. 'De la Galicia romana: Ara de Parga dedicada a Conventina', *Archivo Español de Arquelogia*, 20, 68–74. Madrid.

Phillips, E.J. 1977. *Corpus signorum imperii Romani* I. 1. Oxford.

Richmond, I.A. 1955. *Roman Britain*. London.

Richmond I.A., and Gillam J.P. 1951. 'The Temple of Mithras at Carrawburgh', *Archaeologia Aeliana* 29, 42–3.

Rivet, A.L.F., and C. Smith 1979. *Place Names of Roman Britain*. London.

Ross, A. 1967. *Pagan Celtic Britain*. London.

—— 1968. 'Shafts, Pits and Wells – Sanctuaries of the Belgic Romans?', in J.M. Coles and D.D.A. Simpson (eds), *Studies in Ancient Europe: Essays presented to Stuart Piggott*. Leicester. 255–85.

Salway, P. 1981. *Roman Britain*. London.

Smith, C.R. 1880. 'The Roman Wall: Procolitia', *Collectanea antiqua* 7, 115–35.

Smith, D.J. 1962. 'The Shrine of the Nymphs and the *Genius Loci* at Carrawburgh', *Archaeologia Aeliana* 40, 59–81.

Vives, J. 1971. *Inscripciones Latinas de la España Romana*. Barcelona.

Wheeler, R.E.M., and T.V. Wheeler 1932. *Report on the Excavations of the Prehistoric, Roman and Post-Roman site in Lydney Park, Gloucestershire*. Oxford.

Wilson, D.R. 1975. 'Roman Britain in 1974', *Britannia* 6, 221–83.

CHAPTER NINE

NEMESIS AND BELLONA: A PRELIMINARY STUDY OF TWO NEGLECTED GODDESSES

——— ·◆· ———

Glenys Lloyd-Morgan

Of the two deities who are the subject of this investigation, Nemesis is the elder. One of the earliest references to her can be found in two lines of Hesiod's *Theogony*, dated to the end of the eighth century BC:

> Then deadly night gave birth to Nemesis,
> that pain to Gods and men.
>
> (Hesiod/Wender 1973: lines 222–3)

Another poem, by the Macedonian Parmenion, dated to around the first century BC, has been preserved in the *Greek Anthology*, no. 16.222 on *The Statue of Nemesis at Rhamnous*:

> I am the stone the Persians put to bear
> their trophy, neatly changed to Nemesis;
> Just Goddess seated on the bank at Rhamnous
> Witness to Athens' Victory and Art.
>
> (Parmenion/Paton 1926: 293)

The story behind the poem is recorded by Pausanias, writing in the second century AD:

> If you are going to Oropas by sea, seven and a half miles from Marathon is Rhamnous. The people there live by the sea, but some little way up from the beach is a sanctuary of Nemesis, the specially implacable goddess to wicked and violent men [i.e. the Persians]. The punishment of this goddess apparently fell on the Marathon landing; they were so sure nothing could stop them from taking Athens that they carried a block of Parian marble to raise the trophy over their accomplishments. Pheidas carved this block to make a statue of Nemesis, with a crown on her head ornamented with deer and tiny Victorias. In one hand she has an apple branch, in the other an engraved bowl with figures of Ethiopians.
>
> (Pausanias/Levi 1971: I, 33.2)

Unfortunately, the statue of Nemesis was carved not by Pheidas but by his pupil Agorakritos of Paros, between 430 and 420 BC (Pliny/Eichholz 1962: 15). Some fragments of the statue, which was made of Parian marble, as noted by Pausanias, still survive in the collections in the National Archaeological Museum, Athens, along with fragments of metopes and cornice sections with lim-headed waterspouts (Rossiter 1967: 102).

The worship of Nemesis appears to have started during the sixth century BC and continued down to 431 BC, when the outbreak of the Peloponnesian War put an end to the construction of the last temple on that particular site. The temple is one of a group of four fifth-century BC temples thought to be the work of one, unnamed architect. The other temples are thought to be that to Hephaistos at Athens, built between 449 and 444 BC; the temple of Ares, also at Athens but originally at Acharnae; and the temple of Poseidon at Sounian, constructed between 444 and 432 BC (Hodge & Tomlinson 1969; Lawrence 1957: 234).

Nemesis was not the only goddess worshipped at Rhamnous. She was described as the 'daughter of Justice' and as the keeper of the scales, holding a middle course between the extremes of behaviour. It is therefore not inappropriate that she should have Themis, the goddess of law and justice associated with her. Indeed, two marble seats, dedicated to Themis and to Nemesis, were found at the site, and are now in Athens (Rossiter 1967: 168). A statue of Themis dating to the early third century BC was found and taken to the Archaeological Museum at Athens (ibid.: 107). Nemesis also appears to have some functions that overlap in part with those of Artemis and Aphrodite, as well as with those of the nymph Adrasteia, who had connections with Cybele (Farnell 1896: II, 488–99, 594–5 nn.).

The connection between Nemesis and Aphrodite at Patrae was noted by Pausanias, writing in the second century AD: 'not far from the theatre is a shrine of Nemesis with another of Aphrodite, with white stone statues of great size' (Pausanias/Levi 1971: 7.20.9). One of the curious aspects of Nemesis is the paired Nemeses found as sculptures on several sites. The most celebrated were the twin wood statues at Smyrna (ibid.: 1971: 1.33.6). Levi in his translation notes that there was a pair of Nemeses at Olympia (ibid.: 469 n. 140). More recently a marble pair of Nemeses has been identified at Tomis in Moesia Inferior, now Constanta in Romania, which has been compared to the Smyrna group and dated to the first half of the second century AD (Doppelfield et al. 1969: 202, cat no. F47).

Like other goddesses, Nemesis has her own specific attributes. These include a winged wheel and tiller, and the gryphon, which she is said to have shared with Apollo and Artemis (Farnell 1896: 4497). On the circular base of a statue of a woman found at Viminiacum in Moesia Superior and dedicated to Deae Sanctae Nemesi, a sphinx has been carved in relief (Mommsen et al. 1863–: III, suppl. 1, 144, no. 8108). An excellent example of a Hadrianic coin minted at Alexandria in AD 137 shows a seated female

Figure 9.1   Altar to the goddess Nemesis, found Hugh Thomson et al. in 1966, in the Nemeseum. (See *Archaeologia* 105 (1976).)

gryphon in a shrine with one paw resting on a wheel, strongly suggesting that the goddess was worshipped in that city (Price and Trell 1977: 222, fig. 494). Coins of other cities in the eastern half of the Empire also show temples and aedicules raised in her honour. These include Nicopolis in Epirus, Sinope in Paphlagonia, Smyrna in Ionia, Mallus in Cicilia, and Nicopolis in Pieria (Price & Trell 1977: 250 no. 141; 256 nos 264, 265; 269 no. 504; 276 no. 638; 279 no. 689; 286 no. 842, fig. 494 respectively).

One of the more interesting connections of Nemesis is with the protagonists in the story of Leda and the swan, with Zeus in one of his many disguises. Although Helen, one of Leda's daughters, is said to have been hatched from an egg, there is a version which suggests that it was Nemesis who may have been her mother (Farnell 1896: II, 489). It is from the inscriptions, however, that one can gain further insight into the attitudes of the worshippers towards their goddess. The main body of evidence has been taken from the inscriptions in the *Corpus inscriptionum Latinarum*, which reveal a variety of honorifics, as follows:

1   Augustae Nemesi Sacrum
2   Deae Nemesi (Figure 9.1)
3   Deae Nemesi Augustae/Reginae/Sacrum
4   Deae Sanctae Nemesi
5   Nemesi Augustae
6   Nemesi Augustae Sacrum
7   Nemesi Reginae/Reginae Sacrum
8   Nemesi Sanctae/Sacrum/Sanctae Sacrum
9   Virgini Victrici Sanctae Deae Nemesi

Of the inscriptions, nos 5 and 6 occur most often. Five inscriptions were set up by priests and related officials. Two Vir Sacerdos are recorded: one, from an altar found in Hadrian's Wall, was set up by Apollonius (Collingwood & Wright 1965: no. 2065; Mommsen et al. 1863–: VII, 125, no. 654); the other, found at Colonia Claudia Savaria in Pannonia Superior, had been gifted by a certain Var. Ursus (ibid.: III, suppl. 1, 1751, no. 10911). Another dedication, from Aquincum in Pannonia Inferior, records the names of C. Jul. Victorianus and T. Fl. Lucianus, who were Duovirs and held the rank of Pontiffs in the colony (ibid.: 1698, no. 10440). The one Haruspex, Caius Julius Valens is recorded at Apulum, Alba Julia in Dacia. The inscription is in four lines, with a small, rather modest representation of Nemesis carved in low relief on the upper section (Doppelfeld et al. 1969: 202, cat. no. F46 Taf. 5); whilst from Ostia comes a certain [...] elicis Q Caecilius Fuscus, an *archigallus* – one of the higher-ranking eunuch priests of Cybele (Mommsen et al. 1863: XIV, 15, no. 34; cf. Farnell 1896: 595 n. 138). Three inscriptions record the building or restoration of, in one case a treasury, and in the other two cases temples, to her name and worship. The sacrarium at Alsó Kosály in Dacia is described as becoming dilapidated through age, and was restored by Cassius Erotianus, a *beneficiarius consularis* (ibid.: III, part 1, 165, no. 825). Aelius Diogenes and Silia Valeria are recorded as building a temple to Nemesis on behalf of themselves and other members of the immediate family in fulfilment of a vow, at Fons Augusta in Dacia (ibid.: 246, no. 1547). The third building, a temple of Nemesis which had, like the Dacian sacrarium, become dilapidated, was restored by the *duovirs* at Colonia Aquincum in Pannonia Inferior, and were named as Aurelius Florus and Mercator, during the consulships of Messalla and Sabinus in the reign of Marcus Aurelius (ibid.: suppl., 1697, no. 10439).

A number of inscriptions dedicated to the goddess specifically note that they had been set up in her honour after a dream (*ex visu*), or by her orders (*ex iussu*), or as the result of a warning given in a dream (*somnio admonitus/monitus*). Two come from Aquileia in north-eastern Italy (ibid.: V, part 1, 92, no. 813; suppl. Italica fasc. 1, 22, no. 167); two others come from the northern frontiers of the Empire – one from Pannonia Superior (ibid.: III, suppl. 2, 2281, no. 14071) and the other from Alba Julia in Dacia (Doppelfeld et al. 1969: 202, cat. no. F46, Taf. 5). One of the more recent finds was discovered in 1966 in the shrine behind the wall of the arena in the amphitheatre at Chester (Thompson 1976: 184, pl. 48a, b). The connection of amphitheatres with Nemesis has been found on sites in Italy, Britain, Pannonia Superior, Dacia and Gallia Belgica. Out of sixty–nine inscriptions relating to the goddess, sixteen (i.e. 23 percent of the total) have been found either in or in close proximity to the various amphitheatres of the northern provinces. Two examples come from Britain. The one from Chester has been noted above; the other is a curse tablet from the amphitheatre at Caerleon, found in 1927 during Sir Mortimer Wheeler's excavations (Wheeler and Wheeler 1928: 120, 158, fig. 12, no. 10). Six examples come from Pannonia: one, from Pannonia Inferior, was found in a shrine in the Aquincum amphitheatre (Mommsen et al.: III, suppl., 1698, no. 10442); the other five, from Pannonia Superior, include four dedications made by members of the Fourteenth Legion Gemina stationed at Carnuntum (ibid.: 1773, no. 11121; suppl. 2, 2281, nos. 14074, 14076, and 2328, no. 14357). The fifth inscription does not mention the status of the donor (ibid.: suppl. 2, 2281, no. 14073). Four inscriptions have been recorded at Sarmizegethusa in Dacia (ibid.: 2248, nos. 13777–80). Another damaged piece comes from Trier and was found in the vicinity of the amphitheatre (ibid.: XIII, part 1, fasc. 2, 594, no. 3661). Three other finds come from Italy – one from Venafrum in Samnite country (ibid.: X, part 1, 163, no. 1408); another from Pola in Istria (ibid.: V, part 1, 8, no. 17). Perhaps the most fascinating inscription comes from Verona and is a memorial to the gladiator Glaucus from Mutina, who won seven fights, but not his eighth, and died aged twenty–three years and five days. The stone was set up by his wife and *amatores huius*, presumably his 'fan club'. However, it is the last part of the inscription that commands attention, and this can be roughly translated as follows: 'I warn/advise you to pay attention to your stars. Have no trust in Nemesis, for I was deceived [by her]. Hail and Farewell.' (Ibid.: 354, no. 3466).

BELLONA

If Nemesis can claim seniority of rank, with her impeccable Greek ancestry going back to the late eighth century BC, if not earlier, Bellona is considerably her junior. The first temple built to her honour had been vowed by Appius Claudius Caecus in 296 BC, during the third Samnite War, waged against the Etruscans and Samnites between 298 and 290, and was situated near the Circus Flaminius (Scullard 1964: 368). The temple was 'just outside the walls of Rome and could be used as a meeting place for the senate for receiving foreign ambassadors who were not to be admitted into the city, or welcoming returning Roman generals' (Scullard 1981: 146). 'In front of the temple stood a little pillar (columella) over which a fetial priest in declaring war on an overseas enemy hurled a spear into "enemy territory". This was first done against Pyrrhus in 208 BC' (ibid.: 30–1). Bellona does not seem to have such a wide congregation as Nemesis, being only a personification of war. She has been identified with Nerio, a cult partner of Mars, and with her Greek equivalent Enyo, the Greek goddess of war (ibid.: 146). Bellona's festival was celebrated each year on 3 June. It is hardly surprising that seven inscriptions have been found in Rome relating to her worship. One of the earlier ones, found in the Forum of Augustus, refers back to the time of the wars with Pyrrhus (see the *Elogia clarorum virorum*, Mommsen et al. 1863–: I, part 1, 192). Five of the inscriptions make reference to *Aedem Bellonae*, Bellona's dwelling or shrine (ibid.: I, part 1, 192; VI, part 1, 92, no. 490; 102, no. 2234; 615, nos. 2232, 2233). The other two inscriptions are partially damaged (ibid.: VI, part 1, 615, no. 2235; 831, no. 3674). Another temple to Bellona is thought to have been outside the area of the fortress and colony at York/Eboracum, with the palace established there by Septimus Severus for his British campaign (Norman 1971: 146; cf. the 'Life of Septimus Severus', *Scriptores historia Augusta* Magie 1922–32: section 23).

At least two priests of Bellona have been recorded from the province of Numidia: one from Rusicade, the other from Sigus (1863–Mommsen et al. 1863–: VIII, part 1, 553, no. 5708; 685, no. 7957). The first inscription noted the renovation of pictures and decorations in the temple. As in the case of Nemesis, a small number of inscriptions have been found dedicated to Bellona with the phrase *ex imperio* (by command), *ex iussu* (by order) or *visu iussus* (as ordered in a dream) (ibid.: X, part 1, 643, no 6482; XIII, part 1, fasc. 2, 590, no. 3637; fasc. 1, 439, no. 2872; V, part 2, 720, no. 6507, respectively).

There are a number of inscriptions which have dedications to Bellona in association with Mars and with Virtus, the personification of all forms of military valour. Mars and Bellona are found on inscriptions from Alesia, Gallia Lugdunensis (ibid.: XIII, part 1, fasc. 1, 439, no. 2872), with two others from Germania Superior. The first is to Mars Cicollui and Bellona, the other to Mars and Bellona (ibid.: part 2, fasc. 1–2, 99, no. 5598; 107, no. 5670, respectively). Virtus and Bellona are honoured on another inscription from Castell Mattiacorum (the present-day Kassel) in Germania Superior, set up during the reign of the Emperor Maximinus, AD 235–8 (ibid.: 412, no. 7281), and on a more modest example from the region of Novaria (ibid.: V, part 2, 720, no. 6507). The close relationship between

Bellona and Virtus is confirmed by a comment of Lactantius, writing between *c.* AD 250 and *c.* 317 AD (Lactantius/Monat 1986: 1.21.16).

CONCLUSIONS

Of the two goddesses, Latin inscriptions referring to Nemesis occur more than twice as frequently as those referring to Bellona. This may be due in part to her greater antiquity. Both goddesses were honoured by named priests, by officials in towns and cities, by military men as well as by private individuals. Much honour was paid to Nemesis by soldiers and civilians in the northern frontier provinces of Pannonia Inferior and Superior, Moesia Inferior and Superior, and Dacia, accounting for some 62 percent of the dedications recorded in the *Corpus inscriptionum Latinarum*. Other provinces may have had some inscriptions devoted to both deities, whilst there are a number of damaged items which may or may not still retain a few letters of their names. The association of Nemesis and other deities with the amphitheatre has been only partially discussed, if at all, by earlier writers. The probability is that in her aspect as Goddess of Justice, keeping the balance between extremes of behaviour, she could be seen to be holding the fate of individuals – gladiators and condemned criminals alike – in her hands. Hence the need to invoke her help, not only in daily life, but also in times of peril. Hence, perhaps, the final words ascribed to the disillusioned gladiator Glaucus at Verona. The lead curse-tablet from the Caerleon amphitheatre asking for her retribution against a thief who had stolen a cloak and pair of boots, does tend to confirm her role as arbiter and mediatrix.

Bellona's connection with Mars and Virtus is specifically orientated towards the army, as is witnessed by the names and ranks of their family. In each case the goddess has worshippers who were prepared to rebuild, restore and renovate her shrines and temples at their own cost, or as a family or social group. Others were willing to fulfil the orders and commands sent in a dream or vision and thus make their peace with their favoured deity and their own consciences.

This survey can only be considered as preliminary, as few Greek texts or inscriptions have been included and a number of provinces seem to have little or no evidence for the worship of either deity. However, the evidence does indicate the widespread acceptance within the empire of both goddesses, from their earliest origins down to the fourth century AD and the rising tide of Christianity.

Table 9.1 Nemesis and Bellona: distribution of *CIL* inscriptions according to province

Province	Nemesis	Amphitheatre Finds	Bellona
Italy	16	3	13
Sicily	1		
Britain	3	2	1
Gallia Belgica	1	1	1
Gallia Lugdunensis			1
Baetica Hispania	1		
Lusitania Hispania	1		1
Mauretania Caesoriensis	2		
Numidia			7
Germania Superior			7
Dalmatia			1
Noricum	1		
Pannonia Inferior	7	1	
Pannonia Superior	13	5	1
Moesia Inferior	2		
Moesia Superior	2		
Dacia	19	4	
TOTAL	69	16	33

REFERENCES

Abbreviation

LCL Loeb Classical Library

Collingwood, R.G., and R.P. Wright, 1965.*The Roman Inscriptions of Britain*. Oxford.
Doppelfeld, O. et al. 1969. *Römer in Rumänien*. Catalogue of the Exhibition held in the Kunsthalle, Cologne 12 February – 18 May 1969. Cologne.
Farnell, L.R. 1896. *The Cults of the Greek States*, II. Oxford.
Hesiod, trans. D. Wender 1973. *Theogony: Works and Days*. Harmondsworth.
Hodge, A.T., and R.A. Tomlinson. 1969. 'Some Notes on the Temple of Nemesis at Rhamnous', *American Journal of Archaeology* 73, 185–92.
Hornum, M. *Nemesis, the Roman State and the Games*. Leiden.
Lactantius, ed. P. Monat 1986. *Divinae institutiones*, I: *Sources chrétiennes*. Paris.

Lawrence, A.W. 1957/1983. *Greek Architecture*, 4th edn, rev. R.A. Tomlinson. Pelican History of Art Series. Harmondsworth.

Mesomedes, ed. K. Horna 1928. *Hymn no. 11: To Nemesis*. Vienna.

Mommsen, T. et al. eds 1863–. *Corpus inscriptionum Latinarum*. Berlin.

Norman, A.F. 1971. 'Religion in Roman York', in R.M. Butler (ed.), *Soldier and Civilian in Roman Yorkshire*. Leicester. 143–54.

Parmenion, trans. A. Elliot. 1973. *The Greek Anthology: Selections*. Harmondsworth.

Parmenion, trans. W.R. Paton. 1926. *The Greek Anthology* V. LCL. London and New York.

Pausanias, trans P. Levi. 1971. *Guide to Greece*. Harmondsworth.

Pliny, trans. D.E. Eichholz 1962. *Natural History* X. LCL. London and Cambridge, Mass.

Price, M.J., and B.A. Trell 1977. *Coins and their Cities*. London.

Rossiter, S. 1967. *The Blue Guide to Greece*. London.

Scriptores historia Augusta, trans. D. Magie 1922–32. LCL. New York.

Scullard, H.H. 1964. *A History of the Roman World from 753–146 BC*. 3rd edn. London.

Scullard, H.H. 1981. *Festivals and Ceremonies of the Roman Republic*. London.

Thompson F.H. 1976. 'The Excavation of the Roman Amphitheatre at Chester', *Archaeologia* 105, 127–39.

Wheeler, R.E.M., and T.V. Wheeler 1928: 'The Roman Amphitheatre at Caerleon, Monmouthshire', *Archaeologia* 78, 111–218.

CHAPTER TEN

FORS FORTUNA
IN ANCIENT ROME

——— •◆• ———

Sandra Billington

The concept of the Goddess is central to this study, for the way Fortuna has been conceived over the centuries has changed according to need or preference. Her subject is complex and obscure, partly because she did not occupy one clear-cut niche in the Roman pantheon: she was not an indigenous deity but was, rather, absorbed from outlying areas soon after Rome was established. Yet from the position of outsider she grew to play a central part in the thinking and customs of the Romans and was worshipped in several aspects, as separate goddesses. I shall begin by recapping the prevalent opinions, and then focus more specifically on those customs that I hope might help clarify how Fors (Chance) Fortuna was thought of in Rome specifically during the later Republican period.

At the end of the nineteenth century, discussions about her developed into two quite opposite views. R. Peter and W. Warde Fowler deduced that Fors Fortuna was inconstant, while G. Wissowa stressed a lucky goddess, protectress of peasants (Champeaux 1982: 225). The later, influential work of Kurt Latte went further in asserting that Fors Fortuna was seen in Rome as a positive force and referred to as such by all the major Roman writers. He says that the impersonal and incalculable nature personified in the Greek Tyche was 'neutralised in that optimistic assumption which characterises Roman religion in general' (Latte 1960: 179–80).[1] He further unequivocally states: 'in early Latin, Fors Fortuna always meant good luck' (ibid.: 180). Since the works of Horace, Livy and Cicero, writing between 40 and 10 BC, do not corroborate this, differentiation between the early and later periods might be significant. Latte cites *The Eunuch*, by the second-century BC author Terence, where one finds the phrase *forte fortuna* twice used to mean 'by good luck' (Terence/Sargeaunt 1912: I, lines 134, 568); and in *Phormio* the slave Geta, exults with the phrase 'O Fortuna, O Fors Fortuna' (ibid.: II, line 841). These usages by lower-class characters do endow her name with positive meaning. Latte's other early citation is, however, more ambiguous. This is from Lucius Accius, who differentiates between a goddess Fortuna and an abstract concept of chance. The piece, from a play about the recapturing of Astynax, reads: 'Ulysses:

Fortunane an forte repertus?' ('Was he through Fortune found or chance?'). A contemporary Latin commentator, Nonius, has added: '"Fors" et "Fortuna" hoc distant: fors est casus temporalis, fortuna dea est ipsa' ('"Fors" and "Fortuna" here differ; "Fors" is a chance event of the moment: "Fortuna" is the goddess herself') (Accius/Warmington 1936: 372-3). Therefore this learned second-century reading of Fors is neutral, allowing for chance to be either good or bad, and it may be possible to suggest a distinction between the views of the proletariat and those of the more educated, who have in fact left most of the evidence. The distinction is necessary because to date the few proletarian comments have outweighed the larger corpus, and the conviction that Fors was always considered good luck – a beneficent fertility goddess in Rome – has coloured twentieth-century studies of her. Yet most of the evidence supports Warde Fowler's opposite observation to Latte's, that Fors Fortuna 'represented chance, that inexplicable power which appealed so strongly to the later sceptical and Graecized Romans' (Fowler 1899: 165).

Frazer's interest in fertility may well have influenced twentieth-century thinking; or the shift of emphasis could have derived from other aspects under which Fortuna was worshipped, some of which *were* benevolent: for example, the highly influential Fortuna Primigenia, first-born daughter of Jove. Romans encountered her a few miles away in the Etruscan city of Praeneste, where she was worshipped, in Jacqueline Champeaux's words, 'as Goddess of female fruitfulness, god-mother; and protectress of child-bearing, young mothers, and of the newly born' (Champeaux 1982: 40). Cicero acknowledged loyalty to the supportive Roman version of Primigenia, who, he says, 'has been with us from our earliest moments' (Cicero/Keyes 1928: 404–5). However, at Praeneste she was a multi-faceted deity. As well as being Jove's daughter, she was worshipped as Jove's mother; Cicero wrote that there: 'Mothers piously revere the child Jupiter, seated with Juno on Fortune's knees and suckled by her' (Cicero/Falconer 1923: 466-7). This duality has provided another problem from the point of view of interpretation (see Champeaux 1982: 240; Ovid/Frazer 1926: III, 260), and Frazer observes that being first-born creates the link with child-birth (1926: III, 258). However, it should also be pointed out that 'firstborn daughter of Jove' expresses the link that was often observed between Chance/Fortune and Jove. The Greek Plutarch saw her as part of the power of Zeus:

> Zeus's name was used as a synonym for the power of Fortune before men used the name 'Fortune' but knew the force of causation as it traverses its irregular and indeterminate course, so strong, so impossible for human reason to guard against, they tried to express it by the name of the gods.
>
> (Plutarch/Babbitt 1927: 123–5)

Horace also inferred close relationship between Jupiter and Fortuna, speaking at one moment of the power that the father of the gods had to abase the mighty and exalt the lowly, and the next of the godddess's identical ability (Horace/Bennett 1914: 90–1). Zeus had ultimate cosmic control over man's destiny but the quality of chance which affected destiny is detached from him by these writers as an independent power. At Praeneste, Primigenia was consulted as an oracle whose answers were determined through a game of chance. Lots contained in a chest were chosen at random by a child, in answer to supplicants' questions (Cicero/Falconer 1923: 468-9). It was, indeed, as an oracle that she gained her international fame and was last remembered; therefore it would appear that her best-known function was not confused by the name Primigenia;[2] rather, it was her aspect as Chance that was understood by it. Two strands of logic, therefore, suggest that it was as Jove's mother that she was the maternal, and as his daughter the oracular, deity.

It has been the aspect of Fors that has proved the most long-lasting. She had the capacity to subsume her father and all the other gods, since her changeability undermined their authority. As the sceptical Pliny put it: 'we are so much at the mercy of chance that Chance herself, by whom God is proved uncertain, takes the place of God' (Pliny/Rackham 1938: 183–5). Peter Walsh has called this 'a revealing passage [which] describes the importance [Pliny's] contemporaries attached to [Fortuna]. She alone in all places and at all times is invoked, praised, and blamed; she is considered blind and fickle' (Walsh 1970: 55). Cicero dismissed belief in several of Fortuna's aspects, but allowed the maternal Primigenia, and also Fors, through whom, he said, 'we remember the uncertainty of future events' (Cicero/Keyes 1928: 405).

When the Praenestean Primigenia was brought into Rome in 194 BC, her attributes appear to have leaned towards the protection of the city and of its high-born citizens. She was known as the Firstborn Fortuna of the Roman People, Public Fortune, and Fortune of the State, with three temples inside the city on the Quirinal Hill looking outwards towards Rome's north approaches. These temples gave the hill the name *tres fortunae* (Ovid/Frazer 1926: III, 256-7; IV, 125; I, 204–5) and provided a strong composite image, illustrating Rome's good fortune in her growing power. This stabilized aspect may have influenced the received opinion of Fors in later centuries, but, I shall be arguing, Public Fortune did not confuse the Romans themselves. For example, to recap Cicero's two references in the *De legibus*, one is to 'Chance Fortune, which refers particularly to the uncertainty of future events [and the other to] First-born Fortune, our companion from birth'.[3] He has complete clarity as to his categories.

One of the most influential books for later study has been Plutarch's *The Fortune of the Romans*, and there is no doubt that he does confuse the issue. It has been suggested by the editors of the Loeb edition that, since Plutarch was Greek, he may have misunderstood the oblique cases of *fors* which appear in phrases such as, *Dies Forti Fortunae* in the Roman Calendar, and *Templum Fortis Fortunae* in references to her place of worship. These two phrases appear more frequently in Roman writings than the word *Fors* itself. *Fortis* as a separate noun of course means strength; therefore Plutarch may have deduced that the goddess was 'strong, valiant or manly' with the 'power to conquer everything' (Plutarch/Page et al. 1936: 337; cf. Gagé 1963: 20). Whatever the reason, in *The Fortune of the Romans*, Plutarch argues that it was her strength, rather than that of Virtue, that had been the support and making of Rome. The figure described at first is winged and stands on a globe, which is the image of Fors, not Primigenia. But, after winning the contest with Virtue, Plutarch's Fortuna abandons these unstable signs to enter Rome with her cornucopia, and herself become a figure of Virtue: 'the sister of Good Order and Persuasion, and the daughter of Foresight' (Plutarch/Babbitt 1927: 331). At the opening of this work, therefore, Plutarch himself reconstructs the Fortuna he wishes to address, after which he concludes that faithful good fortune came to Rome's aid on several occasions. The wolf who found the infants Romulus and Remus happened to be full of milk and needing to suckle (instead of hungry and needing to eat). She even rescued the city in 'times of the greatest disaster', such as 390 BC, when the Gauls conquered and threatened the Capitol itself. Without mentioning the horror of the sack of Rome, Plutarch isolates the famous incident of the geese which gave warning of the intruders on the Capitol (ibid.: 347–69).

It is possible that Plutarch's purpose was to demonstrate his skill in rhetoric rather than to present received ideas, for the Roman historian Livy includes many moments when Fortuna withdrew her cornucopia; most graphically in his description of the same Gallic sack of Rome. Livy was just as sure as was Plutarch that this was Fortuna's doing, but treacherously, against the city. As the Gauls approached, he wrote, a series of events was misunderstood by the defenders, 'such is the blindness Fortune visits on men's minds when she would have her gathering might meet with no check' (Livy/Foster 1924–6: III, 127). And, instead of being a haven, the Capitoline Hill is incorporated into Fortuna's malevolent wish to force the refugees watch the destruction of their city from her lofty theatre:

> Wherever the shouting of the invaders, the lamentations of the women and children, the crackling of the flames, and the crash of falling buildings drew their attention . . . they turned their thoughts and their gaze that way, as though Fortune had placed them there to witness the pageant of their dying country.
>
> (ibid.: 143–5)

Even when not specified as Fors or Chance, it is to the abstract concept

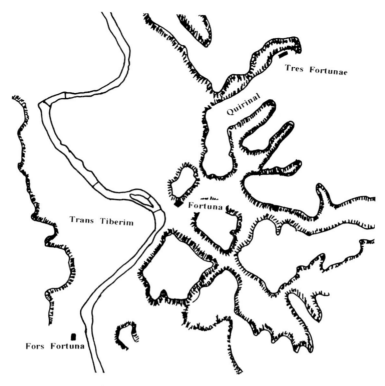

Figure 10.1 The temple site for Fors Fortuna in Ancient Rome

that Roman writers refer most, and, apart from Plutarch, they rarely if ever have anything good to say of her.

The subject of Fors itself contains its own complexities, ranging from debates today about the meaning of the word (Champeaux 1982: 209–10; Dumézil 1975: 245), to those on customs surrounding her, which are the concern here. The two temples mentioned in Roman Calendars were outside the city, on the right bank of the Tiber, an area known as *Trans Tiberim* or, in Italian, Trastevere (Figure 10.1).[4] The first temple dedicated to Fors was attributed to the Etruscan Servius Tullius, who ruled Rome in the sixth century BC,[5] while the second is known to have been built in 293 BC as the fulfilment of a promise made during later Etruscan wars (Livy/Foster 1929: 539). If the date of the first is approximately correct, then Fors was the first aspect of Fortuna to be worshipped at Rome (see Savage 1940: 31). Trastevere was home to several cults with only tenuous links to those publicly worshipped inside the city. One of the most extensive sites was to Sol, where an altar inscribed to Sol Sanctissimus 'betrays [its] Syrian origins' (ibid.: 53). The close proximity of Fors to this and other rites such as the July *Ludi Piscatorum* has supported arguments that she also derived from an agrarian deity, although Champeaux acknowledges that 'the personality of Fortuna and her divine connections are complex enough for multiple interpretations' (Champeaux 1982: 225).

The date of dedication of her temples was 24 June, or Midsummer's Day, when celebrants annually floated to them downstream from the city. After undisclosed rituals they then rowed back, garlanded and inebriated. No contemporary reason is given for the mid-point of the year, other than that it was the alleged choice of Tullius, and some scholars, even as late as the 1980s, have argued that 24 June was accidental rather than integral.[6] However, there is considerable evidence pointing to an integration between Fors Fortuna and the solar crisis. The problem that arises though is how does one interpret the crisis?

Champeaux, following Latte, pursues the agrarian connections, and a conviction that 'the original definition of Fors Fortuna was as a giver of life' (Champeaux 1982: 224). She sees the Roman midsummer cult as one *only* for the plebs: 'Magistrates of the plebs, her aediles and tribunes, men who had achieved *nobilitas* . . . without doubt they had nothing but disdain or at least condescension for [the cult of Fors] Fortuna, freqented as it was by the common people from whom promotion had separated them.'[7] This view is essential to her theory that the cult was one which celebrated a beneficent deity: a 'pre-urban divinity of the Italian countryside [and] protectress of the common people' (ibid.: 243), who, she implies, retained closer links to such agrarian rituals than did those promoted into an urban society. The cult as recorded by Ovid and Cicero, she argues, had once been a water-purification ceremony to encourage rain, such as is found in other parts of the Mediterranean at midsummer, and the description we have of it shows how this had then degenerated. The crisis for the Romans, and particularly for agriculture, she continues, was to do not with the imminent decline of the sun but with its destructive power and the resulting lack of water, which, she argues, was the real agricultural concern at this time of year.

Much about this argument is attractive, yet the custom recorded by Ovid and Cicero was certainly not weak or dying. It even seems to have been adopted in Rome's twin city of Lyons (see Guigue 1887). Also, all the evidence given by Roman writers reveals a celebration focused on ambivalence, therefore a festival which closely reflected the meaning of Fors. To begin with, one may consider Columella's famous observation from his work on agriculture that cultivators should take their wares to market on the longest days of the year and, once these were sold, sing praises to Fors Fortuna and go home rejoicing (Columella/Heffner and Foster 1955: 36–7). To Champeaux this is more evidence of Fors being celebrated as a fertility goddess at midsummer (Champeaux 1982: 225). However, Savage writes:

'There was reason for devotion from such a group, whose livelihood depended very much upon the caprices of the weather' (Savage 1940: 32). Even when Fortune is considered as an agrarian goddess, chance enters in, and one could argue that if it was a need for water that was ritually expressed at midsummer, then this was also in terms of appeasing a capricious goddess rather than rejoicing in a protective one.

The more important drawback to Champeaux's water-purification theory is that at Rome the participants did not bathe or even wash in the Tiber, which is essential to such a rite, and several pages are needed to account for the lack in terms of the degeneracy of Rome's custom. She concludes, unconvincingly I think, 'rowing on the river is one form of contact with the water' (Champeaux 1982: 221).

Rather than look at what is lacking within an agrarian cult, it proves to be more productive to look at what *was* there at Rome in terms of a cult to change, or to the passing of time. On 24 June wheel-shaped cakes, called *Summanalia* were distributed. According to Michael York, the name translates as 'the highest place' or 'the supreme dawn', signifying a day unsurpassed in greatness. He points out that

> the wheel, a possible solar symbol, belongs also to the goddess Fortuna [and] the coincidence of the deity presiding over the turning wheel of fortune, with the date of the turning point of the sun can only reveal that the solstice [was] in some way ritually noted.
> (York 1986: 134–5; see Figure 10.2).

There is substantial evidence for wheels as sun-symbols in Romano-Celtic Europe (Green 1984), and Hilda Ellis Davidson has also seen a possible connection between whirling discs found on some Roman tombstones and the passage of time: 'a symbol of the cosmos, based partly . . . on the turning circle through which the sun and moon pass . . . an image of time's passing and therefore of the power of fate' (Davidson 1988: 169). It would seem to be more than coincidental that the opening of Ovid's account of the midsummer festival in fact focuses on just such mutability. This section is not considered by Latte and Champeaux:

Figure 10.2 Folius Galerius (reverse side): Fors Fortuna with wheel and rudder. (By permission of the British Museum.)

Time slips away, and we grow old with silent lapse of years; there is no
bridle that can curb the flying days. How quickly has come
round the festival of Fors Fortuna! Yet seven days and June will be over.
(Ovid/Frazer 1926: I, 353)

There is here no hint here of purification, but instead an anticipation of
the subsequent decline of summer and the reminder that mankind too, after
a period of rejoicing, will grow old. The present celebration is only a stage
in the season's and man's progress through time. But celebration is to be
made. Ovid continues:

Come, Quirites, celebrate with joy the goddess Fors! On Tiber's
banks she has her royal foundations. Speed some of you on foot, and
some in the swift boat, and think no shame to return tipsy home from
your ramble.
(ibid.)

This contradicts Champeax's assertion that the *nobilitas* did not take
part[8]. The Quirites were the three Primigenia goddesses on the Quirinal
hill, and Ovid tells their representatives that on this day they may lay aside
the dignity which Champeaux emphasizes for them, and behave with
licence. The word 'royal' addressed to them in connection with Fors would
also seem to be added as a suitable attraction for Rome's higher ranks.
Finally, Ovid writes:

The common folk worship this goddess because the founder of her
temple is said to have been of their number and to have risen to the
crown from humble rank. Her worship is also appropriate for slaves,
because Tullius ... was born of a slave woman.
(ibid.: 355)

Tullius' phenomenal achievement of rising from birth to an Etruscan
slave to kingship over Rome appears to have provided a connection between
the highest and the lowest in Rome. On the central day of the year all
Romans could come together in celebration. The plebs' view of Fors, here,
does appear positive, and there is no reason to dismiss the optimism behind
such a celebration for those with nothing to lose. Ovid, however, adds the
word *dubiae* or fickle – casting his own personal doubt on the reliability
of such trust.

The second piece of source-material (not included by Latte and
Champeaux) comes from Cicero's *De finibus bonorum et malorum*, where
there is a brief allusion to the custom in a section on the happiness brought
by Virtue. At first glance the Fors Fortuna reference appears to support
the theory of beneficence. Cicero begins:

What devotee of pleasure, though consumed by most glowing
passions, can be supposed to feel such transports of rapture in winning

his keenest desires, as were felt by the elder Africanus upon the defeat of Hannibal, or by the younger at the overthrow of Carthage? Who ever experienced so much delight from the voyage down the Tiber on the day of the festival as Lucius Paulus felt when he sailed up the river leading King [Perseus] in his train?

These are glowing moments of triumph, but the paragraph ends:

Come now, my dear Lucius, build in your imagination the lofty and towering structure of the virtues; then you will feel no doubt that those who achieve them ... are always happy; realizing as they do that all the vicissitudes of fortune, the ebb and flow of time and circumstance, will be trifling and feeble.

(Cicero/Rackham 1914: 473)

The elation of the river journey down the Tiber, and the greater excitement of conquest, are in a context where triumph is not the end of the matter. The vicissitudes of fortune and the ebb of time will follow, and Cicero's balancing of the two incorporates Fors' dual nature. His view of the festival finally concurs with that of Ovid.

It is possible that we need also to consider the role of the River Tiber. To date, scholars looking for fertility have been baffled as to the purpose of rowing on the river, but if one looks from the perspective of mutability the Tiber itself becomes significant. I would like to suggest that, like Fors, she was both Rome's greatest blessing and her greatest curse. Strabo relates that 'Rome is the only city built on the Tiber ... its position was fixed not by choice but by necessity ... and those who attempted to enlarge it were not at liberty to select a better site, being prevented by what was already built' (Strabo/Jones 1927: II, 349). Because of the river, Rome survived drought, since corn could be moved up- or downstream. She could trade with the rest of the world, which was the reason for her wealth and power, and being upstream meant she was protected from coastal pirates. On the other hand, whenever the Tiber flooded the destruction of the city itself was threatened. Livy's history is full of such moments, particularly between 365 and 189 BC, and these were inevitably seen as ill-fated events. In 193 'there were great floods ... and the Tiber overflowed the flat part of the city ... certain buildings even collapsed. Because of this and other prodigies a nine-day sacrifice was performed ... and the city purified' (Livy/Sage 1935: 23).

The extremes of good and bad which the river was capable of were very like those of Fors herself, and it seems not impossible that the parallel was incorporated in the choice of the river for her commemoration. The name of the celebration was *Tiberina Descensio*, which makes the river central to the event, and one can point out that floating downstream to the temples and returning upstream enacts the two sides of Chance Fortune: an easy passage is followed by a more difficult one. It is hard to believe that those taking part could fail to be aware of the comparison. Finally, it may not be entirely fanciful to observe that *descensio* recalls the imminent decline of the sun.

Therefore, instead of arguing that Fors Fortuna was worshipped in Rome as though she were a fertility-goddess, I would suggest that what might have been an earlier fertility ritual was adapted by the Romans into a more precise reflection of their understanding of Fors Fortuna. The evidence provided by Ovid, Cicero and the wheel-cakes supports the conclusion that midsummer was the time to celebrate mutable Fors as a part of, or respon-sible for, the mutability of the seasons and of life. Before a city vulnerable to the river was built, there could have been a water-purification ceremony as Champeaux argues. But the cult Ovid and Cicero wrote about, and which was practised in Rome between 10 BC and AD 50, is in honour of an ambivalent goddess on an ambivalent day of the year.[9] It is possible that the plebs retained greater trust in her, yet the festival was celebrated by all Romans – Cicero in his *De finibus* implies that he and his reader are fully conversant with the custom – and the dominant perspective of her cannot be interpreted as anything other than celebration of a fickle goddess. The plebs may have appreciated Tullius' extraordinary achievement, but the thought never seems to have been far away that

> 'it is quite the way of Fortune to confound human calculations by surprises; and when she has helped a man for a time, and caused her balance to incline in his favour, to turn round upon him as though she repented, throw her weight into the opposite scale, and mar all his successes'.
>
> (Polybius /Shuckburgh 1889: II, 401)

If the fortunate Tullius was the founder of the first temple to Fors Fortuna, his dedication was more likely to have been to prevent a reversal, than to triumph in his success.

NOTES

1   Translation by Betty Knott-Sharpe, University of Glasgow. I am grateful to Peter G. Walsh for making this available to me.
2   Champeaux simply accepts the two aspects and argues for more attention to be paid to the maternal (Champeaux 1982: 55).
3   'Fors, inquo incerti casus significatur magis, vel Primigenia, a gignendo comes' (Cicero/Keyes 1928: 404–5).
4   Debate continues as to whether or not there were more than two Temples: see Champeaux 1982: 201; Savage 1940: 55.
5   Livy/Foster 1929: 539. There is no evidence for this attribution.
6   'The day of the festival happened to be Midsummer's Day, the summer solstice,

but attempts to find a connection in the ritual are not convincing' (Scullard 1981: 156; cf. Savage 1940: 34).

7   'Les magistrats de la plèbe, ses édiles, ses tribuns, ses hommes nouveaux qui accédaient à la *nobilitas* ... n'avaient sans doute que dédain, ou moins condescendance, pour [le rite de Fors Fortuna], fréquenté par un menu peuple dont leur ascension les séparés' (Champeaux 1982: 239).

8   Savage too believes that the 'followers were rowdy plebeians' (Savage 1940: 31). However, even if Servius Tullius' foundation is myth only, the second by the senator Carvilius proves observance of Fors Fortuna by the leaders of the city.

9   Savage also sees the ceremony during the Roman Republic as distinct from a simple water festival (Savage 1940: 34).

REFERENCES

Abbreviation

LCL   Loeb Classical Library

Accius, L., trans. & ed. E.H. Warmington 1936. 'Astynax', in *Remains of Old Latin*, II. LCL. London and Cambridge, Mass.

Champeaux, J. 1982. *Fortvna*. Rome.

Cicero, trans. H. Rackham 1914. *De finibus bonorum et malorum*. LCL. London and New York.

—— trans. W.A. Falconer 1923. *De senectute; De amicitia; De divinatione*, LCL. London and New York.

—— trans. C.W. Keyes 1928. *De re publica; De legibus*. LCL. London and New York.

—— trans. H. Rackham 1933: *Academica*. LCL. London and New York.

Columella, ed. and trans. E.H. Heffner & E.S. Forster 1955. *De re rustica* III. LCL. London and Cambridge, Mass.

Davidson, H.E. 1988. *Myths and Symbols*. Manchester.

Dumézil, G. 1975. *Fêtes Romaines de l'été et d'automne*. Paris.

Fowler, W.W. 1899. *The Roman Festivals of the Period of the Republic*. London.

Gagé, J. 1963. *Matronalia: Essai sur les dévotions et les organisations cultuelle des femmes dans l'ancienne Rome*. Collection Latomus 40. Brussels.

Green, M.J. 1984. *The Wheel as a Cult-Symbol*. Latomus revue d'Études Latines 183. Brussels.

Guigue, M.C. 1887. *Recherches sur les merveilles: Fête antique et populaire de la ville de Lyon*. Lyons.

Horace, trans. C.E. Bennett 1914. *The Odes and Epodes*. LCL. London and New York.

Latte, K. 1960. *Römische Religionsgeschichte*. Munich.

Livy, trans. B.O. Foster 1924–6. *From the Founding of the City*. III and IV. LCL. London and New York.

—— trans. B.O. Foster 1929. *From the Founding of the City* X. LCL. London and New York.

—— trans. E.T. Sage 1935. *From the Founding of the City* X. LCL. London and Cambridge, Mass.

Ovid, trans. & ed. J.G. Frazer 1926. *Publii Ovidii Nasonis Fastorum libri sex: The Fasti of Ovid*, 5 vols. London.

Pliny, trans. H. Rackham 1938. *Natural History* I. LCL. London and Cambridge, Mass.

Plutarch, trans. F.C. Babbitt 1927. *The Moralia: How to Study Poetry* I. LCL. London and New York.

Plutarch, ed. T.E. Page, E. Capps and W.H.D. Rowse; trans. F.C. Babbitt 1936. *The Fortunes of the Romans, Moralia* IV. LCL. London and Cambridge, Mass.

Polybius, trans. E.S. Shuckburgh 1889. *The Histories of Polybius* II. London.

Savage, S.M. 1940. 'The Cults of Ancient Trastevere', *Memoirs of the American Academy at Rome* 17, 26–38.

Scullard, J.J. 1981. *Festivals and Ceremonies of the Roman Republic*. London.

Strabo, trans. H.L. Jones 1927. *The Geography of Strabo* II. LCL. London and New York.

Terence, trans J. Sargeaunt 1912. *The Works of Terence*. 2 vols. LCL. London and New York.

Walsh, P.G. 1970. *Livy: His Historical Aims and Methods*. Cambridge.

Wissowa, G. 1904. *Gesammelte Abhandlungenzur Römanischen Religions*. Munich.

—— 1912. *Religion und Kultus der Römer*. Munich.

York, M. 1986. *The Roman Festival Calendar*. New York.

CHAPTER ELEVEN

TRANSMUTATIONS OF AN IRISH GODDESS

———— •◆• ————

Máire Herbert

Our sources of information about early Irish female divinities are narrative texts which treat of the legendary past, but which were written in the Christian period, mainly between the eighth and the twelfth century AD. In these works, mythic concern with the sacred has become a historical concern with age-old events. It has been aptly remarked that 'in the case of early Irish narrative, the hypothesis is that we are dealing with mythology refracted through literature' (ÓCathasaigh 1993: 128). The literary texts do not provide access to a systematic view of the Irish mythic universe; rather, they allow glimpses of the manner in which the supernatural was represented in story.

My purpose here is to survey anew the evidence of Irish literary texts regarding female divinities said to be associated with warfare and death. The first major discussion of the subject was an article, published in 1870 by W. M. Hennessy, entitled 'The ancient Irish Goddess of War' (1870: 32–57; 1872: 489–92), a work to which much subsequent scholarship has been indebted. The title implies a single supernatural being with a clearly defined area of operation. Was this the case? A book published in 1983, *Mórrígan–Bodb–Macha: La souveraineté guerrière de l'Irlande* (Le Roux & Guyonvar'ch 1983), appears by its title to propose an alternative view. Do we have a trio of goddesses, or a goddess with a threefold aspect? Does female divine power combine sovereignty and martial aspects?

A survey of secondary material reveals much of current scholarly interest (see Sjoestedt 1940; Ross 1973; Bhreathnach 1982; Carey 1983), but ultimately what is necessary is to return to the primary sources without prejudgement about the divinity's function or plurality. Evidence regarding female supernatural figures is found in a wide range of Irish narratives, in tales which are overtly 'mythological' in that they are concerned with supernatural beings and with the time of beginnings, as well as in epic, in tales of the heroic Ulster Cycle. I take all this textual material as my field of enquiry. It constitutes a comprehensive and coherent body of data which is to be scrutinized within its own cultural context, without the introduction of external *comparanda*.[1]

In the study of narrative evidence of Irish mythology, a source of first recourse is usually *Lebor Gabála Érenn* (literally, 'The Book of the Taking of Ireland'), a text in which cosmogonic traditions of the formation and peopling of the country have been historicized as a series of invasions (Macalister 1938–42; Carey 1993). Notable among pagan supernatural beings represented here as prehistoric populations are the Tuatha Dé Danann, among whom we find the names of many female divinities. The *Lebor Gabála* tends to group these divinities genealogically, and we find the names of the goddesses associated with war listed as three sisters, the daughters of Ernmas (Carey 1983: 269–70). But we must bear in mind that *Lebor Gabála* is an eleventh-century work of synthesis, as we note discrepancies between its various versions in the naming of the trio (ibid.: 269. 34). The names which occur most frequently are the Mórrígan, Badb and Macha. If we accept the *Lebor Gabála* version of their relationship, we should then expect to find these three supernatural females featuring together in other sources. Yet this is not the case. Their association as a triad occurs only in one late, and evidently derivative, narrative (Fraser 1915: 27, section 29, and 45, section 48; Murphy 1954: 191–8).

In fact, freed from the schematization of eleventh-century scholars, the sum of evidence points to contextual affinity between the names of the Mórrígan and Badb in various texts, while traditions regarding the third member of the sisterhood, Macha, are quite separate and distinct. The present study, therefore, will focus on the representations of female divinity named in the literature as the Mórrígan and as Badb. The evidence regarding Macha requires its own interpretative structure, and I leave this material for future investigation.

The Mórrígan is the name which is most dominant in our survey. As a proper name may be regarded as itself a mythic unit, albeit the smallest possible one, what does this name of the Irish supernatural female reveal? *Rígan*, the second element, is the noun meaning 'queen'. The first element has been variously interpreted, but I believe that the sum of evidence indicates that it should be read as the adjective *mór* (great) (see Le Roux & Guyonvar'ch 1983: 97–102). Hence, the name Mórrígan may be rendered as 'Great Queen'. From name we proceed to narrative, beginning with tales of the Irish mythological cycle.

One of the most significant sources of mythic evidence is the tale of the battle of Mag Tuired, a historicized account of contest between two groups of divinities for possession of the country (Gray 1982). Here we find the goddess depicted as washing at a river, with one foot to the south of the water, and the other to the north. The Dagda, literally the 'Good God', father-figure among the divine race of Tuatha Dé Danann, has a sexual encounter with her. Thereafter she offers assistance to his people in the forthcoming battle, promising to deprive the enemy leader of 'the blood of his heart and the kidneys of his valour' (Gray 1982: 44–5). In the repre-

Figure 11.1   Dá Chich Ananu (the Paps of Anu), Co. Kerry.

sentation in this text we are particularly aware of the female divinity's dominance over the landscape as she straddles the river, and of her evident ability
to influence the fortunes of those seeking control of the land.

The place of the encounter of the Mórrígan, the 'Great Queen' and the
Dagda, the 'Good God', is said to have been named the 'Bed of the Couple'.
The *Dindshenchas* (The Lore of Places), a compilation credited with
preserving some of the mythic geography of Ireland, names 'the bed of the
Dagda' and 'the two breasts of the Mórrígan' among the famous places of
Bruig na Bóinne, the Otherworld dwelling which Irish tradition identifies
with the great prehistoric tumulus of Newgrange (Gwynn 1906: 10–11,
18–19; Stokes 1894: 292–3. The conjunction of place-names reinforces the
previous evidence of association between the female and male divine figures.
The manner of naming places for the deities, moreover, is also significant.
In the case of the Mórrígan, an equation seems to be made between the
body of the goddess and the contours of the earth (Figure 11.1). That the
female is implicated in landscape formation is further suggested by the identification of two of the area's hills as 'Comb and Casket of the Dagda's
wife' (Stokes 1894: 292–3). The indications are, therefore, that the Mórrígan
is identified with the feminized earth. Furthermore, we find that other Irish
place-names are designated by their nomenclature as her property or place
of frequentation (see Hennessy 1870: 54–5; Hogan 1910). Thus, the 'Great
Queen' of the supernatural world appears to have the attributes of a goddess
of the land.

Moreover, her power in the earthly and supernatural worlds is linked with possession of cattle. An onomastic tale in the *Dindshenchas* tells of an Otherworld bride who refused to be parted from the calf which was her coeval. Her human suitor besought the Mórrígan, who 'was good unto him', arranging that the Otherworld herd should be transferred to the mortal world (Stokes 1892: 470–1). Not all encounters were equally benevolent, however. A further onomastic tale recounts how the Mórrígan's Otherworld bull impregnated a cow of an earthly herd and led it away to the supernatural realm. Its female owner went in pursuit but was turned into a pool of water by the vengeful deity (Gwynn 1906–24: IV, 196–201).

Indeed, in the heroic literature of the Ulster Cycle, the Mórrígan's herding tends to be presented as arbitrary interference in warrior society. Cattle acquisition and cattle-raiding play an important part in the early Irish heroic tradition, but the narrative emphasis is concentrated on the deeds of the warrior-heroes rather than on the supernatural aspect of control of animal resources. Thus we find ambivalence, even hostility, in the representation of relations between the female divinity and the male warrior. In the tale of 'The Adventures of Nera', we are told that the Mórrígan took the cow of Nera's son, and mated it with the Brown Bull of Cuailnge, one of the animals fought over in the great epic *Táin Bó Cúailnge*. Thereafter, the goddess was overtaken by Cú Chulainn, the hero of Ulster, who demanded, and apparently secured, the return of the cow (Meyer 1889: 212–28; 1890: 209–10). That the encounter between goddess and hero was more complex, however, is implied by a related narrative.

In the tale called *Táin Bó Regamna* (Corthals 1987), the Mórrígan appears before Cú Chulainn as a red woman, in a chariot drawn by a single red, one-legged horse, and accompanied by a man driving a cow. A debate ensues about the cow, as the Mórrígan refutes Cú Chulainn's assertion that all the cows of Ulster belonged to him. His threats of violence are of no avail. Suddenly, woman, chariot, man and cow disappear. Then Cú Chulainn sees her as a black bird on the branch beside him. The Mórrígan states that she has brought the cow from the Otherworld to mate with the Brown Bull, and she prophesies that Cú Chulainn's life will end when the calf which the cow is carrying will be a yearling. Still the hero is defiant towards the goddess. He views the prophesied battle over the bull as a means of achieving fame, while the Mórrígan threatens to hinder his battle-prowess by coming to him in the form of an eel, a grey she-wolf, and a white, red-eared heifer. They part in mutual recrimination, and the goddess and her cow return to the Otherworld.

We return again to this material in Ireland's chief epic tale, *Táin Bó Cuailnge*, (O'Rahilly 1976), the battle for possession of the Brown Bull. In keeping with the heroic portrayal of Cú Chulainn in this work, he is revealed as triumphant over the Mórrígan, whom he encounters in the various guises threatened in the tale of *Táin Bó Regamna* (O'Rahilly 1976:

lines 1845–71, 1982–2025). What we have here, however, seems to be merely derivative narrative, the verbal conflict of the previous tale rewritten for heroic effect. There follows a further episode in which an exhausted Cú Chulainn comes upon the Mórrígan disguised as a lame, one-eyed crone, milking a cow with three teats. Three times, in response to his demand, she gives him the milk of one teat. On each occasion, as he blesses her, one of her bodily deformities is made whole (ibid.: lines 2038–55). The compiler of the *Táin* interprets this as Cú Chulainn's unwitting healing of the wounds which he has just inflicted on the goddess. But the episode belongs in a sequence which has the narrative agenda of demonstrating Cú Chulainn's triumph over the deity. Freed from the compiler's exegesis, one may see the fatigued hero in the role of suppliant, receiving succour from the disguised goddess, who reveals herself in a process of transformation.

Certainly metamorphosis is a striking attribute of the Mórrígan. We have seen her represented in various female forms and have noted her threats of serial shape-shifting, into an eel, a wolf and a heifer. We have noted also how she assumes the form of a black bird in the course of her meeting with Cú Chulainn in *Táin Bó Regamna*. Moreover, the text makes it clear that it is through this transformation that the hero recognises his interlocutor (*Táin Bó Regamna*/Corthals 1987: 54, lines 55–60). This is a significant revelation. The black bird (*badhbh*), the scald-crow which hovered over the field of battle (see Tymoczko 1990: 151–71, Lysaght, p. 154ff below), is shown to be the most characteristic form in which the Mórrígan might appear to a warrior (Figures 11.2 and 11.3).

In *Táin Bó Cuailnge*, it is the cry of the Badb from amidst the corpses that rouses the young Cú Chulainn as he is laid low on a battle-field, and her taunt about his lack of warrior potential incites him to renewed action (*Táin Bó Cúailnge*/O'Rahilly 1976: lines 498–502). The deity also comes in her avian identity to deliver a cryptic warning to the Brown Bull, the animal being fought over in the *Táin* (ibid.: lines 954–66). In the latter episode an onomastic point is underlined. The goddess is introduced as 'the Mórrígan in the form of a bird', but in the poetic utterance ascribed to her she refers to herself as Badb (ibid.: line 960). The latter name, therefore, clearly had specific reference to the bird metamorphosis of the 'Great Queen'. The distinction failed to be maintained over time, however, and medieval scribes came to regard Badb and the Mórrígan as entirely interchangeable names (*DIL*: S.M. Mórrígan, lines 62–9).

Whatever her *alter ego*, the evidence so far indicates that war *per se* is not a primary aspect of the role of the goddess. She has significant associations with the earth and with the cattle-resources of a pastoral people. Her activities have a tutelary character. She oversees the land, its stock and its society. Her shape-shifting is an expression of her affinity with the whole living universe of creatures, bird, animal and human. This broad concern also expresses itself in prophecies ascribed to the Mórrígan at the end of

Figure 11.2   Reverse of Turones gold stater.

the tale of the Battle of Mag Tuired, when she foretells the future in terms which relate to both the natural and the human worlds (*Cath Maige Tuired*/Gray 1982: 70–3).

Epic literature may be seen to depict her relations with the warrior as adversarial. Yet we must be mindful that in all mythic interactions of immortals and mortals tension is inherent in the asymetry of the relationship. In a key statement in *Táin Bó Regamna* the Mórrígan reminds Cú Chulainn that she is guardian of his death (*Táin Bó Regamna*/Corthals 1987: 55, lines 63–4). Viewed in the light of this evidence, her interventions may be interpreted as ensuring that the hero properly fulfils his life-tasks before the end, of which she has foreknowledge. Indeed, the earliest version of the tale of the death of Cú Chulainn relates that, far from rejoicing in his downfall, the Mórrígan breaks the warrior's chariot in an effort to delay his departure on his final, fatal expedition (*Book of Leinster*/Best & O'Brien 1956: lines 13, 814–16; Tymoczko 1981: 42).

That the goddess's tutelary activity is linked with prescience regarding the fates of those in her guardianship is well attested elsewhere. The Mórrígan is depicted as pronouncing on the collective destinies of those involved in the battle of Mag Tuired and in the conflicts in the *Táin Bó Cuailnge* (*Cath Maige Tuired*/Gray 1982: 71–3; *Táin Bó Cúailnge*/

Figure 11.3 Stone statue of bird of prey, from the third-century BC Roquepertuse Sanctuary (Bouches du Rhône). (Musée de la Vieille Charité, Marseilles.)

O'Rahilly 1976: lines 3877–83). The most striking representations, however, are of the deity actively confronting a prominent individual with his impending doom. In the tale of Da Choca's Hostel, Cormac Conloinges, setting out on an ill-fated expedition, comes upon the gruesome tableau of the goddess as a red woman washing a chariot and equipment at the edge of a ford, making the whole river run red with gore. Her prophecy is verbal as well as visual, for she announces: 'I wash the war-gear of a king who will perish' (Stokes 1900: 156–7). The king is again faced with his future in a second appearance of the divinity, this time as a swarthy, lame and squinting hag. She leans her shoulder against the doorpost of the house which he has just entered, and prophesies an approaching time of mangled, bloodied, and headless bodies on the floor (Stokes 1900: 314–15).[2] Similarly, in the tale of the killing of another king, Conaire, in 'Da Derga's Hostel', the goddess, in the guise of a hideous crone, enters the house after sunset, and proclaims to the king: 'Neither body nor flesh of yours will escape from the place to which you have come, save what birds will carry off in their claws' (Stokes 1901: 56–9).[3]

Though the goddess in all these instances is the harbinger of doom rather than its instigator, we find that the horror instilled by the message attaches itself also to the medium. In a ninth-century poem, a vision of the Mórrígan in her guise as washer of battle-remains elicits these sentiments: 'Many are the spoils she washes, dreadful the twisted laugh she laughs ... the heart ... hates her' (Green & O'Connor 1967: 86–92, no. 19). From her role as seer and manifestation of dread fate, therefore, the goddess herself may be regarded as terrifying and malevolent.

Moreover, it is the antipathetic aspect of the goddess that is stressed by certain clerical writers. While euhemerization is the usual mode of representation of pre-Christian deities in Irish narrative literature, some ecclesiastics take the more overt approach of portraying representatives of the pagan supernatural as demonic beings. An Irish gloss on Latin *lamia* in the Bible text of Isaiah 34:14 reads: 'Monstrum in femine figura .i. mórrígan' (Stokes & Strachan 1901: 2, lines 6–7). Thus the name of the 'Great Queen' becomes a term for a sinister apparition. Similarly, the ninth-century episcopal glossator Cormac mac Cuileannáin, equates the Irish term *gúdemain* (fraudulent evil spirits) with *uatha ocus morrignae* (spectres and mórrígans) (*Sanas Cormaic*/Meyer 1912: 58, entry 697).

Classical epic also became an influence on the representation of the Irish supernatural female. The translation into Irish of Latin works such as the *Aeneid*, the *Thebaid* of Statius, and Lucan's *Pharsalia* appear to date from about the tenth century onward (see Stanford 1970: 13–91). In the process, the translators borrow Irish terminology for use in reference to female figures. Thus, *mórrígan* in the demoted sense of 'witch' or 'demon' is used to refer to Jocasta (Calder 1922: lines 87–8). The term *badhbh* or *badbh chatha* is interchangeable with *fúir* (Fury), and *bandea* (goddess) in connection with Tesiphone (ibid.: lines 151–2, 181–2, 194–5, 3447, 3468, 4313). Another Irish expression used of goddesses implicated in warfare is *Bé Néit* (literally 'Woman/Goddess of Battle'), a term which seems to have derived from the Glossary of Cormac mac Cuileannáin (ibid.: lines 3246–7, 4448. See *Sanas Cormaic*/Meyer 1912: 16, entry 168, and n. 46).

Terminology is not to be dissociated from ideology. The portrayal in contemporary classical translations of scheming, strife-causing goddesses, vengeful Furies and terror-inducing female demons, designated by terms used of Irish supernatural females, undoubtedly in turn influenced representations in vernacular Irish narrative from about the tenth century onwards. The earliest surviving text of the epic *Táin Bó Cuailnge* is a compilation redacted in the eleventh century on the basis of earlier source-material. We may see the contribution of the eleventh-century redactor in a reference to the Mórrígan which equates her with Alecto, one of the Furies of Latin literature (O'Rahilly 1976: lines 954–5). The text also makes reference to a supernatural being called in-Némain (literally, 'Battle-Terror') depicted as causing havoc among the hosts (ibid.: lines 210, 2084–5, 3537). Elsewhere in the text a triad of supernatural figures, named as Badb, Bé Néit and Némain is depicted as having a similar effect (ibid.: lines 3942, 4033). Native and classical traditions fuse in these representations. The Irish goddess in her guise as *badhbh*, the scald-crow, is associated with two figures whose names, 'Woman/Goddess of Battle' and 'Battle-Terror' indicate that they are essentially personified abstractions.[4] The trio functions like the malevolent apparitions of classical literature, as an intimation of horror and dread. The role of the Irish *badhbh* becomes assimilated in a generalized portrayal of attendant demons of the battle-field.

Yet it has been proposed that a connection exists between such Irish battle-field spirits and the Valkyries. A long-held thesis holds that significant parallels exist between the Irish representations and those of Germanic mythology, and that these parallels originate in a context of ancient Celto-Germanic connections in continental Europe (Lottner 1870: 55–7; Donahue 1941: 1–12). The thesis of related mythic ideas, however, rests on an *a priori* assumption that Irish goddesses were 'dreadful, witch-like beings, associated with birds of prey, who prophesied of battles' (Donahue 1941: 5). In other words, conclusions have been drawn on a limited basis of Irish evidence. As we have seen, the full range of Irish narrative testimony undermines such a characterization of the Mórrígan in any of her transmutations. Yet the thesis has been influential, even in the formulation of the long-held etymology of the first element in the name of the Mórrígan as a cognate of the Germanic *mara/mare* (see Vendryes 1960: s.v. *mórrigan*; cf. Raudvere, p. 42ff above).

All our Irish sources have indicated, however, that the early Irish Mórrígan was neither valkyrie nor war-goddess but, rather, a multi-aspected deity whose very name implies a role of power and guardianship. She oversees the animal and human populations of the land, which is her personification or place of frequentation. She has knowledge of life and death, a knowledge which may be transmitted to a chosen mortal in the form of a horrifying prefiguration of approaching doom. To what extent do these representations which we have surveyed influence later Irish attitudes to the female supernatural? On the narrative level, it is notable that, in the wake of the classical adaptations, the inclusion in battle-accounts of spectres, spirits and demonic hosts, called *badba* and a variety of other names, becomes a literary commonplace in medieval Irish narrative (see Sayers 1991: 45–55). But these supernatural figures function as single-dimensional apparitions, portents usually lacking a very distinguishable feminine identity. More significant at the conceptual level is the continued portrayal of female supernatural figures as harbingers of death. While the role attributed to divine power in the governance of the earth and its resources diminishes over time, the fate of human life itself continues to be perceived as being beyond mortal control. Even in a Christianized Irish society, mythic omens of doom retain their efficacy, as man seeks to penetrate the mystery of his unforeseen end. Messengers of mortality retain a female aspect. A fourteenth-century account of warfare still depicts the dreaded washerwoman of the slain at her gory task (O'Grady 1929: I, 104–5, 140–1;

II, 93–4, 124–5). It is the dark side of the Mórrígan's power that has the most enduring impact.

NOTES

1 The present work marks the beginning of reappraisal of evidences regarding Irish female supernatural figures; hence the importance of delineating the evidence without the imposition of inferences drawn either from cognate Celtic sources or from comparative mythology.
2 In both instances the name of the supernatural female is given as 'the Badb'.
3 Here, the female visitant lists a series of her names, which includes Badb.
4 The glossator, Cormac, hazards the explanation that Nemon was wife of Néit, characterized as 'god of war among the Irish' (*Sanas Cormaic*/Meyer 1912: entries 181, 965). There is no evidence in vernacular Irish literature to support this. Reference elsewhere by Cormac to Mars as god of war (ibid.: entry 892) indicates that Cormac was influenced by the classical model in his interpretation of Irish evidence of deities. The *Lebor Gabála* tradition pairs Nemaind with Fea in one instance, with Babd in another, as wives of Néit (see Best & O'Brien 1956: I, lines 1183, 1412–13).

REFERENCES

Abbreviation

D.I.L   Dictionary of the Irish Language. Royal Irish Academy. Dublin.

Best, R.I., and M.A. O'Brien eds 1956. *The Book of Leinster, formerly Lebar na Núachongbála* II. Dublin.
Bhreathnach, M. 1982. 'The Sovereignty Goddess as Goddess of Death?' *Zeitschrift für celtische Philologie* 39, 243–60.
Calder, G. ed. 1922. *Togail na Tebe: The Thebaid of Statius*. Cambridge.
Carey, J. 1983. 'Notes on the Irish War-Goddess', *Éigse* 19, 263–75.
—— 1993. 'A New Introduction to *Lebor Gabála Érenn: The Book of the Taking of Ireland*' , in R.A.S. Macalister (ed.), *Lebor Gabála Érenn* I–V. Irish Texts Society. Dublin.
Corthals, J. ed. 1987. *Táin Bó Regamna: Eine Vorersahlung zur Táin Bó Cúailnge*. Vienna.
Donahue, C. 1941. 'The Valkyries and the Irish War-Goddesses', *Publications of the Modern Language Association of America* 56, 1–12.
Fraser, J. 1915. 'The First Battle of Moytura', *Ériu* 8, 1–63.
Gort na Morrignai, Lis na Morríghna: see Hogan, 1910.
Gray, E.A. ed. 1982. *Cath Maige Tuired: the Second Battle of Mag Tuired*. Irish Texts Society. Dublin.
Green, D. and F. O'Connor eds 1967. *A Golden Treasury of Irish Poetry* AD 600 *to 1200*. London.
Gwynn, E. 1906–24. *The Metrical Dindshenchas*, II and IV. Dublin.
Hennessy, W.M. 1870–2. 'The Ancient Irish Goddess of War', *Revue celtique* 1 (1870), 32–55. Corrections and additions, ibid. 2 (1872), 489–92.
Hogan, E. 1910. *Onomasticon Goedelicum*. Dublin & London.

Le Roux, F. & C-J. Guyonvar'ch 1983. *Mórrigan–Bodb–Macha: La souveraineté guerrière de l'Irlonde.* Rennes.

Lottner, C. 1870. [Addendum to Hennessy 1870], *Revue celtique* 1, 55–7.

Macalister, R.A.S. ed. 1938–42. *Lebor Gabála Érenn*, I–V. Irish Texts Society (repr. 1993). Dublin.

Meyer, K. 1889–90. 'The Adventures of Nera', *Revue celtique* 10 (1889), 212–81; 11 (1890), 209–10.

—— ed. 1912. *Sanas Cormaic: An Old-Irish Glossary compiled by Cormac úa Cuilennáin, King-Bishop of Cashel in the Ninth Century.* Anecdota from Irish Manuscripts 4. Halle & Dublin.

Murphy, G. 1954. 'Notes on Cath Maige Tuired', *Éigse* 7, 191–8.

Ó Cathasaigh, T. 1993. 'Mythology in Táin Bó Cúailnge', in H.L.C. Tristram (ed.), *Studien zur Táin Bó Cúailnge.* Tübingen. 114–32.

O'Grady, S.H. ed. 1929. *Caithreeim Thoirdhealbhaigh: The Triumphs of Turlough*, 2 vols. Irish Texts Society. Dublin.

O'Rahilly, C. ed. 1976. *Táin Bó Cúailnge: Recension 1.* Dublin.

Ross, A. 1973. 'The Divine Hag of the Pagan Celts', in V. Newall (ed.), *The Witch Figure.* London & Boston, Mass. 139–64.

Sayers, W. 1991. '*Airdrech, Sirite* and Other Early Irish Battlefield Spirits.' *Éigse* 25, 45–55.

Sjoestedt, M-L. 1940. *Gods and Heroes of the Celts.* Paris. (Repr. Berkeley, Calif., 1982.)

Stanford, W.B. 1970. 'Towards a History of Classical Influences in Ireland', *Proceedings of the Royal Irish Academy* 70 C 1. Dublin.

Stokes, W. 1892. 'The Bodleian Dinnshenchas', *Folk-Lore* 3, 470–1.

—— 1894. 'The Prose Tales in the Rennes Dindshenchas', *Revue celtique* 15, 292–3.

—— 1900. 'Da Choca's Hostel', *Revue celtique* 21, 149–65, 312–27, 388–402.

—— 1901–2. 'The Destruction of Da Derga's Hostel', *Revue celtique* 22 (1901), 9–16, 165–215, 282–329, 390–437; 23 (1902), 56–9, 88.

Stokes, W. & J. Strachan, 1901. *Thesaurus Palaeohibernicus* I. Dublin. (Repr. Dublin 1975.).

Tymoczko, M. 1981. *Two Death-Tales from the Ulster Cycle: The Death of Cú Roi and the Death of Cú Chulainn.* Dublin.

—— 1990. The Semantic Fields of Early Irish Terms for Black Birds and their Implications for Species Taxonomy', in A.T.E. Matonio and D.F. Melia (eds), *Celtic Language, Celtic Culture: A Festschrift for Eric P. Hamp.* Van Nuys, Calif. 151–71.

Vendryes, J. 1960. *Lexique étymologique de l'Irlandais ancien: M N O P.* Paris.

CHAPTER TWELVE

ASPECTS OF THE EARTH-GODDESS IN THE TRADITIONS OF THE BANSHEE IN IRELAND

—— •◆• ——

Patricia Lysaght

... Not for the mean-spirited
Money-grabbing hucksters
She calls.
Sons of uncertain fathers
No banshee ever keened your kind!
She follows the true family.

A solitary
A lone one
Small woman
Dressed in white
To kill?
Ugly–beautiful
Youthfully old
Small and tall
in a dark bright dress..
      Seóirse Bodley, *The Banshee*

I

Few folk beliefs have survived in Ireland with the same tenacity as that of a supernatural female being connected with death in certain families, and popularly called the banshee. She is known by a number of names, however, and here she will be referred to by the generic term '(supernatural) death-messenger', since various strands in the traditions about her which are important in tracing her origin, are specifically linked to the different names by which she is known – and the question of origin is of importance in attempting to find echoes of the land-goddess in the modern folk-traditions of the death-messenger. Some few tradition-bearers and commentators have occasionally looked to fairylore and ghostlore to explain her origin, tending to view her simply as either a fairy woman, or just a restless female spirit in some way connected to the family for which she forebodes or proclaims death (Lysaght 1986: 43–6, 49–50). Both fairylore and ghostlore, as well as other tradition complexes such as that concerned with the human keening women, have indeed influenced aspects of the supernatural death-messenger tradition. However, closer analysis highlights folk-perceptions and traits which point to another, and quite different, complex as the most likely main source of the supernatural death-messenger belief. Certain core elements seem to indicate that the supernatural death-messenger of folk tradition can be related – in cultural terms – to various goddess-figures who play such an important and prominent role in early Irish mythology. What are these core elements, and how are they to be understood?

II

The large corpus of folk beliefs and memorates about the supernatural death-messenger in the archives of the Department of Irish Folklore, University College Dublin, together with the many literary references to her both in Irish and English (Lysaght 1986: 321–64), enable us to identify the main elements of the supernatural death-messenger belief of Irish folk tradition current in the last three centuries. These include the traditional names for the supernatural death-messenger, the role or roles attributed to her, her role-behaviour and traditional images, and ideas about her origin. Since I have already discussed all these aspects in detail in an earlier work (Lysaght 1986), they will be dealt with only briefly here.

III

All the names for the supernatural death-messenger are in the Irish language, indicating that the beliefs about her, whatever their ultimate origin, were fully developed in Gaelic Ireland. These names help to explain aspects of her image, her function and her role-behaviour, and also offer important clues about her origin. The most common name in the whole distribution-area of the death-messenger belief is 'banshee', the anglicized form of Irish *bean sí* (earlier *ben síde*), and in the death-messenger context it means 'woman of the Otherworld' (Byrne 1973: 20, Ó Cathasaigh 1977–8: 137–55; cf. Sims-Williams 1990: 60–81; Carey 1991: 154–9), rather than 'fairy woman', which would also be correct from an etymological point of view. Although influenced by fairylore, the set of beliefs connected with the banshee is intrinsically different. Fairies are imagined to be social beings living in communities, and often have relationships with human beings, and their world is thought to be akin to the human world to a large extent (Ó Súilleabháin 1967: 82–6). The death-proclaiming *bean sí*, however, is a solitary being *par préférence*: the names for her include the definite article *an*/the, indicating that, although each family followed has its own particular death-messenger, they are never imagined to associate with one another or to form communities like the fairy race in general. Though the name also links her to other Otherworld female beings – mainly emanations of the earth-goddess – in the early Irish myths and sagas, the banshee/*bean sí*, essentially denotes a solitary female being of supernatural character (Lysaght 1986: 28–32).

An important alternative name for the death-messenger is *badhbh* – occurring in various dialect forms in the south-east of Ireland – though it is not exclusive in that area, as the term *bean sí*/banshee is also widely known there (ibid.: 34–9). This name also links the death-messenger to a goddess figure, since it is a survival of the name *badhbh*/Badb, the designation of a goddess, usually a goddess of war (Mac Cana 1973: 86), occurring in early Irish literature. This name, therefore, provides another important clue to the origin of the death-messenger of folk tradition and will be dealt with in detail below.

The remaining traditional name for the death-messenger is *bean chaointe* (keening woman), and it describes her role-behaviour, rather than her origin or dwelling-place. It is the name that most closely links her with the human keening women – on whom her appearance and behaviour are sometimes modelled – and she may to some extent be regarded as a supernatural counterpart to those keeners (Lysaght 1986: 32–3).

A central aspect of the death-messenger belief, and one of particular importance in tracing its origin and assessing its cultural significance, is the connection of the *bean sí*/banshee, *badhbh* or *bean chaointe* with certain families. The families she is said to attend or 'follow' are those with Ó or Mac in their surnames: that is, families of noble Irish descent, or families so considered. Not all such families are imagined to be followed by her, however, but only particular ones. And the death-messenger is also said to favour the male members, or even the most prominent male members, of those families. Traces of an aristocratic being attached primarily to noble and illustrious Gaelic families, and in particular to their chieftains or heads, is discernible in the folk-traditions of the death-messenger. Her connection with a family is viewed in an ancestral light – she is regarded as an ancestress of that family (ibid.: 53–63). Further, she would also seem to be concerned with the fortunes of the family, and thus also with the ownership and fertility of land.

The most powerful modern evocation of that sort of connection with families occurs in the poetic reaction to the cultural upheaval, and the forfeitures and confiscations of land, in sixteenth- and seventeenth-century

Ireland, by the English government.[1] Families of English origin who settled in Ireland on land obtained as a result of these measures are essentially excluded from the attentions of the supernatural death-messenger (ibid.: 58, 259–81). The nobleman-poet of Norman extraction, Piaras Feiritéar from the Dingle Peninsula in Co. Kerry, who had fought for many years against the Cromwellian army, wrote in the early 1640s that banshees do not cry for the merchants and hucksters of the area but only for noble families like the Fitzgeralds (Ua Duinnín 1934, 74, lines 29–32; cf. Mac Erlean 1910–17: I, 36–9; Dunne 1980: 20–5). In refusing the death-messenger to foreigners and intruders – the new, largely merchant, class – the poet is, in effect, symbolically denying their title to Irish land. In the seventeenth century in particular, therefore, the death-messenger is viewed as a patroness of distinctively Irish families, and as a symbol and protectress of their land. The special significance accorded to the ancestral home in the death-messenger belief, preserved in recent folk tradition, is also significant in this context: even if the old family home is in ruins, or indeed if nothing is left but 'the track of the house', she will come and cry there – the ancestral cry emanating from the *petite patrie* (Lysaght 1986: 124). The connection of the death-messenger with families and the ancestral home is undoubtedly an echo of a persistent theme in Irish tradition – that of sovereignty – signifying the mythic union between the goddess of the land and its proper sovereign. Further examples of the representation of this theme in the death-messenger tradition will be introduced and discussed below.

Since the basic role of the supernatural death-messenger of Irish folk tradition is to proclaim deaths which are imminent in particular Irish families, the question arises as to how she performs this function. That she does so by means of lamentation is evident from the collective tradition. Sorrow and grief are the key elements in the majority of the terms used to describe her lamenting, indicating that she is – as one might expect of an ancestress – friendly and sympathetic towards the person who is dying, and that she shares, as it were, the grief of relatives and friends (ibid.: 67–9). However, in the south-east of Ireland, where the death-messenger is widely known as the *badhbh*, the terms used to describe her death-foreboding sound express a more fierce and frightening side to her character. They include, for example, 'roar', 'scream', 'screech' and 'shriek', connoting loud, sharp and shrill sounds suggestive of the realms of wild animals or dangerous and hostile supernatural beings, rather than the human sphere. The image of an aggressive, threatening supernatural death-messenger is thus quite strong in this area (ibid.: 69–70). This duality of aspects calls to mind certain characteristics of goddess-figures of early Irish mythology (Carey 1983: 263–75): on the one hand she is benign and sympathetic towards the family and the person who is dying, while on the other she is depicted as a frightening and threatening being (Lysaght 1986: 85), though not actively promoting the person's death.

The death-messenger is imagined to be visible, and to appear in female shape, in most parts of Ireland (ibid.: Lysaght 1986: ch. 5). There has been no established folk tradition within living memory in Ireland that the death-messenger – banshee or *badhbh* – appeared in the shape of any bird, despite the fact that she is commonly known in the south-east of Ireland by the name *badhbh*, which is the Irish word for 'scaldcrow', the form most frequently ascribed to *badhbh*/Badb, goddess of war in the early literature (RIA Dictionary 1913–76: s.v. *badb, bodb*; Mac Cana 1973: 86, Ó Domhnaill 1977, s. v. *badhbh*; Green 1992, 38). Nor is she imagined to appear in the shape of any animal or insect (Lysaght 1986: 107–11). There are also dual aspects to her appearance according to the collective tradition. On the one hand she is generally described as an old, small and somewhat ugly woman with long white hair which, in the eastern part of Ireland, she is said to be continually combing.[2] Although generally said to be dressed in white, the colour red is also mentioned – though to a more limited extent (ibid.: 102–3). Its associations with blood may have rendered it appropriate in the past when the death-messenger appeared in connection with violent deaths, it being also the colour associated with the *badhbh*, goddess of war, in early Irish mythology (Stokes 1900: 156; Knott n.d.: 107; Windisch 1887: 242, line 17). She is also imagined as a young, tall, beautiful and vigorous woman, especially in the south-east of Ireland, where she is known both as banshee and as *badhbh*. Her contrasting attributes – old, small, ugly / young, tall, beautiful – are very clearly signalled in this region (Lysaght 1986: 87–95, 101–3, 105), and they also apply to goddess-figures in Irish literature (Carey 1983: 268, 274–5), who may be regarded as predecessors of the death-messenger of folk tradition.

Other aspects of the death-messenger's traditional manifestation which are of considerable importance in tracing her ultimate origin are her connection with water, and her washing activity. Although never thought of as a water being, she is, like other female beings in Irish literature from an early period (Lysaght 1986: 197–201), commonly imagined to appear close to water – at rivers, wells and lakes – indicating her supernatural origin, since one of the main locations of 'the Otherworld' in medieval Irish literature was under the ground, including beneath lakes and springs (Sims-Williams 1990: 60). In the south-east of Ireland, where she is known as *badhbh*, her association with water, like that of the ancient war-goddess, is very strong – her connection with wells being particularly pronounced, especially in Co. Waterford, where the place-name Tobar na Baidhbe (the Badhbh's Well) indicates that the association is of considerable antiquity in this south-eastern area (Lysaght 1986: 127–130).

The appearance of the death-messenger close to a lake or river must also be considered in relation to a special activity sometimes ascribed to her: namely, her washing,[3] an activity particularly associated with the goddess of war – Mór-Ríoghain or Badb – in early Irish literature (ibid.: 197–201).

Its ascription to the death-messenger further links her to those beings, and it is also paralleled in the washing activity of the *bean-nighe*, the supernatural washerwoman foreboding death in Scottish-Gaelic tradition (ibid.: 133, 387–8n. 49, 50, 400n. 79). One might expect to find particular emphasis on the washing activity of the death-messenger in areas where she is widely known as *badhbh*, and where her connection with water is particularly strong. Distribution data, however, show that the core area of this activity is in Co. Galway and the border regions of neighbouring counties (ibid.: 128–33), and some suggestions why this is so will be presented later. Significantly, it is from within this core area that what appears to be the only reference so far from the oral tradition of a woman foreboding violent death in a battle context has come. The conflict referred to is the Battle of Aughrim 1691, the last battle of the Williamite campaign in Ireland, in which the Jacobite army was decisively defeated (Hayes-McCoy 1980: 238–72). This Irish-language account collected from a Menlo, Co. Galway, story-teller in the 1930s (Ó Broin 1957: 10–11), tells that when the earl of Clanricarde of Tirellan Castle (near Galway city) and his servant approached the battlefield of Aughrim, they saw a loud-lamenting woman in a boghole (a large stretch of bog did in fact separate the opposing armies: Hayes-McCoy 1980: 241). The servant asked her why she cried, and she then foretold the violent death in battle of both Burke and himself. She is not, however, at all hostile to them – unlike many of the *badhbh*-figures in the early literature. One is tempted to view the foreboding woman at the Battle of Aughrim as a 'washer at the ford' (Motif D 1812.5.1.1.7* (in Cross 1952), and thus as a remarkable survival of this age-old motif, in its ancient context, in twentieth-century Irish oral tradition.

IV

In the foregoing summary of the main elements of the supernatural death-messenger belief, connections between the supernatural death-foreboder of folk tradition, and certain goddess-figures in early Irish literary texts who are, in one way or another, associated with the deaths of noble personages, were suggested. Like the death-messenger, these female divinities may be classified as favourable or threatening beings – though their disposition is not unrelated to the contexts and literary genres in which they appear. The eighth-century story of the hero Fraoch mac Idath, whose imminent death is announced by the cries of Otherworld women (*mná síde*), belongs to the benign strand of the tradition. He is cried for by the divine women of the Boyne and especially by his mother, the divine Bé Find, sister of Bóinn, the eponymous goddess of the River Boyne (Meid 1967: 9–10; Lysaght 1986: 193–4).

Mór Mumhan ('Mór of [the province of] Munster), who is depicted in a late medieval tale as weeping over the grave of her late husband, the former king of Munster (Mac Cana 1955–6: 79), is also a sympathetic being. The title 'Mór' was originally a designation for the land-goddess, and in this text Mór personifies the land of Munster. Thus, in accordance with the age-old convention of sacral kingship, she represents the sovereignty of the region, and the dead king was her mystical spouse (ibid.: 80–90).

The theme of the marriage of the land-goddess to the proper ruler of a territory, thus ensuring his sovereignty, is a perennial one in Irish tradition (Breatnach 1953; Mac Cana 1955–6; 1958–9; Byrne 1973; Ní Bhrolcháin 1980; Doan 1984; Herbert 1992). That the land of Ireland and its local divisions were each identified with their appropriate goddesses has long been recognized as a feature of early Irish belief (Mac Cana 1955–6: 76). Thus the king of Tara (or Ireland) was symbolically espoused to the land-goddess Ériu, representing the sovereignty of the whole of Ireland, on attaining the kingship, and lesser kings were likewise espoused to local territorial goddesses, representing local or divisional sovereignty (ibid.: 77, 90). One such local divinity was Aoibheall of Craig Liath or Craiglea, near Killaloe in Co. Clare, who appears to have been originally territorial goddess of east Clare and the north-west of Co. Tipperary, and later patroness and protectress of the Dál gCais sept in Co. Clare (Ó hÓgáin 1990: 38). According to a twelfth-century account of the Battle of Clontarf (1014) – which is conventionally taken to mark the end of the Viking wars and power in Ireland – Aoibheall appeared to Brian Ború, high-king of Ireland, the night before the battle and foretold that he would be killed in that conflict the following day and that the first of his sons he saw on that day would gain the kingship of Ireland after his death (Todd 1867: 200–1). Aoibheall was thus clearly acting in the capacity of goddess of sovereignty and her foreboding of death was an aspect of that role.

Another local territorial goddess appearing in the role of death-foreboder and ancestress to an illustrious individual and sept – Áine Cliar, said to reside in Cnoc Áine, the hill of Knockainey, rising above the rich pasture lands of the Munster plain (Figure 12.1) – can clearly be regarded as a manifestation of the land-goddess. An association with the Eoganacht, the dominant Munster sept, is already clearly expressed in the eighth century; she was considered the ancestress of that sept, and symbol of its sovereignty, thus stressing its right to the kingship of Munster (Ó hÓgáin 1990: 182–3). Like the Eoganacht, the powerful Norman Geraldines, as the new overlords of Munster in the Middle Ages, also claimed descent from Áine, regarding her as a symbol of their sovereignty (ibid.: 21) and thus culturally legitimizing their right to the territory of Desmond. In later tradition Áine functions as a death-foreboder for the Fitzgeralds; she is depicted as a weeping *bean sí* in a seventeenth-century elegy by the poet Piaras Feiritéar for a member of the noble Fitzgerald family (Ua Duinnín 1934: 73, lines 17–20).

Figure 12.1   Cnoc Áine (Knockainey), Co. Limerick.

Áine has survived as a latter-day figure of the land-goddess and as a banshee, not only in the folk tradition of Munster but in widely scattered areas throughout Ireland. Áine of Cnoc Áine, parish of Lissan (Irish: Lios Áine, 'Áine's fort'), Co. Derry, is said in folk tradition to be the ancestress of the local Corr family, and their banshee, her crying presaging the death of members of that family (Ó hÓgáin 1990: 21).

The goddess Clíona, associated with Carraig Chlíona, the 'Rock of Clíona' in Co. Cork, and sometimes referred to as Clíona Ceannfhionn (Fair-haired Clíona), was considered one of the principal Otherworld women of the province of Munster in literature and folklore, and, in the folk tradition, was regarded as an ancestress of the Ó Caoimh sept (ibid.: 91). Like Áine, she functions as a *bean sí* foreboding death in later tradition. A contemporary lament depicts Clíona foretelling by her crying the death in 1726 of the bishop of Cork, and while lamenting she wrings her hands, and her long hair hangs long and loose in sorrow (Ua Duinnín 1902: 49–50: lines 1172–84).

These figures – like the death-messenger of folk tradition – have, in one way or another, associations with water: Mór Mumhan with the streams on Mám Clasach, Dingle peninsula, Co. Kerry (Curtin 1894: xli–xliii); Áine with Lough Gur and the Camóg River, Co. Limerick; Clíona with Tonn Chlíona or the 'Wave of Clíona', Glandore strand, Co. Cork; and Aoibheall with Tobar Aoibhill, 'Aoibheall's Well', near Killaloe, Co. Clare (Lysaght 1986: 400n., 76, 77).

The divine beings mentioned in the foregoing texts, especially in the earlier ones, can, despite some differences in detail, be regarded as generic predecessors of the death-messenger of folk tradition. They are connected with, and are favourably disposed to, aristocratic and politically important individuals and families. As land-goddesses or patronesses of sovereignty, they are not solely associated with foreboding or lamenting death but have a range of functions in relation to the rulers and inhabitants of their areas. In the literature, for example, the Otherworld woman, the *bean sí* or *sí bhean* of eighteenth-century Aisling or Vision poetry, is usually depicted as lamenting a dead leader (de Bhaldraithe 1944: 214–5), while in the folk tradition it is the role of foreboder of death that is emphasized.

V

In addition to benign patron-goddesses foreboding and lamenting the death of their rulers or leaders, divine female beings provoking, as well as foreboding, the death of the king or leader are also met with in the early literature. Resembling the death-messenger of folk tradition in some respects, they differ radically from her in others; her foreboding means that death is imminent and inevitable, but she is never considered an agent of death. In a number of the more notable death-tales of kings in Old Irish literature, however, the approaching death of the king is prophesied by a woman who has an intimate connection with him and who can be identified by her characteristics with the sovereignty-goddess of the accession tales. By contrast to her happier role in those tales, her function in the death-tales is as a death-goddess who is instrumental in the downfall and death of the unjust king whose reign has ceased to be productive, and who thus can no longer be her mystical spouse.

In these tales she is perceived either as a beautiful woman or as a horrible, loathsome hag – attributes which find some correspondence in the traditions of the death-messenger. In the death-tale of Muircheartach Mac Earca (high-king of Ireland c. 513–34),[4] composed in or about the eleventh century (Ó hÓgáin 1990: 310), the sovereignty-figure (in her role as goddess of death) foreboding his violent death appears as a beautiful woman, while in the death-tale of Conaire Mór,[5] mythical king of Tara – 'the primordial just king who unwittingly breaks his *gessa* or taboos and is hounded inexorably to his doom' (Byrne 1973: 59) – the woman who is promoting and foreboding his death is a loathsome hag and sorceress, who is comparable with the *puella senilis* of the accession tales. She is admitted to the *bruidhean* after sunset in violation of the last of Conaire's *geasa* and thus seals his fate (Bhreathnach 1982: 243–60; Rees and Rees 1961: 327–30).

Both her name and aspects of her behaviour link the hag in the foregoing tale to the loathsome female sorceress, also named Badhbh, appearing in the death-tale of Cormac Conn Loingeas,[6] the aspiring king of Ulster. She causes him to break prohibitions or taboos, this leading inevitably to his violent death, and also *forebodes* his death in the familiar war-goddess guise of the grim 'washer at the ford' (Stokes 1900: 156; Lysaght 1986: 199–200). The *badhbh* in this text might be identified with the territorial goddess of Ulster who is denying the sovereignty of the province to Cormac Conn Loingeas.

In the death-tale of Cú Chulainn, compiled at the end of the Middle Ages, the *badhbh*, as she seeks his death, appears in a number of guises, such as a scaldcrow (*feannóg*), and a hag roasting dog-meat on a spit (Van Hamel 1933: 82, 98) – which is *geis* (taboo) for him to eat and *geis* for him to refuse (Rees and Rees 1961: 327). However, it is as a beautiful maiden that he encounters her as he sets out for his final fateful battle. She is lamenting and moaning as she washes hacked wounded spoils in cold water, thus foreboding violent death (Van Hamel 1933: 95–6; Lysaght 1986: 198). Here the additional death-messenger-like element of lamentation is included.

Badhbh/Badb is the most common alternative name for the war-goddess, the Mór-Ríoghain, who appears as a 'washer at the ford' under that name in a text from the Old Irish period. The text is concerned with the violent death of the mythic warrior Fothad Cannaine, and contains the following reference to the Mór-Ríoghain – 'horrible are the huge entrails which the Mórrígan washes . . . many are the spoils she washes' (Meyer 1910: 16–17; Lysaght 1986: 199). This type of portrayal of the war-goddess became almost customary in the literature, and, as we shall see below, it appears in the accounts of battles fought in the fourteenth century.

The *badhbh*-figures in the foregoing texts represent the goddess of war; and the supernatural death-messenger of folk tradition, on analogy with these beings, may also, in broad terms, be considered a descendant of the ancient war-goddess as depicted in the older literature. An aspect of the war-goddess that remains to be considered, however, is the element of fierce hostility displayed by her, in her various manifestations, towards the person whose death is imminent, in the early literature. Although there are echoes of this hostility in the folk tradition in the south-east of Ireland, where the death-messenger is known as *badhbh*, it is, nevertheless, essentially as a being favourable to the person who is dying that she is depicted even in that region. That favourable attributes were also characteristic of the war-goddess is, however, evident from the early literature.

The Mór-Ríoghain 'phantom queen' emerges in the tradition as the goddess of war *par excellence*, and this primary role has coloured her portrayal in the literature, where she appears hostile to the personages whose deaths she is foreboding. That she is, however, an emanation from the earth-goddess (representing her war-function), is evident from her intimate association with the landscape and fertility, which is indicated by place-names such as Gort na Morrígna (the Morrígan's Field) in Co. Louth, dá chích na Morrígna (Paps of the Mórrígan) near Newgrange, Co. Meath (cf., however, Carey 1983: 274 n. 56), and the designation of large ancient cooking-sites as *Fulacht na Morrígna* (the Morrígan's Hearth) (Hennessy 1870–2: 54–5). Her connection with the land is further indicated by her identification with Anu, *mater deorum Hibernensium* and goddess of prosperity of the land of Munster, after whom two Kerry hills, Dá Chích Anann (The Paps of Anu; Figure 11.1) are named (ibid.: 37; Mac Cana 1973: 85, 94; Carey 1983: 269–75), and with Macha, whose name means 'pasture'. In addition, an older strand of the tradition indicating the Mór-Ríoghain's protective role is also discernible in the literature. For example, the account of the Second Battle of Moytirra depicts her as a goddess of fertility as well as of war, and as a protectress of her people's interests (Stokes 1891: 85; Mac Cana 1973: 66; Gray 1982: 240–1). Other examples also point to the protective role of the Mór-Ríoghain: for example, as a young beautiful woman she offers help to Cú Chulainn in the *Táin Bó Cúailgne* (but reverts to type when he refuses because he does not wish to be helped by a woman) (*Táin Bó Cúailnge*/O'Rahilly 1976: 57–8; Mac Cana 1973: 90); she unyokes his chariot the night before his final fatal battle in an attempt to stop his departure ((*Táin Bó Cúailnge*/Best and O'Brien 1956: 443); and the war-goddess trio (representing the triplication of a single deity, the Mór-Ríoghain) shrieks over Meadhbh's army during the *Táin*, causing confusion and death among some of the Connachtmen, thus protecting the men of Ulster (*Táin Bó Cúailnge*/Best and O'Brien 1976: 118).

As the centuries wear on, the protective or caring role of the war-goddess becomes more obvious – even in what is, perhaps, her most repulsive manifestation, that of a woman washing mangled corpses prior to battle. In a mid-fourteenth-century account of the Battle of Corcomroe Abbey – fought in the year 1317 between Donnchadh Ó Briain and the faction of Toirdhealbach Ó Briain, led by Murchadh Ó Briain, for supremacy in Thomond – Donnchadh, on his way to battle, encounters a hideous and loathsome 'washer at the ford', who foretells his own and his followers' deaths in the forthcoming battle. Donnchadh recognizes her as the friendly and protecting *badhbh* of his opponents, and her foreboding is vindicated when Donnchadh and his kinsmen are mortally defeated in the battle (O'Grady 1929: I, 104–5; II, 93–4). This *badhbh*-figure again favoured clan Toirdhealbhach at the Battle of Dysert O'Dea (1318), when she foreboded by her bloody washing at the River Fergus (ibid.: I, 140–1; II, 124-5), the decisive defeat of the Norman army under Richard de Clare, thus giving the O'Briens a supremacy in old Thomond lying north of the Shannon, which they retained for the Gaelic order until the sixteenth century (Hayes-McCoy 1980: 38–9, 45). This 'protecting *badhbh*' of clan Toirdhealbhach Ó Briain represents the sovereignty- and war-functions of the territorial goddess of Thomond.

The generative force of the 'washer at the ford' motif seems to have been lost to Irish literature and language after the fourteenth century, but this may be due to the rigidity and exclusiveness of the bardic order and literature. It was used creatively in the English language by some nineteenth-century writers drawing on translations of Irish texts by the noted Gaelic scholar John O'Donovan (Lysaght 1986: 397–8 n. 41). It remained, however, a dynamic element of the oral tradition of the supernatural death-messenger into the twentieth century, though connected only with 'non-violent' deaths in the changed political and social climate. It survived, and survives, most vigorously in areas where the Gaelic language and traditions were, and are, strong enough to nourish and support such a powerful and ancient cultural motif. Thus it is no longer part of the racial and cultural repertoire of the province of Leinster, where a Gaelic culture in decline since the twelfth-century Anglo-Norman invasion, and in substantial retreat in most parts of the province from the seventeenth century onwards, could not sustain it (ibid.: 209–11, Ó Cuív 1951: 15–32).[7] It was, however, undoubtedly in the conflict associated with the change of land-ownership due to confiscations in this prosperous region, especially in the seventeenth century, that the name *badhbh* became so firmly rooted in the area, and that the modern reflex of the *badhbh*-tradition developed, particularly the emphasis on a connection with distinctively Gaelic families, which was an expression of the age-old concept, sovereignty. That the *badhbh* was associated with particular Irish families as death-foreboder and was considered simply an Otherworld woman, a *ben síde/bean sí*, is clearly evident in eighteenth-century lexicographical and poetic works (Lysaght 1986: 34, 210, 215, 402 n. 96). It was, and is, the benign and caring aspects of the ancestral goddess that prevailed, but the names banshee and *badhbh* remind us that echoes of the sovereignty- and war-functions of the earth-goddess survive in the supernatural death-messenger-belief of twentieth-century Ireland.

NOTES

1   The response of the colonized Gaelic population is found mainly in the Gaelic poetry of the period because of the paucity of other evidence. The anguish of colonialism was most clearly expressed in the passionate verse of Dáibhí Ó Bruadair (*c.* 1625–97) – e.g. Mac Erlean, 1910–17: I, 36–9. The Irish poets attack the ignorant boorishness and cruelty of the Cromwellians, whose names they frequently ridicule in their poetry (ibid.: 37–8 nn. 2, 3). For a discussion of Ó Bruadair and other poets of the seventeeth and eighteenth centuries whose work may be used to chronicle the effects of the colonial process on native Irish culture, see Dunne 1980: 7–30.
2   The combing-motif in the death-messenger context, and in relation to other female supernatural beings, is dealt with in detail in Lysaght 1986: 95–101, 154–81, 401–2, nn. 91, 92, 94, 96. A description of the hair of the woman whom

the poet sees in his vision is a standard feature of the Irish-language allegorical *Aisling*, or 'Vision', poems of the eighteenth century. The woman may be Ireland or a *sí-bhean*, an 'Otherworld' woman, such as Aoibheall, Áine or Clíona, former land-goddesses of the province of Munster. In just four lines of one such poem, the Kerry poet Eoghan Rua Ó Súilleabháin (Ua Duinnín 1901: I, lines 5–8) uses more than a dozen adjectives to describe the woman's long, flowing, thick masses of fair wavy hair, which touches the ground.

3   Other supernatural washerwomen not specifically connected with foreboding death are also dealt with in Lysaght 1986: 132–3, 387 n. 48.

4   Nic Dhonnchadha 1964.

5   The principal text concerning Conaire is *Togail Bruidue Da Derga* ('The Destruction of Da Derga's Hostel'): see Stokes 1902; Knott 1936.

6   This is the text *Togail Bruidue Da Choca* ('The Destruction of Da Choca's Hostel'), which was composed in or around the ninth century (Ó hÓgain 1990: 120); see also Stokes 1900; Knott n.d.

7   The Gaelic culture of Leinster progressively weakened as a result of the continuing decline of the Gaelic language after the Anglo-Norman invasion of the twelfth century, native population deplacement as a result of land confiscations, and the advent of English settlers with their language and culture, especially in the seventeenth century.

REFERENCES

Bhreathnach, M. 1982. 'The Sovereignty Goddess as Goddess of Death?', *Zeitschrift für celtische Philologie* 39, 243–60.

Breatnach, R.A. 1953. 'The Lady and the King: A Theme of Irish Literature', *Studies: An Irish Quarterly Review* 42, 321–36.

Byrne, F.J. 1973. *Irish Kings and High Kings*. London.

Carey. J. 1983. 'Notes on the Irish War-Goddess', *Éigse* 19, 263–75.

—— 1991. 'The Irish "Otherworld": Hiberno-Latin Perspectives', *Éigse* 25, 154–9.

Cross, T. P. 1952. *Motif-Index of Early Irish Literature*. Bloomington, Ind.

Curtin, J. 1894. *Hero-Tales of Ireland*. London.

de Bhaldraithe, T. 1944. 'Nótaí ar an Aisling Fháithchiallaigh', in S. O'Brien, OFM (ed.), *Measgra i gCuimhne Mhichíl Uí Chléirigh, eag.* Dublin. 210–19.

Doan, J.E. 1984. *Sovereignty Aspects in the Roles of Women in Medieval Irish and Welsh Society*. Boston, Mass.

Dunne, T. J. 1980. 'The Gaelic Response to Conquest and Colonisation: The Evidence of Poetry', *Studia Hibernica* 20, 7–30.

Gray, E.A. 1982. *Cath Muige Tuired*. Dublin.

Green, M.J. 1992. *Dictionary of Celtic Myth and Legend*. London.

Hayes-McCoy, G.A. 1980. *Irish Battles*. London.

Hennessy, W.M. 1870–2. 'The Ancient Irish Goddess of War', *Revue celtique* 1, 32–55.

Herbert, M. 1992. 'Goddess and King: The Sacred Marriage in Early Ireland', in L.A. Fradenburg (ed.), *Women and Sovereignty* (*Cosmos: The Yearbook of the Traditional Cosmology Society* 7). 264–75.

Knott, E. 1936. *Togail Bruidne Da Derga*. Dublin.

—— n.d. 'The Destruction of Dá Chóca's Hostel', in *The Golden Legends of the Gael*, I, 104–15. Dublin and Cork.

Lysaght, P. 1986. *The Banshee: The Irish Supernatural Death-Messenger*. Dublin.

Mac Cana, P. 1955–6, 1958–9. 'Aspects of the Theme of King and Goddess in Irish Literature', *Etudes celtiques* 7 (1955–6), 76–114, 356–413; 8 (1958–9), 59–65.
—— 1973. *Celtic Mythology*. London and New York.
—— 1980. *The Learned Tales of Medieval Ireland*. Dublin.
Mac Erlean, J.C. 1910–17. *Duanaire Dháibhidh Uí Bhruadair* I–III. Irish Texts Society. London.
Meid, W. 1967. *Táin Bó Fraích*. Dublin.
Meyer, K. 1910. 'Reicne Fothaid Canainne', *Fianaigecht*, RIA Todd Lecture Series 16. Dublin.
Ní Bhrolcháin, M. 1980. 'Women in Early Irish Myths and Sagas', *The Crane Bag* 4: 1, 12–19.
Nic Dhonnchadha, L. ed. 1964. *Aided Muirchertaig meicErca*. Dublin.
Ó Broin, T. ed. 1957. *Scéaltaí Tíre: Bailiúchán Seanchais ó Ghaillimh*. Baile Átha Cliath.
Ó Cathasaigh, T. 1977–8. 'The Semantics of "Síd"', *Éigse* 17, 137–55.
Ó Cuív, B. 1951. *Irish Dialects and Irish-Speaking Districts*. Dublin.
Ó Domhnaill, N. ed. 1977. *Faclóir Gaeilge-Bearla*. Baile Átha Cliath.
O'Grady, S.H ed. 1929. *Caithréim Thoirdhealbhaigh/The Triumphs of Turlough*, 2 vols. London.
Ó hÓgáin, D. 1990. *Myth, Legend and Romance*. London.
Ó Súilleabháin, S. 1967. *Irish Folk Custom and Belief*. Dublin.
RIA Dictionary 1913–76. *Contributions to a Dictionary of the Irish Language*. Dublin.
Rees, A. and B. 1961. *Celtic Heritage*. London.
Sims-Williams, P. 1990: 'Some Celtic Otherworld Terms', in A.T.E. Matonis and D.F. Melia (eds), *Celtic Language, Celtic Culture: A Festschrift for Eric P. Hamp*. Van Nuys, California. 6–81.
Schoepperle, G. 1919. 'The Washer of the Ford', *Journal of English and Germanic Philology* 18, 60–6. Bloomington, Ind.
Stokes, W. ed. 1891. 'The Second Battle of Moyturra', *Revue celtique* 12, 52–130, 306–8.
—— ed. 1900. 'Da Choca's Hostel', *Revue celtique* 21, 149–65, 312–27, 388–402.
—— ed. 1902. *The Destruction of Dá Derga's Hostel*. Paris.
Táin Bó Cúailnge, ed. R.I. Best & M.A. O'Brien 1956. *The Book of Leinster* II. Dublin.
Táin Bó Cúailnge, ed. C. O'Rahilly 1976. Recension 1. Dublin.
Táin Bó Regamain, ed. E. Windisch 1887. Inische Texte. 2. Serie 2. Leipzig.
Todd, J.H. ed. 1867. *Cogadh Gaedhel re Gallaibh/The War of the Gaedhil with the Gaill*. London.
Ua Duinnín, An tAth P. ed. 1901. *Amhráin Eoghain Ruaidh Uí Shúilleabháin*. Dublin.
—— ed. 1902. *Amhráin Sheagháin Chláraigh Mhic Dhomhnaill*. Dublin.
—— ed. 1934. *Dánta Phiarais Feiritéir*, 2nd edn. Dublin.
Van Hamel, A.G. ed. 1933. 'Aided Con Culainn', *Compert Con Culainn*. Dublin.

CHAPTER THIRTEEN

THE CAUCASIAN HUNTING-DIVINITY, MALE AND FEMALE: TRACES OF THE HUNTING-GODDESS IN OSSETIC FOLKLORE[1]

—— •✦• ——

Anna Chaudhri

THE MALE HUNTING-DIVINITY: OSSETIC ÆFSATI

> Æfsati, give to us, give, for you have many,
> One of the big ones of those with worn-out horns.
> If you do not give one of this type, then give us
> One of their smaller ones from the rhododendron grove.
> O Æfsati, there is no firewood but
> Grant that we may come across a rhododendron bush, Æfsati.
> O heroic Divine George, you too ask Æfsati, on our behalf,
> That our path may be straight,
> That the hunter may not die in vain.
> The four-eyed, the five-legged
> Are under your control, Æfsati.
> O Æfsati, then give to us, give us one of these.

This short hymn was recorded from an elderly inhabitant of the Ossetic village of Nar in 1932 (Salagaeva, 1961: II, 448). It is addressed to Æfsati, the lord of wild beasts and patron-deity of the Ossetic hunter.

Hunting has always been a vital and highly esteemed activity in the mountainous areas of the Caucasus, a region of dramatic alpine scenery and a rich variety of wildlife. Until comparatively recently hunting would have provided a major means of subsistence, particularly for the inhabitants of the least-accessible highland areas. It is not surprising, therefore, to find a concentration of hunting-divinities and associated beliefs and practices amid the rich hunting-lore of the region. In spite of the ethnic and linguistic diversity of the Caucasian peoples, certain features of their hunting-cults are remarkably similar: the sacredness of the hunt is an ancient and basic element of Caucasian culture (Kaloev 1971: 249).

Among the Ossetes of central Caucasus, Æfsati has long been the only recognized deity of the hunt, and he is always regarded as male. He belongs to an ancient pagan pantheon which has been influenced by some aspects of Christianity and constitutes the traditional religion of the Ossetes. Many of the old beliefs have died out by now, but some elderly inhabitants in rural villages still show a good knowledge of the old religion, and a brief account of Æfsati provides an illustration of a typical Caucasian hunting-divinity.

The hymn cited above would have been handed down for generations in a purely oral tradition, sung by hunters when setting out on the chase. The words describe Æfsati's sovereignty over all the wild beasts, particularly the many varieties of deer and mountain goat, much sought by the hunter. Success in the hunt would depend entirely on the goodwill of Æfsati; therefore the hunter begged to be allowed to kill an animal, a member of Æfsati's flock. If the god did grant him such a gift, the hunter would offer thanks by setting aside a roasted kebab of the heart and liver of the slain animal, in honour of Æfsati. There were no particular shrines dedicated to the Ossetic hunting-divinity; rather, the whole territory where game was hunted was regarded as sacred. Once in Æfsati's domain, the hunter was obliged to abide by strict rules; he would seek a spot in the forest where the hunt was to begin and there make an offering of three cheese pies, baked by his wife or mother on the preceding evening, and pray to Æfsati for success in the hunt. If a party of hunters was involved, then strict order of age or rank would be observed in the division of the kill. Hunters were expected to share their meat with any stranger they might meet, giving him the right haunch of the slain animal. On their return home, they would further share their meat with family, friends and neighbours. Any neglect of these duties would result in future failure on the hunt because of the abuse of the hunting-divinity's gift (Kaloev 1971: 249–50).

While on the chase Ossetic hunters used a secret hunting-language, examples of which can be found in the above hymn to Æfsati. They would refer to their weapons and to the beasts they hoped to shoot by special names, with the aim of deceiving the game and its divine shepherd (Dirr 1915: 9–11; 1925: 146–7; Kaloev 1971: 250). Such names might be descriptive euphemisms, such as the 'big ones with worn-out horns' (Ossetic: *ikhsyd særtæj se'styrtæj*), which appears to be a reference to stags or rams with horns damaged from continuous combat with rivals. The 'four-eyed, the five-legged' (*tsyppærdzæstyg fondzk'akhygon*) appear to be supernatural epithets applied to Æfsati's animals by the hunters (Salagaeva 1961: II, 655). Such hunting-languages are thought to have existed in the past among several other Caucasian peoples, notably the Abkhaz and the Circassians (Dirr 1915: 10–11; 1925: 146–7; Kaloev 1971: 250).

The Ossetic hunting-divinity is often portrayed as old, bearded, and blind or one-eyed. He is the subject of many popular hunting-tales and traditions, according to which he dwells alone or with his wife and children in the depths of the mountain forests. He is said to show particular favour to poor huntsmen, occasionally allowing them to marry his beautiful daughters (Salagaeva 1961: II, 448–62, poems 2–8).

Æfsati was known to Caucasian peoples other than the Ossetes; in Svanetia he was known as Apsat', and, among the Balkars and Karachai, as Absaty or Apsaty. Typically close to Æfsati was the Abkhaz divinity of the hunt, Azhweypshaa. He too is represented as old and blind, dwelling in a hut in the forest with his attractive daughters, who milk the female wild beasts. These daughters were also said to enter intimate relationships with mortal hunters (Bgazhba 1965: 26–31). Azhweypshaa was said to allow the hunters to kill only those animals which he himself had first eaten; he would collect all the bones of the dead animal into its skin and bring it back to life (Dirr 1915: 1; 1925: 139). The Chechens and Ingush also recognized a male patron of the hunt, whom they called Elta. The beasts of Elta's flock were thought to bear the god's special mark, and sometimes Elta himself appeared in the guise of a white stag or ram (Dalgat 1908: 1070–1). Among the Chechens and Ingush, as among other peoples of the Caucasus, the killing of, or attempt to kill, a white animal was regarded as especially unlucky. White animals were regarded as sacred, the animal guardians of the flock (Virsaladze 1976: 33).

The blindness, and occasionally deafness, of the male hunting divinity is an interesting characteristic. According to one tradition, Elta lost the sight of one of his eyes because he defied the supreme god's wishes and helped a poor man to raise a harvest (Dalgat 1972: 258–60). In Ossetia a tradition exists regarding another divine patron of animals, namely Fælværa, protector of domestic animals. Fælværa is said to have been blinded in one eye by a blow from the wolf-god. As a result of this, the wolves who creep up on Fælværa's blind side will be successful in stealing a sheep (Gatiev 1876: 40). Perhaps Caucasian hunters were likewise able to take advantage when the hunting divinity turned a blind eye.

THE FEMALE DIVINITY

In a book devoted to the Goddess, it may seem strange to spend so many words on the male hunting-divinity, but in the Caucasus it is impossible to consider the hunting-goddess without her male counterpart. Hunting-divinities of both sexes are known among the Caucasian peoples, and the fundamental concepts of sovereignty over the wild beasts, the sacredness of the domain of the divinity, and the treatment of a slain animal as a gift to the hunter, remain the same, regardless of the sex of the divinity. There are, however, certain features which belong to the hunting-goddess alone and which have permeated Caucasian folklore even in areas where the patron-deity of the hunter has long been regarded as male.

The Caucasian female guardians of the game seem to have been regarded as zealous in the discharge of their duty. Among some peoples of eastern Georgia, the duties of the sovereign of the game were undertaken by a pair of divinities, one male and one female, who operated in alternate seasons. During the boy's turn of duty it was said that the hunters had an easy time; the boy was lazy and so the hunters were allowed to kill many animals. When it was the girl's turn, however, few or no animals at all were granted to the huntsmen, so protective was she of her charges (Dirr 1915: 5; 1925: 143[2]; Virsaladze 1976: 34). This use of the pair of divinities illustrates the inherent ambivalence in the nature of the animal guardian: on the one hand a patron of the hunters who frequented his or her domain, and, on the other, the protector of the hunted. It may also illustrate the sexual ambivalence of this ancient figure. Among the Circassians certain groups regarded the divinity of the hunt, Mezytkha, as male, others as female. And in a rare fragment of a Kabard hymn addressed to Mezytkha it is said that 'the childless young wife remains long on her knees before you', indicating that Mezytkha was also a patron of human fertility, a particularly feminine characteristic (Talpa 1936: 79, 589).

The figure of the female animal guardian and hunting-goddess is preserved particularly clearly in the hunting-lore of some of the mountain peoples of western Georgia. The Mingrelians called her T'qashi Map'a, the 'Sovereign of the Forest', and among the Svans she is perhaps best remembered under the name Dali. However, Dali is only one of the divine patrons which were once revered in Svanetia. Apsat' has already been mentioned; he was thought to have dominion over birds and fish, and Dzhgyrag (the Svan name for St George) was the patron of hunters and wolves. *Cxek'ish angelwez* (the Angel of the Forest) ruled over the animals of the forest, such as bears, foxes and jackals, while Dali was responsible for the hoofed and horned animals of the mountain, the deer and mountain goats. These four divine beings assisted *Ber Shishvlish* (the Lord of the Bare Mountain) (Charachidzé 1968: 482–3).

The figure of the goddess Dali has also inspired a rich heritage of hunting-traditions and poetry. She was thought to dwell high among the rocks in a cave or mountain hut, where she would tend and milk her wild flock. She liked to assume the form of a member of her own flock, in which guise she would often attract the attention of hunters. This animal form of the goddess was often distinguished by some peculiar characteristic such as a pure white colour or the possession of a single golden horn. Not only a shape-shifter, the female animal guardian was also thought by some peoples to be able to alter her size. Virsaladze recalls a tradition from eastern Georgia according to which hunters would leave a tiny pair of shoes among the rocks for the diminutive hunting-goddess. At other times, however, the goddess might appear in the form of an enormous ibex (Virsaladze 1976: 36).

Unlike the old male hunting-divinities described above, the goddess was usually thought to be youthful and beautiful. She wandered the mountains naked, clothed only in her abundant, ankle-length, golden or black hair. Her body was of such a pure whiteness that it dazzled the beholder. Her beauty was both irresistible and terrible, so that a mortal huntsman dreaded an encounter with her, fearing that a man might be driven mad if he entered into conversation with her. Hunters were traditionally counselled to talk to no one on the road and to reveal the route of their hunt to no one, mortal or otherwise (ibid.: 29, 71).

As in the case of the male divinities, the entire domain of the hunting-goddess was considered sacred, and the hunter would be subject to strict taboos and codes of behaviour when entering upon the hunt. He would be bound to make an offering and to pray to the goddess that she might grant him one of her flock; he would also be bound to thank her if he were successful and to share his meat accordingly. On the eve of the hunt, hunters were required to keep themselves pure for the sacred activity of the hunt. They were to avoid intercourse with any woman, even their own wives. Contact with any menstruating or pregnant women was regarded as particularly impure, and such women would not be allowed any share of the hunters' meat (ibid.: 29, 74).

A unique feature of the female hunting-divinity was her relationship with the mortal huntsman, which is vividly described in the hunting-traditions and poetry of Georgia. The hunter, entering the sacred realm of the goddess, meets her face to face. The goddess offers the hunter her sexual favours and if he agrees she grants him great success on the hunt. If the hunter dares to refuse, then it is sure to end badly for him. At the very least, on his return home he might sicken and die. As a token of their special understanding, the goddess sometimes gives the hunter a gift, such as a necklace, a ring or an arrow-tip, the possession of which will ensure his success. The hunter, however, is strictly forbidden to reveal the source of his success to anyone or to have sexual relations with any mortal woman. Any breach of these prohibitions will result in the hunter's death. For example, while out hunting he might be enticed by the goddess in animal form to some dangerous precipice, or else he might be injured or killed by one or more of her animals. The Mingrelian *Tqashi Map'a* (Sovereign of the Forest) was thought to have the power to turn a transgressing hunter to stone (ibid.: 71–2).

Dali was, however, thought to mourn for the hunters she killed. According to Virsaladze, the Svans believed that Dali would come to perform mourning rites over a dead hunter, and so, in some cases, they stood guard over a newly interred corpse to prevent the goddess from exhuming him to this end. According to another tradition, the family were supposed to leave the corpse of a dead hunter alone in the house for a while, in order to allow Dali to enter and mourn and to clothe him as she liked (ibid.: 72–3).

Some of the finest illustrations of this uneasy relationship between the hunter and his female patron are to be found in the poems concerning the dying hunter which have been collected by scholars in various parts of Georgia over the past 150 years. The lament for Qursha is one such, an ancient ritual, choral poem, of which several versions have been recorded. In Ratcha, in western Georgia, it was performed annually on the third Monday after Easter near the village of Ghebi, at the foot of the mountain from which the hero of the poem is reputed to have fallen to his death (ibid.: 51, 67). Virsaladze compares versions of this with other, closely related poems and, in spite of the fragmentary nature of some of the poetry, nevertheless demonstrates its essential subject-matter. In a dramatic, conversational form, the poems lament the evil fate of the miraculous hunting-dog Qursha, which, with its master, has become stranded on a rock from which there is no possible descent. The two arrived there by following the trail of a mountain goat. The hunter ascends the rock on steps of snow and manages to kill a number of mountain goats, throwing their carcases down for later collection, but all in vain. Suddenly he finds that the snow has melted and he is stranded, desperately clinging to the rock. In some versions the starving hunter is said to slay his faithful hound, but he is unable to eat it. In others, the hound is urged to bark or run home to summon help. When the family and friends arrive to help, they bring the hunter's beloved. She challenges her lover to leap without fear from the rock but, when he does so, nothing can break his fall and he is dashed to pieces.

At first glance, the choral tradition of Qursha appears to have little connection with the beliefs associated with the hunting-goddess. Virsaladze points out, however, that the lament for Qursha is related to the Svan ritual lament for the hunter Betkil. This choral poem was performed annually in February at the foot of a mountain designated his place of death (Virsaladze 1976: 67). Some versions open with a description of a performed ritual dance; an ibex lures Betkil away from the dance, up a steep rock. Once near the top, the ibex assumes another form, that of Dali herself. She is angry at the hunter for having revealed her gift to a mortal woman, named Tamar. In several versions of the poem, Tamar is said to be the hunter's sister-in-law, but in at least one it is said that she allowed the hunter to go on the hunt 'impure', implying, perhaps, a breach of more than just the taboo of silence (ibid.: 62, 235, 328 n. 1). Once again a mortal woman is, in some measure, responsible for the hunter's death, but the power behind his fate is revealed in these Svan poems as Dali herself. It is she, in her favourite animal form, who has lured the offending hunter into her own enchanted realm, so that she may exert her full power over him. She causes the rock to behave strangely: the hunter's path disappears behind him, and when the villagers try to help by throwing ropes, the rock rises and rises into the sky. Inevitably the hunter plunges to his death, indicting Tamar as he does so.

TRACES OF THE FEMALE HUNTING-DIVINITY IN OSSETIC FOLKLORE

A prose version of this powerful story of the fatally stranded hunter was recorded among the South Ossetes, in the village of Ruch', in 1930, from the words of the narrator Plity Shalik'o (Tybylty 1931: 44–6). This is a good opportunity to provide a full translation of the previously untranslated text, keeping as close as possible to the vivid narrative style of the original.

The Tale of Lord Egor

Lord Egor was a good huntsman. He destroyed many good species of game. Early one morning he set out to hunt. On the way a witch met him and so he turned back again. On the following morning, very early, he prepared provisions, which were tasty to eat, light to carry. Day was just breaking. The birds were waking. On the way again the witch met him and again the hunter was worried.

'Ah, see, again the witch has met me, so now what should I do? If I turn back again, then I shall disgrace myself a second time. Let us go; I shall go on; there is no other escape from her.' Lord Egor said angrily, 'What evil fortune brings you before me every time? Are you afraid of nothing at all at night?' Then she replied to him, 'What is your business here? Go elsewhere on your way! Do you no longer allow me to watch over my road?' Then the hunter said to her, 'What is your watching? What are you yourself? What is your foot?' She said to him, 'Go, then, and may a treacherous beast encounter you!'

The man set off full of rage and went to the Black Mountain. In the early morning Lord Egor began to look this way and that; he rubs his eyes and the cracking sounds of the rock come to his ears. Meanwhile a great ibex came running towards him, bleating, and suddenly stopped. As soon as it stopped, Egor caught sight of it and shot. He hit the ibex between the two horns and it rolled away downwards. Then he said to himself, 'Nothing has come of the words of that witch, rather I have found a good route.'

The hunter followed the blood trail of the beast down. The beast got stuck on a rock. Once the ibex had become stuck on the rock, then he threw it off but there was no way down for him. Happily he was running back upwards but the mountain blocked his way. Then there was no longer an escape for Egor in any direction and he brushed away his tears. He sat down beneath the rock and said, 'Alas, I have not ended up in a good place after all!'

He remained there over night. In the morning the village raised the alarm but they found nothing. The next day too they raised the alarm but again they found nothing anywhere. Meanwhile he wrapped himself in his black felt cloak and when they saw him, then they shouted to him, 'Come down, Egor!' Egor sobbed and he says in a tearful voice, 'Where is my freedom to come down?' The people who had raised the alarm worried the whole day long but they found no means of help; they returned to the village.

The village assembled and began to discuss, saying, 'So what action shall we take to help him?' One old man said, 'His sister, the Lady Azau, the dark beauty, is a wife of the Water Guardians and it is necessary to explain things to her.'

When they explained to his sister, then she came in a golden phaeton. Lady Azau calls up to him from below, 'What have you done, my only brother?' Lord Egor wraps himself up in his felt cloak and weeps. Then Azau also wails, she slashes her cheeks and tears her hair.

The sun was about to set. Lady Azau says to him, 'Throw yourself down, Egor! There is no longer any other way for you!' Of course the good hunter tries to do so but he could not bring himself to and once again he wrapped himself in his felt cloak and lay down. Lady Azau weeps and wails, she tears out clumps of hair and again she says to him, 'Throw yourself down. I shall not let you fall to the ground.' Egor tries to but, no, he cannot. Azau spread out mattresses and carpets worked with gold beneath him and again she says to him, 'Throw yourself down on to this soft spot. I shall not let you hit the ground.'

Egor threw himself down but Lady Azau could not catch him and he was dashed to pieces in the gorge. Lady Azau, with her golden thread and needle, sewed the fragments of his bones together, then she placed him in her golden phaeton and she dragged him away. She had a deep, broad grave dug.

The elders of the village said, 'We have lived long lives but we have never seen such a broad, deep grave.' Then Lady Azau told them, 'It is because he was dashed to pieces, it is so that his bones will rest in peace.' When they laid him on the edge of the grave, Lady Azau shot herself with a pistol. An old man said, 'Did I not tell you I had never seen such a grave being dug?' So they buried the two of them there.

Virsaladze observes that she is familiar with at least one Georgian account of the fatally stranded hunter in which the hunter's name is also Egor (1976: 60). In the past, there were close cultural links between the southern Ossetes and their Georgian neighbours. The above version of the stranded-hunter story is told as a folktale and therefore lacks the ritual significance of the poetic Georgian laments. It is nevertheless full of interesting detail. The old figure of the hunting-goddess is thinly disguised as a 'witch', but there is no doubt that the young hunter at once recognizes her power and menace. The text does not describe her appearance at all, but the hunter does mention her foot. Perhaps the foot of the witch is a hoof, since one of the favourite guises of the hunting-divinity was as a deer or mountain goat. The witch's curse is that Egor should encounter a bad beast; in the texts from Georgia the beast that leads the hunter astray is the goddess herself in animal form. The rock upon which the poor hunter is eventually stranded is enchanted and changes its behaviour once he has shot the ibex: in the texts from Georgia the deadly rock is within the sacred realm of the hunting-goddess. The motive for the witch's curse is interesting: at the very beginning of the text it is stated that Egor was a good hunter who had destroyed many species of wild beasts; the implication is undoubtedly that he has killed excessively, thus breaking one of the great taboos of the hunting-cult. Like the Georgian accounts, the Ossetic story introduces another woman to the scene of the hunter's death. She is the sister of the hunter, a wife in the family of Water Guardians (Ossetic: *Donbettyrtæ*), who frequently interact with human heroes in Ossetic folklore. As soon as she sees her brother, she realizes that his situation is hopeless; they both recognize that he is in the thrall of some superior power. Egor himself cries out, 'Where is my freedom to come down?' Finally the sister persuades her brother to jump and after commits suicide at his grave, perhaps as an act of grief or because she feels guilt at having been powerless to prevent the fatality. Her presence in the Ossetic version reminds one of the more culpable role of the hunter's sister-in-law in the poems from Svanetia.

The influence of belief in the old hunting-goddess on the folklore of Ossetia is felt elsewhere. Hunting-beliefs form an important part of the background to the Ossetic Nart Epos, and the powerful witch-figure – apparently fulfilling functions of the goddess – occurs in several Nart legends. One of these, the Digoron (western Ossetic) version of the story of Ækhsaræ and Ækhsærtæg, has already been discussed in a previous paper, in the context of the international tale of the Two Brothers, with special reference to the incident of the binding of the hunter's dogs with the witch's hair (Davidson and Chaudhri 1993).

A long Digoron account of the lives of the Nart heroes Khæmits and Batraz opens with a short hunting-tale (Salagaeva 1961: I, 198–9). Khæmits has shot a chamois but, in breach of strict hunting-etiquette, whereby he should share his good fortune with his neighbours, he neglects to give any of the meat to the local witch. The witch casts a spell on him: she secretly takes away the pieces of skin and the bones of the chamois and pours them on to her fire, while expressing the curse that Khæmits shall no longer even catch sight of one of Æfsati's animals, let alone kill one. The spell binds the hero, and he can only extricate himself by making the ritual offering of three cheese-pies at a suitable spot in the forest. The nature of the witch's magic is reminiscent of the way in which the Abkhaz hunting-divinity also performs miracles with the skin and bones of the dead animal. In spite of the fact that she acknowledges Æfsati's sovereignty over the beasts, the witch is nevertheless able to exert great power over the fate of the hunter.

A very popular tale, widespread in Ossetia and frequently told in the context of the Nart Epos (e.g. Gardanti 1927, 38–40[3]; Salagaeva 1961: I, 315–16) is that of the hunter transformed into a dog. The hunter is lured by a fine deer, which keeps itself just out of his firing-range, to a lonely house in the forest. There the deer assumes the form of a beautiful woman. She treats the hunter kindly, offering him food and a bed. When she lies down to sleep near him, the hunter cannot resist and touches her. Indignantly the woman strikes the man with a magic whip and changes him into a bitch. In time the enchanted bitch gives birth to pups. Then the woman strikes the bitch again with the whip and this time it changes into a mare which, in time, gives birth to foals. Eventually the transformed hunter manages to reverse the magic and, gaining control of the magic whip, transforms the enchantress into a donkey.

In this tale the dazzling beauty of the enchantress is stressed. In a South Ossetic variant she is actually married to the hunter, and she lights his path home from his night raids by the radiance of her body. When she transfers her affections to his father, however, he is forced to stumble home in the dark, and then the disastrous chain of events begins whereby the hunter is transformed into a mare and a bitch (Tybylty 1931: 40–3). That particular version of the story is prefaced by another popular hunting-motif of the hunter who becomes stranded on a high rock but manages to kill an animal. He follows the animal-track down from the rock, thus escaping the first predicament. When, however, he has prepared the carcase for cooking, the animal proves to be enchanted. It becomes whole again and runs away, telling him to seek the Ingush hunter Tsopan, to whom more extraordinary things have happened.

In these few examples of Ossetic hunting-tales the features and influence of the old hunting-goddess are clear to see in the nature of the witch who is constantly interfering in the exploits of the hunter. Similar supernatural women, with attributes of the goddess, are to be found among the neighbours of the Ossetes, such as the Chechens and Ingush, who also traditionally recognized a male divinity of the hunt, Elta, but also preserve numerous hunting-tales in which a powerful female figure is dominant.

Among them, this figure is known as the Almas. She is usually represented as very beautiful, but she can sometimes be grotesquely large and ugly, representing the two aspects of the old goddess-figure, the beauty and the hag. According to one tradition noted by Virsaladze, the goddess Dali is said to be both an angel and a demon (Virsaladze 1976: 135, 252). The Almas of the Chechens and Ingush sometimes intermarries with mortal hunters or else leads them astray in the forest, assuming the form of an animal. Once the hunter reaches the dwelling of the Almas, who lives alone or with her sisters, she regales him kindly and makes him spend the night with her. She resurrects the animal she has killed for their supper with the usual trick of the skin and bones and on the following day the hunter is often allowed to kill that very animal again. The animal is clearly one of the wild flock of the Almas (Dalgat 1908: 1069–70). The hunter involved with these women is sometimes the Ingush Chopa who appears to be the hero of the South Ossetic tale of the transformed hunter mentioned above (the Ingush Tsopan). In one story, the Almas and her sisters, represented as giant , forest-dwelling sorceresses, terrify the hunters, who are forced to spend the night at their cave, by their dancing after supper, during which they fling their huge breasts back over their shoulders. Nevertheless, no harm comes to the hunters and they are allowed to go on their way in peace in the morning (Dalgat 1972: 265–6).

Occasionally the Almas can be represented as male, in which case he is always covered with hair and very frightening to behold. He carries a great axe at his breast and will kill unsuspecting hunters (Dalgat 1908: 1069; 1972: 264). In one story, the female Almas comes to mourn her beloved mortal hunter, who has been killed by her fearsome brother (Dalgat 1972: 262–3).

Representations of dangerous forest people of both sexes, feared and appeased by huntsmen, are very common in Caucasian folklore. The close connection between these forest folk and the traditions of the sovereign of the game in the Caucasus has been observed by W. Feuerstein in an article on a Laz 'Forest Man' (1988: 81). This connection can be seen well beyond the boundaries of the Caucasus in the many supernatural inhabitants of the forest who exert power over the forest itself and all the wild animals therein. Examples can be found all over Europe, from the Lyeshy, the treacherous wood-sprite of Russian folklore, to the Scandinavian Skogsrå.

The hunting-divinity, male and female, forms a fundamental part of Caucasian culture. The divinity is patron of both the hunter and the hunted, and the female in particular is a jealous guardian of her wild flock. The most striking features of the female divinity are her intense but terrifying beauty and her fatal love for the mortal hunter and all its tragic consequences. Even in areas where the male divinity has long dominated the hunting-cult, the figure of the old goddess, often modified into an enchantress, has proved a popular and durable subject of folklore. It is not difficult to understand why.

NOTES

1 I should like to thank Dr Ilya Gershevitch for his help in checking my Ossetic–English translations in this paper.
2 A slightly extended version of his 1915 article. Unfortunately, the footnotes after no. 25 were lost.
3 Recorder of the Ossetic texts.

REFERENCES

Bgazhba, Kh.S. 1965. *Abkhazskie Skazki*. Sukhumi.
Charachidzé, G. 1968. *Le Système religieux de la Géorgie paienne*. Paris.
Dalgat, B. 1908. 'Die alte Religion der Tschetschenen', *Anthropos* 3, 729–40, 1050–76.
Dalgat, U.B. 1972. *Geroicheskij Epos Chechentsev i Ingushej*. Studies and Texts. Moscow.
Davidson, H.E., & Chaudhri, A. 1993. 'The Hair and the Dog', in *Folklore* 104, 151–63.
Dirr, A.M. 1915. 'Bozhestva okhoty i okhotnichij iazyk u Kavkaztsev' in *Sbornik materialov dlia opisaniia mestnostej i plemen Kavkaza* 44: 4, 1–16.
—— 1925. 'Der kaukasische Wild- und Jagdgott', *Anthropos* 20, Vienna.
Feuerstein, W. 1988. 'Die Gestalt des Waldmenschen (*Germakoçi*) im Volksglauben der Lazen', in F. Thordarson (ed.) *Studia Caucasologica* I. Proceedings of the 3rd Caucasian Colloquium. Oslo. 69–86.
Gardanti, M. 1927. *Pamiatniki narodnogo tvorchestva Osetin*, II. A collection of Ossetic folklore, with notes and Russian trans. by G. Dzagurti. Vladikavkaz.
Gatiev, B. 1876. 'Sueveriia i Predrasudki u Osetin', *Sbornik materialov dliia opisaniia mestnostej i plemen Kavkaza*, 9: 3, 1–83.
Kaloev, B.A. 1971. *Osetiny*, 2nd edn. Moscow.
Salagaeva, Z.M. comp. 1961. *Iron Adæmy Sfældystad*. [A two-volume collection of Ossetic folklore.] Ordzhonikidze.
Talpa, M.E. comp. 1936. *Kabardinskij Fol'klor*. Moscow and Leningrad.
Tybylty, A. 1931. *Khussar Irystony Adæmy Uatsmystæ*. [Vol. III of a three-volume collection of South Ossetic folklore.] Tskhinval.
Virsaladze, E.B. 1961. 'Die Amiranisage und das grusinische Jagdepos', *Acta Ethnographica Academiae Scientiarum Hungaricae* 10, 363–87.
Virsaladze, E.B. 1976. *Gruzinskij okhotnichij Mif i Poeziia*. Moscow.

help to Yamanokami that she was safely delivered of her child. As a reward, she gave him and his descendants permission to hunt game on her mountain.

Another version of the story describes how a famous archer called Manzaburō was besought by the goddess of Mount Nikkō for help against a divinity of a neighbouring mountain who was threatening her in the form of a giant centipede. Manzaburō, with unerring aim, shot the centipede, thus delivering the goddess from her plight. Here, too, she rewarded him by giving permission to him and his descendants to hunt on her holy mountain (*NMJ* 1978: 762). The *matagi* hunters who hunt bear, boar, deer and other animals on mountains known to be sacred to Yamanokami can thus by such legends always justify their forays. They claim descent from Banzaburō or Manzaburō or some other ancestor who long ago was thus rewarded by Yamanokami for help in distress.

Such permission, however, was by no means unconditional. If the hunters are to keep the favour of Yamanokami, they must take care to obey her rules and rituals and to make every allowance for her capricious and volatile temperament. For if she is flouted or offended in any way, she will forget the favour granted to their ancestor, and mete out *tatari* to the offenders as virulently as she might to any unauthorized trespasser.

What, then, are the peculiar traits of her temperament that hunters must bear in mind if they are to be successful in their chase and safe from accident or death? What are the special exigencies of her cult?

First, Yamanokami is a protean shape-shifter. Like many Japanese divinities, she has a 'true form', or *shōtai*, by which she manifests herself to the human eye, together with a number of *keshin*, or temporary transformations or disguises. Whereas other divinities confine themselves to one or two disguises – an old man, for example, or a miraculous child – Yamanokami is apt to appear in a baffling and bewildering number of shapes and likenesses. She may appear in the form of one of her own subject animals, a bear, wolf or deer, but is always to be distinguished from her subjects by a shape that is large, royal, mysteriously majestic and of a pure and holy whiteness. She may, on the other hand, choose to appear in a more monstrous and terrifying form: a dragon, a red-faced demon, or the sinister goblin with beak and wings known as a *tengu*. A further shape she is apt to assume in the north of Japan is that of a pair of figures, man and woman together, with distinctively red faces. Anyone treating such a pair with rudeness or aggression may expect to be knocked unconscious and either die in a few days or remain an idiot for the rest of his life.[2]

Her *shōtai* or true form, is, however, is always that of a woman. But even here her penchant for volatile shape-shifting persists, for the woman-form itself tends to be ambivalent and 'split'. The goddess tends to show two faces of her woman-form, contrary and opposed. When she chooses she can appear as young, beautiful, compassionate, protective and maternal. But in a flash the face can switch to its other aspect, an old, hideous, malicious hag, with a mouth that splits open in a terrifying manner from ear to ear. This dark form of Yamanokami is given a special name, *yamauba*, the old woman of the mountain, a shape which haunts much of Japanese folklore and even psychic experience well outside the domain of Yamanokami.[3]

The next distinctive trait which hunters must take account of in their dealings with Yamanokami is her virulent dislike and jealousy of women. So fiercely does she detest women that a powerful taboo prevails against any woman setting foot on a mountain in her territory. No article belonging to a woman, not even a towel, may be taken on to the mountain, nor may the name of a woman be so much as mentioned. Bawdy talk, needless to say, is utterly prohibited at any time during the hunt, and it is even considered inadvisable to allow a newly married man to join the hunting-party, for fear that his thoughts may run too much on his wife. The goddess's dislike of women is said to be particularly spiteful on her festival day, the twelfth day of the twelfth month – so much so that women in many *matagi* villages deem it advisable to stay indoors on that day.

A further odd feature of the goddess's character which hunters must bear in mind if their luck is to last is her jealous appropriation of the number twelve. Her festival, as we have seen, falls on the twelfth day of the twelfth month; in some districts she is believed to bear twelve children every year, and in Gumma prefecture she is given the alternative name of Jūnisama, Mistress Twelve. It follows that on her mountain no one else may use this number, and hunters must take care that their party never numbers a round dozen. If by an oversight they find themselves, on arrival at the mountain hut, to consist of twelve men, they must quickly fashion a doll, or effigy, often called Sansuke, which will bring their number up to a safe thirteen.

A fourth peculiarity of Yamanokami is her liking for the dried fish known as *okoze*. She is said to 'love' this creature, which is ugly, so full of bones as to be inedible, and prickly, with poisonous spines on its dorsal fins. It is a rare fish, being found only over a limited stretch of the Japanese coast. But so fond is Yamanokami of the *okoze* that the *matagi* will always try to procure some to take with them to the hunt, in the hopes of promoting the success of the chase (Yanagita 1963: 441-8; Hori 1962; Naumann 1963).

The rules and rituals imposed on the hunters by this capricious divinity further extend to the words they may use while on her territory. While they are on her holy ground they must take care to use the special vocabulary of words that she requires. These words are known in general as *yamakotoba*, mountain words, and used to be a secret language, known only to the *matagi* and never divulged to outsiders and women.

Yamakotoba are a variety of what in Japan are called *imikotoba*, words which you must avoid using in a sacred place or at a sacred time because they will pollute and weaken, or result in a supernatural curse. There are certain words, for example, that fishermen will avoid using when at sea, and for which they must hence find substitutes. As early as the ninth century the *Engishiki* records fourteen words which must not be used at the Grand Shrine of Ise, and for which substitutes must be used. The 'mountain words' must be used by the *matagi* instead of ordinary language as soon as they cross the boundary, often marked by a stone, between the human world and the goddess's mountain. If they inadvertently use an ordinary word on the mountain, they must take immediate steps to remove the pollution by performing an approved act of purification, such as a cold-water ablution. The same penalty should follow from a careless use of a mountain word in the village below.

Most of these 'mountain words' refer to animals, to the parts of their bodies used for food or medicine, to their special habits and to the instruments used for cutting up and cooking the body. Many of the terms differ from one district to another, but some have been discovered to be common to all parts of Japan. These include the term *seta* for a dog, *wakka* for water, and *hedari* for blood. Such words have been recognized as deriving from the language of the Ainu, suggesting possible affinities between the cult of the goddess and the aboriginal Ainu people.

In some cases the 'avoiding language' is accomplished, not by substituting a new set of 'foreign words', but simply by using the name of another animal for the one which is to be avoided. In Akita prefecture for example, you cannot call a bear a bear: you must call it a weasel. A bear is not *kuma* but *itachi*. In Echigo prefecture the bear is called a 'four-legged animal' (*shishi*), while its own name (*kuma*), is applied to a saucepan. The Winchester College 'notions', where the loo becomes 'the seethers', is a possible parallel.[4]

Such rules of speech must be observed especially strictly in the mountain hut (*yamagoya*) where the hunters live for the duration of their chase. Yamanokami is apt to make sudden brief appearances in these huts, often in her old-woman form, to warm herself in front of the fire. Special precautions are therefore needed. Hunters must never sing or whistle while in the hut, or consume alcohol or tobacco. The taboo on bawdy talk is of course strictly enforced.

The hunt itself is likewise governed by strict rules. The season when animals may be taken is prescribed, as are the manner in which the body is dismembered, and the spells and invocations which must be uttered during the operation. A pregnant bear must never be killed, nor any animal which has taken refuge in a place on the mountain known to be a sacred asylum. Once they have killed their bear, the hunters must first offer thanks to Yamanokami for her gift. Then they must turn the bear's head to the north, cut the body in one stroke from stomach to throat, then cut off the left legs before the right. The heart and the liver must be extracted to a prescribed formula of words, and the soul of the animal set to rest by another. A final 'grace' to Yamanokami completes the rite.

The chief quarry of the hunter has always been the bear, for the reason that from its liver or gall-bladder *kumanoi* a medicine of unrivalled efficacy may be concocted. The potion used to be greatly prized throughout Japan, fetching such high prices, especially in the mansions of feudal lords, that for four months of the year the *matagi* made a handsome living by turning pedlar. Wearing a special distinctive garb, they would travel great distances throughout Japan to sell the precious recipe, venturing even further afield after 1870, to Korea and the Ryūkyū islands. The medicinal properties of the bear's liver have long been recognized in the Chinese pharmacopia. *Hsiung-tan* is recommended in the celebrated sixteenth-century Chinese herbal *Pen-tsao Kang-mu* as efficacious for curing fevers, poor eyesight, heart disease and tapeworms.[5] In Japan it was valued chiefly as a panacea for stomach disorders, in some districts so greatly that the local hunting communities enjoyed a special protection from the feudal lord to ensure that he received a regular supply.

It was not only the liver of the bear, however, that was prized. Medicinal remedies could also be extracted from the tongue, paws, blood, genitals and intestines. Nothing, indeed, not the smallest scrap of the bear's body, the paramount and crowning gift of Yamanokami, should be wasted or profaned. Any part of the body that was of no medicinal use was eaten by the *matagi*.

The diet of the *matagi* must certainly have been enough in former times to set them apart from the people on the flat land to whom four-legged meat was polluting and abhorrent. They ate monkey, rabbit and wild boar. They drank bear's blood as an energizing tonic. They ate bear's entrails seasoned with salt, and bear's brains raw after the kill. Even the excrement of animals, particularly if herbivorous animals, did not deter them. Old *matagi*, indeed, are still alive who recall that in the *fun*, or excrement, of deer, extracted from the entrails, a distinct and delicious flavour was detectable of the leaves that the creature had eaten (see Ōta 1979: 140–57 for a full account of their diet and cuisine).

The survival of Yamanokami from an age which may well predate agriculture thus provides a fascinating example of the peculiar power in Japan for ancient cults to persist in remote places and under new names. In this enigmatic goddess, who owns the animals, birds and trees on her mountain, who is fiercely hostile to women, who requires a secret language to be spoken on her own ground, and who appears in a bewildering number of different disguises, we may well see an archaic remnant of a continental component which in prehistoric times formed part of the ethnic endowment of the Japanese people.

NOTES

1 This paper is concerned only with Yamanokami in her older, feminine form. The later development of a male divinity, worshipped by agricultural people, who descends from the mountain in spring to become the rice-field god Tanokami and returns to the mountain in autumn, is not relevant to this theme. For the two types, see the clear account in Earhart 1970: 12–16.

2 See, for example, the tales called *Tono Monogatari* which Yanagita Kunio collected from an informant from the village of Tōno in north-eastern Japan as early as 1910, and which include several descriptions of Yamanokami in various guises: translated in Morse 1975.

3 An example is the story rife in girls' primary schools in Japan about ten years ago. On your way home from school you are likely to meet a strange woman with a dead white face who accosts you demanding, 'Am I pretty?' If you dither in your reply, she whips off her white mask, to reveal the face of a malignant hag, with glaring eyes and a mouth which splits open from ear to ear. The figure of *yamauba* is well described in Miyata 1990: 19–33.

4 Surviving 'mountain words' include the term *ichigo-otoshi* which means the habit of mother-bears of taking their two-year-old cubs to a strawberry bed on the mountain and there abandoning them while they are absorbed in eating strawberries. See Chiba 1975: 273–5; Ōta 1979: 230–308 for a full vocabulary.

5 The *Pen-tsao Kang-mu* was completed between 1550 and 1590 and presented to the Ming emperor in 1596. In the eleventh-century work *Hsin T'ang Shu*, it is stated that Liu Chung-ying owed his success in life to the bear's-liver pills he took every night on his mother's instructions, to stimulate diligence.

Bear's liver is still so much prized in China that a ruthless slaughter of 'moon-bears' for commercial purposes threatens the species' extinction. The IFAW charity has recently organized a 'Save the Bears' campaign to rescue these unfortunate animals from a horrible death imprisoned in small cages, 'with the bile drained from their bodies through a crude metal tube.'

REFERENCES

Abbreviations

TYKS *Teihon Yanagita Kunio Shū*
NMJ *Nihon Mukashibanashi Jiten*

Note

Japanese surnames come before the given name.

Chiba Tokuji 1975. *Shuryō Denshō*. Tokyo.
Earhart, H.B. 1970. *A Religious Study of the Mount Haguro Sect of Shugendō*. Tokyo.
Hori Ichirō 1962. 'Shokugyō no Kami', in *Nihon Minzokugaku Taikei* VIII. Tokyo.
Hultkrantz, A. ed. 1961. *The Supernatural Owners of Nature: Nordic Symposium on the Religious Concepts of Ruling Spirits (Genius Loci, Genius Speciae) and Allied Concepts*. Stockholm Studies in Comparative Religion. Stockholm.
La Barre, W. 1972. *The Ghost Dance*. London.

Miyata Noboru 1990. *Yōkai no Minzokugaku*. Tokyo.
Morse, R. 1975. *The Legends of Tōno*. Tokyo.
Naora Nobuo 1968. *Shuryō*. Tokyo.
Naumann, N. 1963. 'Yama no Kami', *Asian Folklore Studies* 22, 133–366.
Nihon Mukashibanashi Jiten 1978. [A Dictionary of Folktale Types and Motifs.]
_ Tokyo.
Ōta Yoshiji 1979. *Matagi: kieyuku yamabito no kiroku*. Tokyo.
Yanagita Kunio 1963a. 'Kami wo tasuketa hanashi' *TYKS* 12, 168–211.
—— 1963b. 'Yamanokami to okoze', *TYKS* 4, 441–8.
—— 1964. 'Nochi no Karikotoba no Ki', *TYKS* 27.

INDEX

———— ◆ ————